VALLE-INCLÁN'S
RUEDO IBÉRICO

A Popular View of Revolution

Alison Sinclair

VALLE-INCLÁN'S
RUEDO IBÉRICO

A Popular View of Revolution

TAMESIS BOOKS LIMITED

LONDON

Colección Támesis
SERIE A – MONOGRAFIAS XLIII
© by Tamesis Books Limited London 1977
ISBN 0 7293 0034 X

Designed and printed by
The Compton Press Ltd.
The Old Brewery
Tisbury, Wilts

for

TAMESIS BOOKS LIMITED
LONDON

For Stewart

Acknowledgements

The completion of this book has left me with a number of debts of different kinds : to the Hemeroteca Municipal and Museo Municipal of Madrid in which the greater part of the popular material was found; to the Señores de Muguruza for their extreme generosity in allowing me access to their Valle-Inclán collection; to Dr Carlos del Valle-Inclán and Don Jaime del Valle-Inclán for the help and information they gave me; to Mrs Helen Grant for her support, encouragement and enthusiasm in supervising the thesis on which this book is based; to Professors Arthur Terry, Geoffrey Ribbans and John Varey for their helpful comments and suggestions about the book; last, but by no means least, to Clare College and Girton College, Cambridge, for the financial support which has made the publication of this book possible. To all these people and institutions I would like to express my thanks.

In addition, I would like to thank the following institutions for their kindness in allowing me to reproduce illustrations : to the Museo Municipal, Madrid, for Plates I, II, III and VIII, to the Hemeroteca Municipal, Madrid, for Plates V, VI and VII, and to the University Library, Cambridge, for Plate IV.

ALISON SINCLAIR

Contents

List of Plates

References

Quotations in the text of this study are taken from the following editions :

Corte : *La corte de los milagros: El ruedo ibérico, I* (Madrid : Austral, 1968)
Viva : *Viva mi dueño: El ruedo ibérico, II* (Madrid : Austral, 1969)
Baza : *Baza de espadas* (Barcelona : AHR, 1958)

The short title is followed immediately by the page number. Reference to other works by Valle-Inclán is, wherever possible, to the Plenitud edition of the *Obras completas* (Madrid, 1954). For other editions, and for other works quoted in the text, see the Bibliography.

Introduction

¡La Historia! ¿Sabes tú quién hace la Historia, hija mía? En
Madrid los periodistas, y en estos pueblos los criados.

Valle-Inclán, *Gerifaltes de antaño*.

The course of Valle-Inclán criticism has been a curious one. Originally a man
who gained a rather shocked renown for the morbid and decadent extravagance
of his early short stories and the *Sonatas*, matched only by the equally shocked
personal renown he gained for his actions as a 'personaje estrafalario', he was
then relegated to comparative neglect for some decades. In more recent years,
and especially since the centenary year of 1966 (centenaries act as a convenient
critic's calendar, ensuring that periodic attention is fairly paid to both major
and minor literary figures), there has emerged a new Valle-Inclán, with a
certain political awareness shown to have succeeded on, or even been co-existent
with, the early aesthetic interests. The new Valle-Inclán, modern apple of the
critic's eye, is however predominantly the Valle-Inclán of the theatre. He has
been placed alongside such apparently different companions as Synge and
Artaud, his dramatic theory dissected, his definitions of a new genre, the
esperpento, re-defined. The *esperpento*, central as it is to his literary output,
has had its sources and ramifications traced in such a way that no part of his
literary work may be declared innocent of it. Much of the tracing has been
salutary in result. The works set in Galicia have rightly been shown to be quite
distant from rural idylls. The *farsas*, light as they are, nonetheless have their
sharp edge of political commentary.

My only justification for adding to this already formidable collection of
Valle-Inclán criticism is that there is a major section of his work which cannot
adequately be dismissed as an extension of the *esperpento*. *El ruedo ibérico*,
which dominated the last years of Valle-Inclán's life, is rich and complex. The
degree of that richness and complexity can, I believe, only really be seen by
setting it firmly in the historical background which constitutes its subject matter.
There are two types of reality which lie behind the *Ruedo*: events which
occurred, and the contemporary versions of those events. Both of these realities
bear a close resemblance to what has, up till now, been labelled as the
'esperpentic' vision of the *Ruedo*. The relationship between these realities and
the fiction of this work may be our only firm basis for speculation about Valle-
Inclán's intentions in writing it. It may also be a measure of his literary
achievement. It would be foolhardy to assert that both intention and achievement are totally distinct from those of the earlier *esperpentos*, but it is equally
foolhardy to assert that they are identical.

The notion of a 'relationship between fact and fiction', however, does not bear too close inspection. We may imagine that there is some absolute type of reality, but since such an absolute is going to be unknowable to the isolated individual, or even to a group, then it is of little use to either critic or reader. We may claim that in many instances written evidence of a particular event exists, but this is no more and no less than a statement by X (possibly corroborated by Y) that such an event took place. It is recounted according to the perceptions and researches of X, an individual who is fallible like the rest of us. There are, of course, the primary sources of history, deeds of sale and laundry lists, royal decrees and love letters, but even they, were we to push our original doubts to their logical conclusion, might well prove to be suspect. The distinction, then, should probably not be between 'fact and fiction', but between different degrees of supposed reliability (which bear no necessarily close relationship to the differing degrees of credibility). Fiction stands on the extremity of such a scale, but not on a scale apart.

In the case of the *Ruedo*, we have a few clear distinctions between fact and fiction. Some characters – politicians, members of the royal family, prominent practitioners of the arts – are taken from reality, and we assume them to have at least some features in common with their historical originals. Other characters bear no resemblance to historical figures that we can identify, and float freely in their fictional world, except for characteristics marking them out as credible creatures of their time. (No character may be safely classified. It is generally assumed that the Torre-Mellada family is fictional, but a brief note in *La Época* of 16 January 1868 makes one wonder : 'Esta noche reanudan los señores condes de Torre-Mata sus agradables reuniones, interrumpidas por las sensibles dolencias que han afligido a entrambos y causando vivo pesar a sus amigos.' Here is not only a remarkable similarity of name, but also a reference to recent family grief which might be related to Gonzalón Torre-Mellada's involvement with the killing of a policeman in *Corte* or his 'vómito de sangre' in *Viva*.) Some events, such as the presentation of the golden rose to Isabel II, are easily verifiable in reliable official sources. Others, such as the 'crimen de Solana', may prove difficult or impossible to verify, although peripheral features of the affair, such as the custom of granting Royal pardons to criminals on certain days of the year, may be traced with little difficulty. Many characters and events must be assumed to be fictional until the time when they can be shown to be otherwise.

Predictably, it is in areas where 'fact' and 'fiction' are most difficult to disentangle that the greatest motivation for disentanglement exists. We have ample evidence that Isabel II existed, but much conflicting and uncertain evidence about the manner of her existence, particularly in her private life. We may be led, by the *Ruedo*, to question whether her life in reality was as absurd, as futile and as vacuous as Valle-Inclán would have us believe. When we try to prove or disprove this by looking at historical evidence, we do not obtain a clear solution. Of the contemporary accounts of the period, the revolutionary but serious ones neglect detailed accounts of Isabel as a person, favouring instead the analysis of state politics. Liberal conservatives or *moderados* paint her as a paragon of Christian charity and generosity, at worst as a weak woman misled by her advisers.

El ruedo ibérico is, of course, not alone in Valle-Inclán's works in the close relationship it bears to a historical reality. Not only was it preceded by the Carlist war trilogy (*Los cruzados de la causa*, 1908, *El resplandor de la hoguera*, 1908-9, *Gerifaltes de antaño*, 1908-9), but the *farsas* and *esperpentos* had clear contemporary reference and significance, despite the fact that they had been written under constraining political circumstances. Alonso Zamora Vicente, José Rubia Barcia and Rodolfo Cardona have led modern criticism in the study of the contemporary significance of *Luces de bohemia* and *Los cuernos de Don Friolera*.[1] When the *Farsa y licencia de la reina castiza*, which first appeared in *La Pluma* (Madrid), nos. 3 and 5, (August and October, 1920), was published in book form in 1922 in Madrid, Valle-Inclán is said to have sent a copy to Alfonso XIII with the following dedication : 'Señor : Tengo el honor de enviaros este libro, estilización del reinado de vuestra abuela Isabel II, y hago votos porque el vuestro no sugiera la misma estilización a los poetas del porvenir.'[2] As for the other *farsas*, one of the best accounts of the political resonances of the *Farsa infantil de la cabeza del dragón* (1910) has been provided by Manuel Bermejo Marcos.[3]

Similarly, the *Ruedo* is not Valle-Inclán's only excursion into the genre of the novel, although it is arguably his most distinguished. There are two main novel-writing phases in his career, the first, 1895-1909, in which collections of short stories, the *Sonatas* and the novels of *La guerra carlista* were written,[4] and the period 1924-36 which sees the publication of the *Ruedo* and *Tirano Banderas*, and in which Valle-Inclán seems to have been uncertain about which works were to be designated as novels and which as theatre.[5] Although the

---

[1] A. Zamora Vicente, *La realidad esperpéntica: (Aproximación a 'Luces de bohemia')*, (Madrid, 1969). This was amplified by his paper at the Association of Hispanists' Conference, Cardiff, March, 1972.
Rodolfo Cardona, 'Los cuernos de don Friolera: estructura y sentido', *Ramón María del Valle-Inclán: An appraisal of his life and works*, edited by A. N. Zahareas, (New York, 1968), pp. 636-71.
J. Rubia Barcia, 'The *esperpentos*: a new novelistic dimension', *Valle-Inclán Centennial Studies*, edited by R. Gullón, (Austin, Texas, 1968), pp. 65-96.
See also Miguel Enguídanos, 'Las raíces históricas del esperpentismo', *Insula*, XXVII, no. 305, (April, 1972), pp. 1, 10, 14.
[2] Melchor Fernández Almagro, *Vida y literatura de Valle-Inclán*, (Madrid, 1943), p. 206.
[3] Manuel Bermejo Marcos, *Valle-Inclán: introducción a su obra*, (Madrid, 1971), pp. 167-73.
[4] *Femeninas* (1895), *Epitalamio* (1897), *Sonata de otoño* (1902), *Jardín umbrío* (1903), *Corte de amor* (1903), *Sonata de estío* (1903), *Sonata de primavera* (1904), *Flor de santidad* (1904), *Sonata de invierno* (1905), *Jardín novelesco* (1905), *Historias perversas* (1907), *El Marqués de Bradomín* (1907), *Una tertulia de antaño* (1908), *Los cruzados de la causa* (1908), *El resplandor de la hoguera* (1908-9), *Gerifaltes de antaño* (1908-9), *Cofre de sándalo* (1909).
[5] *Tirano Banderas* (1925-6, in *El Estudiante*, Salamanca, then Madrid), *La corte de los milagros* (1927), *Viva mi dueño* (1928).
El terno del difunto (1926, later to become *Las Galas del difunto*) was called a novel, and *La rosa de papel* and *La cabeza del Bautista* were published under the title of *novelas*

novels of *La guerra carlista* have a tenuous link with the *Ruedo* via fictional
characters and subject matter, in their over-riding concern with Carlism they
lack the general perspective of the later novels. Contrary to expectation, the
view of Carlism presented in them is not totally unalloyed in its admiration.
It is a political credo best suited to the museum ('Yo hallé siempre más bella
la majestad caída que sentada en el trono, y fui defensor de la tradición por
estética' asserts Bradomín, the universal character[6]). Furthermore, considerable
emphasis is laid on the cruelty and violence of Santa Cruz at the same time
as his energy and force of character is displayed. By the importance of
Bradomín as a character and the incidence of 'courtly' and 'noble' detail in
these novels, the trilogy has more in common with the contemporary group of
the *Sonatas* than with the *Ruedo*, the product of a man with over a decade of
further experience and scepticism.

The selection of 1868 as the period in which to set his final work constitutes
a return for Valle-Inclán to the area of Spanish history already explored in the
Farsa y licencia de la reina castiza. The return brings a more complex approach.
The scandals of Isabel II's household are now set in the context of the general
political scandals of the country, and new social areas are explored and related
to the aristocratic centre.

Part of the change between the *Farsa* and the *Ruedo*, and indeed between
La guerra carlista and the *Ruedo*, is explained by Valle-Inclán's shift in attitude
to the novel, or rather, the shift he perceives in novel writing, and in which he
participates. The shift was expressed in an interview of 1925 : for Valle-Inclán,
the novel of the individual (and presumably this includes the Bradomín of the
Sonatas and the individuals of *La guerra carlista*) had come to an end, but not
so the genre itself :

> Creo que empieza un período que pudiéramos llamar de novela de masas
> en contraposición al de novela individualista . . . La causa de esta
> transformación es muy honda, está en el cambio total, respecto al interés
> que despiertan las cosas. Por de pronto, ha dejado de interesarnos el
> individuo, al menos se ha borrado el primer término, ante el interés mayor
> que despiertan en nosotros las colectividades, la Nación, el hecho social.[7]

In moving away from the novels of the individual, Valle-Inclán is departing

---

macabras in 1924. The main bulk of the material produced between 1925 and 1936 is in
novel form, either in complete novels or texts of novelette size which are later incorporated,
with certain changes, into the *Ruedo*, or, like *Fin de un revolucionario* (1928) which deals
with the death of Vallín, were almost certainly intended for future novels of the cycle which
were never completed. Fragments connected with the *Ruedo* which were published
separately at this time are : *Cartel de ferias*, (Madrid, 10 January 1925), *Ecos de Asmodeo*,
(Madrid, 1926), *La rosa de oro*, (Madrid, 1927), *Fin de un revolucionario*, (Madrid, 15
March 1928), *Teatrillo de enredo*, (Madrid, 28 June 1928), *Las reales antecámaras*,
(Madrid, 12 October 1928), *Otra castiza de Samaria*, (Madrid, 15 November 1929), *Vísperas
de la gloriosa*, (Madrid, 16 May 1930), *Correo diplomático*, in *Ahora*, (Madrid, 12, 19 March
1935), *El trueno dorado*, in *Ahora*, (Madrid, 19, 26 March, 2, 9, 16, 23 April 1936), *La
jaula del pájaro*, (Barcelona, 1957) – presumably a reprint of an earlier edition.

[6] *Sonata de invierno, Obras completas*, II, 237.

[7] Interview of 1925 reprinted in *Primer Acto*, no. 32, 1967.

not only from his own previous practice, but also from that of his contemporary Baroja, whose *Memorias de un hombre de acción* (1913–35) were individual-orientated novels par excellence, and that of his predecessor Galdós, who, while treating a broad span of Spanish history in the *Episodios nacionales*, used a series of fictional characters in order to engage, focus and maintain his reader's attention. He was also flying in the face of the strictures of Ortega, whose *Ideas sobre la novela* (1925) showed such pronounced scepticism about the viability of the historical novel as a genre. Believing as he did, that 'la materia de la novela es propiamente psicología imaginaria',[8] and maintaining, as ever, a strict elitist sense of categories, Ortega was bound to react strongly against a genre in which 'no se deja al lector soñar tranquilo la novela, ni pensar rigorosamente la historia'.[9] His assumption that there are two distinct worlds to fuse or unite, that of fiction and the imagination, and that of fact or history, is one which shows a great deal more confidence in the separateness of the two worlds than was felt by Valle-Inclán and perhaps by any novelist who recognises the very imprecise nature of reality, and thereby the folly of raising history to a status of superior validity when placed alongside a work of fiction.[10]

[8] Ortega y Gasset, *Ideas sobre la novela, Obras completas*, 11 vols., (Madrid, 1957-69), III, (fourth edition, 1957), 416.

[9] ibid., p. 411.

[10] Space does not permit further discussion here of theoretical distinctions between 'fact' and 'fiction', 'illusion' and 'reality', and contingent general problems posed by the genre of the historical novel. These are topics deserving extensive and detailed treatment, which they have received elsewhere. The reader might like to refer to J. P. Stern, *On Realism*, (London, 1973), particularly Chapter 8, 'Description and evaluation', (pp. 129-41), and to W. J. Harvey, *Character and the Novel*, (London, 1965), particularly Chapter 1, 'Illusion and reality', (pp. 11-29).

I

The Setting of the *Ruedo*:
A Specialised View of Nineteenth-Century Spain

El viejo pardo, por el hilo de sus cavilaciones y recelos, deducía el
monstruo de una revolución social. En aquella hora española, el
pueblo labraba este concepto, desde los latifundios alcarreños a la
Sierra Penibética.

Valle-Inclán, *La corte de los milagros.*

El ruedo ibérico comes as close as is possible to challenging the validity of the
historical novel as a genre. The problems provoked by this hybrid or bastard
offspring of two disciplines, or of a creative activity which has had a passing
flirtation with a discipline now made attractive by its clothing in anecdotal
rather than formal fact, have partly been avoided, partly solved, partly re-posed
with dogged insistence. How is the necessary historical information to be
provided? What constitutes 'necessary' information in this context? Should the
historical element be merely the source of picturesque background? Of the
historical element and the literary, which should be the medium and which the
content? Perhaps Ortega was right to have warned novelists to leave well alone,
and to concentrate upon a narrowly-defined trade.

The solution adopted by the *Ruedo*, to take history as both content and
medium, and the novel as both content and medium, is perhaps the most
elegant, but also the most problematic. We may blush at the obvious way in
which Galdós will stage a discussion of contemporary or past events, showing
a historical awareness which undermines the credibility of many characters as
simple folk who are the natural salt of the earth, but we are at least provided
with a solid corpus of facts to guide us through the novel. Valle-Inclán, by
contrast, plays a game of intellectual one-upmanship with the reader. The novels
of the *Ruedo* demand not only that the reader should be well acquainted with
nineteenth-century Spanish history, but that he should be prepared to pick his
way through an obstacle-course of nicknames, rumours, and informal references,
hindered additionally by the occasional chronological disjunction, and the
over-riding determination of the author that he should not be allowed to read
the novels comfortably.

The result of this tantalising and uncompromising attitude of Valle-Inclán
is that either the reader gives up, or he reconciles himself to reading the *Ruedo*
as a series of unconnected and frequently enigmatic sketches. Perhaps only a
fully annotated critical edition of the *Ruedo* will finally give the reader the tool
he requires, and presumably if such an edition existed, it would frustrate

the author's intentions of teasing and bewildering his readers so that they are in the same state of ill-comprehension as were the contemporary spectators of the 1868 revolution. If, however, the alternative to this frustration is to have a reduced and irritated body of readers, there seems to be some case for at least giving the average reader orientation in the Iberian arena. This chapter discusses some of the particular historical background to that arena, and what we know of Valle-Inclán's attitude to it, while the following one looks more closely at the arena itself, and the way it is constructed.

The historical background

The range of factors which one needs to take into account in reading the *Ruedo* extend from a recognition of social changes and movements in nine-teenth-century Spain to an understanding of the political complexities surround-ing the succession of Isabel II to the Spanish throne. Thus the expansion of the 'clases acomodadas' accounts partially for the moral and financial dependence of Torre-Mellada on his steward Don Segis, and for the importance of Salamanca, and initial liberal support for Isabel as Queen accounts for later tension in the government about her ecclesiastic advisers. The background to Isabel's accession to the throne is also the background to her removal from it : the same problems and dynastic quarrels are ready to emerge on her departure.

Isabel II had succeeded her father, Ferdinand VII, at his death in 1833, although Spain was ruled first by her mother, María Cristina, then Espartero, as regents, until 1843. She was supported principally by liberals who were in inevitable opposition to the Carlist claim to the throne, since the latter aimed at an absolutist theocratic type of regime which would have been incompatible with constitutionalism. The 1834 constitution assured a certain measure of liberal support for Isabel, but when the more radical *exaltados* returned from exile after Christmas 1834, the liberals split into two streams : *progresistas* and *moderados*, tending to the left and right respectively.

Whatever the limitations of Spanish liberalism of the nineteenth century when compared with what we understand by liberalism today, it did at least aim at the recognition of a new structure of society in which trade and finance held high place, thus opposing the rather primitive traditionalism of the Carlists. But since many liberals belonged to the middle class, which in addition to its growing importance in society in economic terms, had also acquired property through the disentailment laws, the type of social progress they envisaged was always likely to be circumscribed by concern for their own vested interests. Carlism, were it to have triumphed, would probably have brought the reversion of land to Church and nobility, and thus was to be opposed on the basis of self-interest as well as on political theory. Yet another factor was involved in this equilibrium : the type of theocratic state sought after by the Carlists was similar to the type of state that the Vatican would have liked to see established in Spain. Moves towards Carlism represented, for the liberals at least, moves towards political submission to the Pope.

Given these conditions, it is easy to see how complex Isabel's situation was. The monarchists had been forced to side with liberals in order to maintain themselves in a position of power, and this had already caused a number of unhappy compromises. When, in addition, Isabel II proved not to be a perfect or even an adequate constitutional monarch, but a weak, rather silly and frivolous woman whose natural urge was to rule by personal whim and not by agreed legislation, tension was bound to result. More complications arose from her ingenuousness, and inability to see repercussions of her actions, both public and private. Not only could she cause embarrassment to her cabinets through direct action, but her superstitious faith and dependence upon religious advisers opened up the possibility that her life, and the political life of Spain, might be brought into line with the wishes of the Vatican. Some cold comfort could however be derived from her very fickleness which made her an unreliable lever for the powers of Rome.

Raymond Carr has indicated the uneasy relationship which existed in Spain between the established forces of the army, the political parties and the Crown, all of which might unite against Carlism or republicanism, or any two of which might unite to oust the third from power.[1] The 1868 revolution showed yet another possible realignment, in the discussion of a union between liberals and Carlists to effect the dethronement of Isabel II. Cabrera, in *Viva* IX.v, points out the disadvantages of such an arrangement. The army was central to any hope of political change, and yet the main paradox of its role as political activator lay within its composition. Although the army contained all classes within its ranks, and was one of the few areas where social rising was clearly possible, the generals, key figures in the mechanics of revolution, tended to come mainly from the landed middle classes or the aristocracy, and as such were unlikely to desire any drastic change in the status quo. Given this, we realise that the type of popular and complete revolution expressly desired by the landless peasants and bandits who occupy the central books of *Corte* and *Viva* is far from the type of revolution they are likely to obtain from the only people powerful enough to bring it about. This need for parties and groups of conflicting views and interests to combine in order to change the government displays the country's political and social fragmentation and is a chronic symptom of its malaise. Since fragmentation was not to disappear, the detailing of political chaos and division in the *Ruedo* was bound to have special point for the reading public of the 1920s and 1930s.

These are the political problems which form both backcloth and substance for the action of the *Ruedo*. They are assumed to form part of the general cultural background of the reader, and are only indicated in the text by oblique reference via reportage of popular rumour and anecdote. The reason for this is simple. Valle-Inclán has no desire to give us a reflection of history, that clear and thoughtfully judged account of events viewed in retrospect by the scholar, but to thrust History before us, that is, events as they might have appeared to those participating or spectating at the time. We are given a re-creation of the mood of the Spanish people in the face of a major political event, revolution, and this is motivated by a clear desire to penetrate the Spanish character : 'Para mí, la sensibilidad del pueblo se refleja y se mide por la forma

[1] Raymond Carr, *España 1808-1939*, (O.U.P., 1966, Spanish edition, Barcelona 1969), p. 211.

de reaccionar ante esos hechos.'[2] Valle-Inclán also considered that man was no longer of a moral stature commensurate with his life, which 'es siempre la misma fatalmente'.[3] In showing how the Spanish people react to revolution, he demonstrates this loss of stature which has occurred since the times of the Conquest, and most noticeably since the recent epic of the struggle against Napoleon.

One of the most striking features of the way this portrayal is realised is the consistent refusal to make direct surmises about personal psychology or motivation : at the most there may be speculation from the outside about the motives of others, and the more subtle communication of the author's judgment about character via the external appearance presented. Occasionally Valle-Inclán does permit himself that authorial omniscience which lets us into the workings of others' minds. We have a direct line to the Queen's mental chaos and to the ambition of Prim. Characters do have some inner processes, but they are reduced to a minimum since the author's assumption is that we are forced inevitably to react to the external appearance of others' actions and apparent motives, and not to what may lie behind them. Since we have no route to their inner workings, they must be negligible in a novel that purports to look at a moment of history as it was experienced, with all its false conceptions and inconsistencies.

This mode of portrayal does not, however, imply either the author's objectivity or his impartiality (unhelpful concepts anyway in the majority of circumstances). It is also simplistic to assume that the *Ruedo* is no more and no less than a fiction (based on fact) about a brief period of Spanish history. The very interest shown in what constitutes the nature of the Spanish people is a general one, although the means employed to explore it are particular. The *Ruedo* could be said to constitute an indirect and artistic way of exploring the 'problema de España' that preoccupied Valle-Inclán's contemporaries, although it was never explicitly labelled as such by the author. The Spain we see in it is a country pervaded by cynicism and materialism, with every social stratum beset with intrigue and hypocrisy. The picture is relieved only occasionally by elements such as the idealism of the anarchists, or the sense of rough social justice among the bandits, and these too are tempered in their impact. Signs of degeneration and disillusion are shown as essential to the period. What matters to our view of Valle-Inclán and his work, is to see the extent to which this mood of degeneration might be considered as an imposition of the author whose gold-rimmed *quevedos* are far from rosy, a judgment on the mood of his own times projected conveniently into the past, and the extent to which it is the reflection of a tangible reality. Our touchstone for the inquiry must be the commentary on the events and characters of 1868 that is provided by contemporary popular literature.

The term 'popular literature' is not without its difficulties. Some of them at least can, I hope, be dispensed with by defining what I intend to include under that heading, as distinct from what might be included under the same heading by others. Since no adequate sociological study yet exists which might indicate for us the total range of reading matter available to the Spanish

[2] Francisco Madrid, *La vida altiva de Valle-Inclán*, (Buenos Aires, 1943), p. 115.
[3] ibid., p. 114.

public in the mid-nineteenth century, we cannot say with certainty what reading matter, if any, was the fodder of the *pueblo*, and whether this was different from what was read by other social classes. Nor can we tell what proportion of the *pueblo* read at all. Although we have some information about the extent of illiteracy in Spain in this period, the ability to both 'deletrear' and to sign one's name on official documents is by no means sufficient qualification for the regular reading of newspapers or novels. We simply have insufficient information to know whether 'illiterate' and 'pueblo' might be co-terminous. One may suspect that they are, but since in the mid-1860s the numbers of literate adults in the population of Spain were approximately double the size of the electorate in the same period, and since the electorate constituted less than 3% of the population, this suggests that the size of the illiterate 'pueblo' was enormous.[4] If we assume (and this may or may not be correct), that very little could be read by the *pueblo* itself, we may ask whether the term 'popular literature' defined as the literature which is read by the *pueblo* can be used at all for this period in Spain. Even making an allowance for the existence of an indirect reading public, consisting of those who would be read to by others, the term 'popular literature' as defined above is likely to be devoid of meaning in this context.

The absence of reliable information about the size and possible social composition of the reading public in nineteenth-century Spain is frustrating in absolute terms, but there are other elements in the situation. Although our ideas about who was doing the reading in this period may be vague, we have more information about what was being read. The sort of distinctions that may be drawn between different types of reading matter have two types of basis : the subject matter itself, whether serious or frivolous in intention, and the manner of publishing, whether in book form or newspaper, ephemeral or regular. Serious reading matter, published in 'serious' and expensive form in books, excludes itself. Within my definition of popular literature I would like then to include the following : all sections of the press that were of a self-confessed festive, satirical or comic nature, the most important group here for our purpose being the satirical political papers; *aleluyas* and broadsides circulated occasionally with the intent of serious comment, but more frequently in the hope of swaying public opinion by ridicule and satire; certain theatrical productions of the 'género chico', parodic anr burlesque in type, apparently crackling with contemporary references which are virtually incomprehensible when separated from their own historical context. This type of reading matter exaggerates, distorts, deflates, parodies its subjects, which it assumes to be already familiar to its readers. Also included, but for slightly different reasons, are the sentimental novels frequently published in serial form in newspapers and other

---

[4] J. Vicens Vives, *Historia económica de España*, third edition, (Barcelona, 1964), p. 567, gives the electorate in 1865 (those paying more than 200 *reales* yearly in direct taxation) as 418,271, less than 3% of the total population of 16,600,000. As Carlo Cipolla, in *Literacy and Development in the West*, (London, 1969), Table 30, gives the number of adult illiterates in Spain in 1860 as 15,673,000, we can assume the number of literate adults (including those who could read but not write) as numbering just over 900,000, that is, somewhat more than twice the electorate.

papers of light entertainment : these novels, and the Romantic drama, provide the hero and heroine prototypes on which so many characters of the *Ruedo* model themselves.

The first category of popular literature, whose nature is of contemporary political and social commentary, pre-supposes that, in the majority of cases, some serious political papers are also read, or at least that the elements of public events are known already in some way to the reader. This is no different from the assumption of *Private Eye* that its readers are acquainted with the news via serious daily papers and other branches of the media. This type of assumption leads us to another one, namely that ephemeral reading matter, sometimes sophisticated, often crude, was probably read by those of a reasonable level of education, with some awareness of politics. This is an assumption based on the nature of the reading matter only and not on any statistical evidence about literacy or population figures. It is worth noting at this stage, however, that there is considerable variation in tone and taste between popular satirical papers of this type, which suggests, again on the basis of the subject matter and the style employed, rather than on any statistical basis, that some of the target audience, some of the time, was intended to be of a social group which was not so elevated as to belong to the electorate, nor even perhaps to belong to a professional class. In spite of this reservation, the principal impression of the political section of the material that I am classifying as 'popular literature' is that it was directed at a body of readers who were relatively well-educated and politically sophisticated, the same type of reading public to which the *Ruedo* itself is directed.

The social scope of the *Ruedo* is wider than the narrow band of those who might be supposed to have formed the readership of popular literature, but not much wider. There is no question of a fair cross-section of Spanish society in 1868 being presented. The novels are devoted to blocks of scenes from different social areas : the court, the Church, the world of journalism, the world of the gypsies and bandits. The inhabitants of the various social spheres express their reaction to the coming political changes. Sometimes they are voicing their own views, but more often they relay popular opinion. They often resort to the simple notion that an event is like a *folletín* or a *farsa*. There is a similar obliquity in the 'direct' narration of the author, since the evocation of events is frequently achieved by a restatement of how they were recorded in the satirical papers and broadsides of the time, already at one step removed and with the judgment of the contemporary spectator already firmly imprinted upon them. This portrayal of pre-digested reaction, which betrays itself in speech by the use of clichés, is not to the total exclusion of serious discussion in the novels. The arguments on politics in *Baza* 'Alta mar', and some of the exchanges about the type of politics needed by Spain in the future (is it a 'carlismo sin sotanas' or democracy?), are refreshingly free of the general tone of cynicism. Outside these rare oases of seriousness, the novels are heavily weighted towards farce and ridicule. Prim, for example, is not allowed to state his aims without it being pointed out that he has an inflated image of himself similar to that of a hero in a Romantic melodrama (*Baza* 164). Such a tipping of the scales implies a sharp division between those who saw themselves as acting out melodramatic plots, and those who, on seeing this, were forced to reactions of cynicism or despair.

Cynicism and despair may be thought to be standard keynotes of Valle-Inclán's writing, but a perusal of the popular literature of the revolutionary period impresses one with the close similarity between its mood and that of the *Ruedo*. What looks like an esperpentic distortion might more accurately be described as a piecing together of the vociferous and biased opinions of those who created History as it was happening. To this, stylisation of structure and speech is added, much of the latter deriving its framework from popular sources. The resulting texture is more dense and varied than in other works of Valle-Inclán.

The idea that there is a link between the *Ruedo* and popular literature is not a new one. The author's awareness of such sources is made abundantly clear by the wealth of reference in the novels to popular papers, nicknames of public figures, *coplas* and *romances*. In 1943 Fernández Almagro pointed to this use of History : 'El contraste es la ley natural del esperpento y nuestro siglo XIX proporciona materia más que bastante para que Valle Inclán no experimentara la necesidad de inventar perfiles grotescos ni de forzar demasiado la línea real de sus modelos. La caricatura está implícita en las crónicas mismas de la época : en discursos, en artículos, en folletos, en coplas, pasquines y carteles.'[5] Although he rightly adds that this treatment of caricature is extended to all the subject matter in the novels, it should be pointed out that the Andalusian episodes have little connection with such sources.[6] Similarly, a link with popular literature is recognised by Zamora Vicente, who in *La realidad esperpéntica de Valle-Inclán* relates *Luces de bohemia* to the satirical press and theatre of Valle-Inclán's lifetime. What he has to say obviously has some relevance for the *Ruedo* in so far as he shows how *Luces* reflects popular attitudes to current events, but there is a difference both in the time-lag between source and text and the type of use which is made of the source.

Valle-Inclán's interest in History as conveyed through popular literature is evident not just from reference in the text, but also from what we know of his reading interests. In 1952 Gaspar Gómez de la Serna published a list of some of the historical works contained in Valle-Inclán's library at Pontevedra.[7] The list is imposing, its most remarkable feature being that most of the works were written at the time of the events dealt with in the *Ruedo*, or shortly afterwards. Many of the contemporary accounts of the background, events and aftermath of the revolution are written by those who had been directly involved in it. Thus Fernando Garrido, for example, a republican (later to become much more socialist in his politics), published his *Historia del reinado del último Borbón de España* in three volumes between 1868 and 1869.

In both form and style these accounts were intended to catch the attention. There appear to have been few historical works without a direct political axe to

---

[5] Fernández Almagro, *Vida y literatura de Valle Inclán*, (Madrid, 1943), p. 252.

[6] According to H. L. Boudreau, the main source for these episodes was Zugasti, *El bandolerismo andaluz*. See Chapter IV, note 7.

[7] Gaspar Gómez de la Serna, 'Las dos Españas de don Ramón María del Valle-Inclán', *Clavileño*, III, no. 17, (September-October, 1952), pp. 17-32.

grind. Some, such as Bermejo's *Estafeta de Palacio*, appeared in serial form, the slant of the title altering with circumstances. Published between 1871 and 1872, the first two volumes of Bermejo's work had the subtitle 'Cartas trascendentales dirigidas a D. Amadeo', whereas the third carried the sign of change : 'Cartas trascendentales dirigidas a S.A.R. El Príncipe D. Alfonso de Borbón.' Other subtitles were more than explicit. Garrido's work declared that it treated of 'los crímenes, apostasías, opresión, corrupción, inmoralidad, despilfarros, hipocresía, crueldad y fanatismo de los gobiernos que han regido a España durante el reinado de Isabel de Borbón'. Such a declaration was clearly an advertising gimmick, since the work in question is far more concerned with the actions of politicians and the development of republicanism than with the personal shortcomings of Isabel II. Its publication had been held up until the revolution occurred : it was advertised in *El Telégrafo* (Barcelona) on 18 October 1868.

Gómez de la Serna's list, though imposing, was not exhaustive. On further enquiry, Dr. Carlos Valle-Inclán, the author's son, showed me two examples of non-printed sources : a longhand biography of Fermín Salvochea, and the longhand memoirs of a general in the Carlist wars. In periodical publications there were two serious omissions from the list. Two periodicals had been named, the *Semanario Pintoresco* and *El Padre Cobos*. The latter was incorrectly listed as complete : the first two series are there, but the third, 25 February to 25 November 1869 is not. The collection also contains five satirical papers of the revolutionary period, all published in Madrid: *La Gorda* (10 November 1868 to 15 June 1869); *El Gato* (19 November 1868 to 5 July 1869); *La Mano Oculta* (10 January to 17 February 1869); *Don Quijote* (5 January to 10 July 1869); *Las Ánimas* (12 April 1869 and 3 May 1869).[8] None of these were complete series. The papers vary in importance, *La Gorda* being the best known. In their politics they are close to one another. *La Gorda, Don Quijote* and *Las Ánimas* were conservative, while *El Gato* and *La Mano Oculta* were Carlist. No republican papers were there, although these could obviously have been consulted by the author at the Biblioteca Nacional, Madrid.

Another, but much more tenuous, indication of Valle-Inclán's contact with the world of the satirical press, is that on visits to Barcelona he habitually stayed at the Hotel Oriente, beneath which was a bookshop founded by Antonio López Bernagossi, the editor of *La Campana de Gracia* and *L'Esquella de la Torratxa* of 1870 and 1872 respectively, both republican, *catalanista* and anti-clerical in nature.[9]

The papers and books which, by their presence in his library, we may perhaps assume to be sources of fact and inspiration for Valle-Inclán belong, with few exceptions, to the post-revolutionary period. In the case of books this is not a motive for surprise, but the case of newspapers requires some explanation about the effect of censorship upon the political press in the pre-revolutionary period.

In the period in which the novels of the *Ruedo* are set, the few months preceding the revolutionary coup of September 1868, censorship in Spain was

[8] In future references to newspapers, the place of publication will only be given if it is not Madrid.

[9] F. Madrid, p. 24.

governed by González Bravo's law of 7 March 1867. *Gil Blas*, on 2 August 1868 (a week before the unsuccessful coup described in *Baza*) commented that, of the fifty-four articles of that law, only the twenty-seventh guaranteed any right of opposition, and this was limited since it permitted one to 'censurar la conducta oficial o los actos de los funcionarios públicos en el ejercicio de sus cargos, si sus escritos estuvieren redactados con decoro y siempre que las imputaciones que se hicieren no fueren calumniosas'.[10] The terminology of this particular law betrays an almost panic-stricken need to keep publication completely under control. It distinguished between an 'impreso' and a 'periódico', the first being 'todo pensamiento manifestado con palabras fijadas sobre cualquier materia por medio de la imprenta, por los de la litografía y fotografía, o por cualquier otro procedimiento' and the second being any item defined as an example of the first which appeared once or twice daily, or at intervals of up to sixty days. Since an 'impreso' could have a 'título constante o variado, o uno diverso en cada número o entrega' the law could reach anyone publishing anything with a vestige of regularity.

Not only was the letter of the law extreme : its application revealed touchiness on the part of the censors. Carlos Rubio tells of an occasion when a literary *folletín* of his, which he asserts was 'completamente literario y completamente tonto acerca del almanaque' was suppressed on account of conclusions that might be drawn from it. The censor, he relates, gave the following justification for his action : 'Usted habla del zodíaco . . . y dice que trae su nombre de una palabra griega que significa animal, porque entre los signos que le componen hay ocho representados por animales; pues bien, esto no puede pasar, porque claro está que cuando el público oiga hablar de ocho animales, comprenderá al momento que se habla de los ocho ministros.' He then cites another case where a short Latin phrase was deleted by the censor : 'También el fiscal esta vez me sacó de apuros diciéndome : – Que él, aunque abogado, no sabía latín, y no podía dejar pasar una frase que no entendía, porque con ella podría inferirse una ofensa al ministerio.'[11]

The change in the press situation when, on 26 October 1868, complete 'Libertad de Imprenta' was declared, and writings in the press became subject only to the penal code, may be imagined. Not only did it become easier actually to go into print, since political papers were no longer required to deposit large sums with the censor before starting publication (the deposit formed the easiest means of extracting fines when press offences were committed), but also it became possible to state much of what had been suppressed in the way of political opinion and public emotion in the pre-revolutionary period. A dramatic change took place in the size of Spanish newspaper production, and in its composition. One of the best guides to periodical publications in Madrid in this period was compiled by Eugenio Hartzenbusch from the holdings of the

[10] P. Gómez Aparicio, *Historia del periodismo español*, 3 vols., (Madrid, 1967-74), I, 81. For a full account of Spanish censorship in this period, see also José Eugenio de Eguizábal, *Apuntes para una historia de la legislación española sobre imprenta desde el año de 1480 al presente*, (Madrid, 1873).

[11] Carlos Rubio, *Historia filósofica de la revolución española de 1868*, 2 vols., (Madrid, 1869), I, 63.

Biblioteca Nacional in Madrid, many of which have now been passed to the Hemeroteca Municipal. Since he also included other papers of which he had report, or which he was able to see in small private collections, his *Apuntes para un catálogo de periódicos madrileños desde el año 1661 al 1870* (Madrid, 1894) is the most complete account of the papers to which we have access. His rough statistical chart included in the volume shows how Spanish newspaper publication expanded rapidly in certain periods. A peak occurs between 1820 and 1823, and a much higher one is reached after the 1868 revolution. By 1870, three hundred and two papers were in print.[12] Another view of the sudden intensification of newspaper activity is given by Antonio Asenjo, one of the past Directors of the Hemeroteca Municipal. He calculates that between October 1868 and the end of 1870 about three hundred and sixty papers appeared, of which sixty made their debut in the last three months of 1868.[13] In passing we may note wryly how this flourishing of journalism in the nineteenth century contrasts with its difficult life later on. Schulte (aided by the data of Hartzenbusch) compares 1944 in Spain when there were nine dailies, a hundred and four periodical publications in Spain and six in the colonies, with a century earlier when there had been three times as many.[14]

The change in character of the press is also important. The crude figures given by Hartzenbusch fail to reveal the enormous increase in papers which were satirical, short-lived, or both. Their festive or satirical nature is revealed in part by the titles they carried. Although the existence of satirical political papers before the revolution was minimal, deflation was a strong note in the publications of 1868. Before the revolution, papers such as *El Quijote, La Flora, El Trancazo, Don Diego de Noche*, and *El Centinela del Pueblo* began their life. After the revolution they were followed by *La Cosa Pública, El Ganso, La Gorda, La Flaca, El Gato, La Píldora, La Seca, La Diosa Razón, El Anti-Cristo, El Capitán Araña, El Juego, El Monaguillo de las Salesas, El Niño Terso* and many more. As in the case of books, subtitles were revealing. *El Despertador* (1868) declared : 'El que quiera comer, que trabaje, Gobierno poco y barato.' *Neo* (Huesca, 1868) described itself as a 'periódico republicano con ínsulas de beato y puntos de republicano'. *El Loro* (Seville, 1868) played upon its title with the phrase 'revista semanal de colores rabiosos escrita por una sociedad de pajarracos'.

The lifting of censorship increased the numbers of papers in print, and the proportion of those that were satirical. It must not be imagined, however, that all new papers supported a revolutionary or republican viewpoint. Since the information we have about many of the shorter-lived papers is scanty, it is not possible to say exactly what the relationship was between the numbers of papers launched to support the revolution, and the numbers of papers which sprang up in a movement of counter-attack. But it is possible to detect some

[12] The achievement of Hartzenbusch is outstanding, but his analysis of the press necessarily limited by the difficulty and tedium of doing a hand-count on his information. A computer-aided study using his data may reveal more interesting fluctuations.

[13] Antonio Asenjo, *La prensa madrileña a través de los siglos: Apuntes para su historia desde el año 1661 al de 1925*, (Madrid, 1933), p. 53.

[14] Henry F. Schulte, *The Spanish Press 1470-1966*, (Chicago, 1968), pp. 20-21.

shift in the proportions. Of the papers listed by Hartzenbusch as newly appeared between the revolution and the end of 1868, the vast majority apparently support the revolution, whereas of the papers which appeared for the first time in 1869 there seems to be a fairly even division between those obviously for the politics resulting from the revolution, those obviously against them, and papers which existed to provide some neutral comment.

Of the papers that came out in the first flush of revolutionary enthusiasm in 1868, many were enthusiastic about the annihilation of the old system. At the same time there was a release of pent-up resentment against the Bourbons, which gave rise to pieces which ranged from the comically absurd to the frankly unsavoury. A similar release is evident in historical accounts published at this time. Changes of mood followed in some papers, enthusiasm giving way to criticism and later disillusion as revolutionary hopes failed to be realised by the military triumvirate of the generals Prim, Serrano and Topete. At the same time, papers of the Right turned the weapons of revolutionaries and republicans back on themselves. Apart from the fact that campaigns of attack or defence might be conducted with a greater or a lesser degree of taste (dependent on the target reading public rather than on the type of politics expressed), newspapers of all persuasions tended to employ the same general technique, that is, concentration upon characteristics and foibles of individuals rather than on the general situation. Most of the papers we may assume to have been founded by those wanting to support a particular line : this is revealed by those they favoured as well as those they attacked. Of the 'candidatos baratos' (those contending for the Spanish throne after the departure of Isabel II), the Duque de Montpensier escaped ridicule in some quarters. According to Schulte, however, (p. 206) he was responsible for founding no less than fourteen dailies and six weeklies in Madrid which defended his claim to the throne. Carlist papers such as *Rigoleto* and *El Papelito* naturally idealised both Carlos VII and his wife, who represented the virtuous alternative to the scandalous household of Isabel II and her Consort.

Given the different targets of the various popular papers and broadsides, it follows that if he was to use them as source or inspiration for a work which would give a general perspective of the situation, Valle-Inclán could not restrict his culling of material to republican publications only. In the case of Prim, for example, although Iris Zavala suggests that the characterisation here was largely inspired by the republican press,[15] it is clear that it is closely related to the attacks made on him by conservative papers. What is not clear is whether Valle-Inclán made any use of the serious political press. While he may have used it for factual documentation, this type of journalism is singularly unrelated to the concepts and style of the *Ruedo*, although allusions to serious papers are naturally included in the novels as part of the historical and intellectual background. Another area of popular documentation is the clandestine press, but this by its very nature is the type of material least likely to find its way

[15] Iris M. Zavala, 'Historia y literatura en *El ruedo ibérico*', *La revolución de 1868: Historia, pensamiento, literatura*, edited by Clara E. Lida and Iris M. Zavala, (New York, 1970), pp. 425-49 (p. 426). *La Gorda* here was included as one of the republican papers, although its character was that of conservative reaction.

into official collections, and consequently is now hard to locate. The relevant clandestine papers that I have seen, *El Relámpago*, *El Murciélago* and *El Centinela del Pueblo*, only appear as odd numbers in libraries. The suggestions and commentaries contained in them are so extreme, intended perhaps to shake the throne by the sheer enormity of the allegations made, that their scarcity is not surprising. *El Centinela del Pueblo* in its early numbers, published in the last months before the revolution, was outrageous. Later numbers were less so. It was still in print in 1870, an unusually long life for a paper with such beginnings.

The extent to which use of the popular press provides a basis for characterisation and style in the *Ruedo* will be dealt with in later chapters, but here it is worth noting some obvious symptoms of an interest in such sources. The titles of the novels themselves have their roots in popular literature. Suggestions have already been made about the origins of *La corte de los milagros* as a title. Julián Marías considers it to be the combination of a hint of the underworld 'Cour des mirâcles' of Victor Hugo's *Notre-Dame de Paris* and a reference to Sor Patrocinio, the miracle-working nun who was a close friend of Isabel II,[16] whereas Boudreau quotes from Rubio's *Historia filosófica de la revolución española* : 'Tengo muchos amigos en la unión liberal, amigos a quienes aprecio individualmente, pero en el conjunto del partido, no puedo ver otra cosa que una *Corte de los Milagros* semejante a la que pintó Victor Hugo en *Nuestra Señora de París*' and suggests that this might have been the source, both historical and literary.[17] There are other possibilities. 'La corte de los milagros' was also the title of a poem which appeared in *Gil Blas* on 2 March 1871. The poem referred to a sharing-out of uniforms of the post-revolutionary period, and hinted that someone was making financial gain out of the operation – a reversion to the pre-revolutionary situation. It was also the rather unlikely title of a play by José Picón, first put on at the Teatro de Variedades on 24 December 1862. Although there seems to be no direct reference to Isabel II in the text of the play, the second edition shows that the censor insisted on various cuts being made because of allusions to contemporary figures. The play is concerned with the honour of Aurora, a girl whose father tries to force her into marriage with Mendoza for financial reasons. One of the suppressions insisted upon was of the final *redondillas*, which argued that it was better to be poor and honourable than rich and ashamed :

> Y así, como en buena ley,
> más vale ante el mundo entero
> la mujer de un carbonero
> que la querida de un rey,
> tambien más vale en conciencia
> el mendigo con honor,
> que el que goza sin rubor
> de una anónima opulencia.[18]

[16] Julián Marías, *Valle-Inclán en el Ruedo ibérico*, (Madrid, 1966), p. 16.
[17] H. L. Boudreau, 'Materials toward an analysis of Valle-Inclán's *Ruedo ibérico*', (unpublished PhD dissertation, University of Wisconsin, 1968), pp. 119-20. The reference is to Rubio's *Historia*, I, 423.

Possibly this suppression was made because the lines were felt to be a reflection on the state of affairs at court.

For *Viva mi dueño*, Valle-Inclán himself indicates one source, saying that it was a motto that used to be engraved on small knives (*Viva* 91). It was also a phrase in vogue at the time of the revolution. It appears in *Don Quijote* of 15 February 1869 as a motto supposedly worn by the police when quelling a riot (a hint of the uncomfortable closeness of official life and banditry), and in *El Papelito* of 25 April 1869, where it is tagged to *La Iberia* (a paper of liberal politics) as a sign of egotism.[19] The title of the third novel of the cycle, *Baza de espadas*, refers to the group of generals planning the revolution, and forms part of a widely used series of playing card images which appear in the popular press.[20]

Titles of individual books within the novels show similar debts to popular literature. *Corte* begins with 'Aires nacionales', a title intended satirically, and used in similar manner for the poems 'Aires nacionales' in *La Gorda* of 11 January 1869, and 'Todo es mentira : Aire nacional' in *El Papel de Estraza* (Valencia) of 11 May 1866. The third book of the novel is 'Ecos de Asmodeo', Asmodeo the court journalist being a minor character who is glimpsed in *Corte* III.xxvii and *Baza* '¿Qué pasa en Cádiz?' ii-vi, xii. We learn that Torre-Mellada is a keen follower of the column of this erstwhile William Hickey in *La Época* (*Corte* 142). Some 'Ecos de Asmodeo' did appear in *La Época*, written by Ramón de Navarrete, but they did not begin until December 1868, whereas in Valle-Inclán's chronology they were in print six months earlier.[21] *Viva* begins with 'Almanaque revolucionario', Book V is 'Cartel de ferias', and it ends on 'Periquito gacetillero' – all three the names of different types of ephemerae. The second series of the cycle was to have been called *Aleluyas de la Gloriosa*, close to the title of a real *aleluya, Historia de la Gloriosa*, produced soon after the revolution.

In addition to this, journalistic life also forms part of the material of the novels. We see the offices of *Gil Blas* (*Viva* VI.xi) and of *El Baluarte de Betis*

---

[18] J. O. Picón, *La corte de los milagros*, second edition, (Madrid, 1863), pp. 83-4.

[19] Valle-Inclán had first used the phrase in 'Palabras de Mal Agüero', *El Universal*, (Mexico), 11 June 1892, collected by William L. Fichter in *Publicaciones periodísticas de Don Ramón de Valle-Inclán anteriores a 1895*, (Mexico 1952), p. 165.

[20] I have discussed this in 'Nineteenth-century popular literature as a source of linguistic enrichment in Valle-Inclán's *Ruedo ibérico*', *Modern Language Review*, vol. 70, no. 1., (January 1975), pp. 84-96.

[21] I owe Asmodeo's real name to Boudreau's census in his dissertation. Asmodeo also appeared as a minor character in *Vivitos y coleando*, (lyrics by Lastra, Ruesga and Prieto, music by Chueca and Valverde). It was first produced at the Teatro de Variedades, 15 March 1884, and ran for 145 performances. His only appearance is in scene xi as a 'niño vestido de diablillo, con lápiz y cuartillas' who states :

> Ayer tarde se casó
> la condesa de Recreo
> con el duque de la O.
> Punto y la firma. Asmodeo.
> No hay cronista como yo.

This accurately pinpoints the tone of the column. This play would almost certainly have come to Valle-Inclán's notice in his time in Madrid.

of Cordoba (*Viva* VII.ii), thus representing journalism in Madrid and in the provinces. We learn how the press can be used to propagate convenient rumours. *El Baluarte* has carried a report of Vallín's taking refuge in the convent (*Viva* V.xxii). Subsequently el Niño de Benamejí instructs its editor to continue the *folletín* of the revolutionary's hideout, even though Vallín is now at large in Cordoba (*Viva* VII.xvi). (This example of misuse of the press is, incidentally, a lesson for us in the need to treat the papers with caution : what may seem to be fact is often opinion or rumour.) We also see how Antonio Guzmán el Tuerto appeals to *El Baluarte* for help after he has been ill-treated by the police, believing that the paper might be able to exert pressure on his behalf. *Corte* IV.xiv-xvi deals with Don Felipito, a blind man who sells *pliegos* and papers of a dangerous nature. We are made fully aware of the constant threats overshadowing those who write and distribute these publications, and of the interest they arouse in both *pueblo* and aristocratic *tertulias* where they are in competition with Asmodeo's court gossip and the latest episode of a *folletín*.

The other types of popular literature included in my definition are more strictly literary. The sentimental *novela por entregas* which provides a framework of imagery for certain character types has attracted a certain amount of critical attention already. To the general studies of Montesinos and Brown has been added the work of Ferreras,[22] and I have discussed imagery based on the novel elsewhere. More central to the imagery and characterisation of the novels is the nineteenth-century theatre in Spain. Because we tend to think of a theatrical perspective as an integral part of Valle-Inclán's style in works written before the *Ruedo*, it is important to realise the extent to which here at least he is using a particular type or types of theatre to achieve a certain moral and stylistic impact as well as an added level of documentation. The two aspects are integrated and complement one another.

In the years which preceded the 1868 revolution two main lines of development in the theatre can be traced : one which sought to make the theatre more morally uplifting, and one which sought to make it more palatable and accessible to the public than it had been previously. López de Ayala and Tamayo y Baus in the 1850s had headed a movement which, like the 'théâtre utile' in France, aimed at portraying on the stage the triumph of duty and highmindedness over instinct and passion. López de Ayala's preface to *Un hombre de estado* (1851) spells this out clearly :

He procurado en éste mi primer ensayo, procuraré lo mismo en cuanto salga de mi pobre pluma, desarrollar un pensamiento moral, profundo y consolador. Todos los hombres desean ser grandes y felices; pero todos buscan esta grandeza y esta felicidad en las circunstancias exteriores; es decir, procurándose aplausos, fortuna y elevados puestos. A muy pocos se les ha ocurrido buscarlos donde exclusivamente se encuentran : en el fondo del corazón, venciendo las pasiones y equilibrando los deseos con los medios de satisfacerlos, sin comprometer la tranquilidad.[23]

[22] Reginald Brown, *La novela española, 1700-1850*, (Madrid, 1953); José F. Montesinos, *Introducción a una historia de la novela en España en el siglo XIX*, (Valencia, 1955); Juan Ignacio Ferreras, *Los orígenes de la novela deciminónica, 1800-1830*, (Madrid, 1973) and *La novela por entregas, 1840-1900*, (Madrid, 1972).

Many of the *arreglos* at this time, also favoured by López de Ayala, were from the French 'théâtre utile' and from Calderonian drama. In the cases of *arreglos* of foreign works sometimes changes were demanded by the censor in order to make the play 'moral'. Ixart recounts that the censor, when faced with *Las circunstancias* (1867) by Gaspar, demanded that a promise of marriage should be made to the *seducida*, 'aunque no era éste el nudo de la trama ni mucho menos'.[24]

This moralising trend in the Spanish theatre is relatively well documented in comparison with the *género chico*, paradoxically so, since this second type of theatre worked on the assumption that the theatre needed to find new life by adapting itself to the criteria of popular demand, and was likely to have reached a wider audience.[25] The Bufos, the most extreme form of the *género chico*, are almost without trace in histories of the theatre, perhaps since they were considered to be a totally degenerate form, typical of the superficial society which delighted in them. They were imported from France by the impresario Arderíus who converted them from the 'opéra Bouffe' into the 'Bufos madrileños'. In this genre, satire and caricature were prominent, although contemporary political comment was, as far as we can tell from the printed text, veiled and incidental until the revolution. It is of course possible that much was conveyed by non-verbal aspects of the performances. The Bufos were inaugurated with a performance at the Teatro de Variedades of *El joven Telémaco* by Eusebio Blasco on 22 September 1866. It recounted the story of Telemachus in mocking and deflating terms. In a post-script to the first edition of this play, Blasco described the aims and origins of the new genre :

> Mucho tiempo hacía que mi íntimo amigo Francisco Arderíus y yo, pensábamos en la necesidad que se sentía en Madrid de *un teatro dedicado exclusivamente a la caricatura.* Hoy la idea está realizada y el éxito ha superado nuestros deseos merced a la buena acogida del ilustrado público de Madrid, que al aceptar el género tal como se le ha ofrecido y al comprenderlo tal como es, ha animado con su constante y decidido apoyo a la empresa y a los autores dramáticos, para que una y otros le ofrezcan en lo sucesivo obras del *género comico exagerado, sin mas pretensiones que la de divertir al espectador.* (italics mine)[26]

The plays generally took some known subject, whether literary, or based on contemporary life, and subjected it to satire. Typical titles of works put on in 1867 and 1868 were *Pablo y Virginia: zarzuela burlesca en dos actos en verso*, *Los novios de Teruel: Drama lírico burlesco en dos cuadros, en verso,* and *¡¡A la humanidad dolente!! Juicio del Año 1868*. Some works, and *El joven Telémaco* is an example of this, went through a further process of satire by later appearing in *aleluya* form.

---

[23] López de Ayala, 'Al lector', preceding *Un hombre de estado* in *Obras completas de D. Adelardo López de Ayala*, 3 vols., *Biblioteca de Autores Españoles*, nos. 180-182, I, 5.

[24] José Ixart, *El arte escénico en España*, (Barcelona, 1894), p. 51.

[25] For information on the *género chico*, see Ixart, pp. 87-93, and José Deleito y Piñuela, *Origen y apogeo del género chico*, (Madrid, 1949).

[26] Eusebio Blasco, postscript to *El joven Telémaco*, (Madrid, 1866).

Both the moralising theatre of López de Ayala and the antidote provided for it by Arderíus figure in the *Ruedo*, supplying contrasting backgrounds and focussing some political and social differences. The former is clearly linked to the movement towards revolution, and López de Ayala himself is given ample space in *Corte* III.xxi to discuss his aim with the liberal-minded Carolina Torre-Mellada. *Corte* III xxii-xxiii then deals with one of his *refundiciones* given as a benefit performance for Julián Romea. By insistence on the serious tone of the theatre and those who admire it, the whole is shown up as a pretentious sham, and by no means a worthwhile alternative to the Bufos. There is an apparent distinction between the two audiences: the first has some concern for public welfare and moral improvement, the second merely goes to the theatre for enjoyment derived from a process of innocent mockery and derision. In life, as distinct from fiction, the first group will pretend to act out serious roles, such as participation in revolutionary politics, the second will show itself to be empty-minded in its attitude to the public power it possesses. In no way can politics or public action be taken seriously:

> ¡Aquí todo es bufo!
> ¡Bufo y trágico!
> ¡Pobre España!
> Dolora de Campoamor.
> *Viva* 24

As later chapters will show further, Valle-Inclán drew on a wealth of historical background material, and considered its smooth insertion into the text as his touchstone for success in this type of work.[27] When writing the *Ruedo*, there was a particular need for sure touch with detail and the evocation of atmosphere. As a statement of 1925 shows, Valle-Inclán thought it crucial to see what the past was like, so that it would act as a warning with possible positive effect. Spain's future might not be quite so bleak

en cuanto sea superado el siglo XIX con su ridículo individualismo, con su criticismo menudo, con su visión detallista de miope y vuelvan a sentir las gentes los hondos y eternos problemas que están en pie, no para resolverlos cosa no concedida al hombre, pero sí para volvernos a ver con una nueva mirada.[28]

---

[27] See p. 103, n. 11.
[28] Interview of 1925 reprinted in *Primer Acto*, no. 32, (1967).

II

Genesis and Structure of *El ruedo ibérico*

> Todo escritor tiene derecho a que busquemos en su obra lo que en
> ella ha querido poner . . . No es lícito censurar a un autor porque
> no abriga las mismas intenciones estéticas que nosotros tenemos.
> Antes de juzgarlo tenemos que entenderlo.
>
> Ortega y Gasset, *Ensayos de crítica*.

El ruedo ibérico was originally intended by its author to be a cycle of nine
historical novels divided into three series :

Los amenes de un reinado
I. *La corte de los milagros*
II. *Viva mi dueño* (original title *Secretos de Estado*)
III. *Baza de espadas*

Aleluyas de la Gloriosa
IV. *España con honra*
V. *Trono en ferias*
VI. *Fueros y cantones*

La restauración Borbónica
VII. *Los salones Alfonsinos*
VIII. *Dios, Patria y Rey*
IX. *Los campos de Cuba*

The period of history the cycle was to cover was from the months preceding
the revolution of 1868, which dethroned Isabel II, through the restoration of
the Bourbons in the person of her son Alfonso XII, to the death of Alfonso in
1885. The text we now have represents less than a third of the projected work.
It dominated the last ten years of Valle-Inclán's life, but as early as 1928 he
realised that he would be unlikely to complete the cycle.[1]

Genesis

The first complete novel of the cycle to be published was *La corte de los
milagros* which appeared in 1927. It was followed in 1928 by *Viva mi dueño*.
The only complete novels of the cycle to appear in book form before Valle-
Inclán's death on 5 January 1936, they were serialised a few years later in
El Sol. Corte was published in this paper between 20 October and 11 December

---

[1] 'En cuanto a *El ruedo ibérico*, es obra a la cual es lo más probable que no pueda darle
fin, ya por su extensión y mis años, ya por sus dificultades', quoted in G. Martínez Sierra,
'Hablando con Valle-Inclán', *ABC*, 7 December 1928.

1931, and *Viva* between 14 January and 25 March 1932. *Viva*, as it appeared in *El Sol*, was little different from the first edition, but there were significant changes in *Corte*. An extra book, 'Aires nacionales', was inserted at the beginning, providing a powerful opening to the whole series. Also, some additions were made to the episodes connected with the death of the policeman in *Corte* III.xiii. This version of *Corte* remained unknown to the general reading public of later years until it was re-published by Austral in 1968.

Part of a third novel, *Baza de espadas*, appeared in the same paper between 7 June and 19 July 1932. It came out in book form finally in 1958, published by AHR of Barcelona. The introduction to this edition stated that the version had been taken from *El Sol*, but also mentioned that part of the novel had been published in the series *La Novela de Hoy*, numbers 392 and 418. No. 392, *Otra castiza de Samaria: Estampas isabelinas*, came out on 15 November 1929, and formed the basis of *Baza* 'Alta mar', chapters xvi forward. Some textual changes, including two substitutions of names, were later made. The man named as Kropotkin in *Otra castiza . . .* became Bakunin in *Baza*, and Pompolio Mela became simply 'El pollo de los brillantes'.[2]

Baza was not the only novel of the *Ruedo* to have appeared partially in fragments. The existence of a large number of separately published fragments of the cycle complicates the study of the novels' genesis, particularly since many are difficult to obtain. Some of them are listed in Rubia Barcia's biobibliography of Valle-Inclán,[3] and a comprehensive article by H. L. Boudreau, 'The metamorphosis of the *Ruedo ibérico*',[4] makes a survey of how the separately published fragments are related to the completed novels, and of the indications this gives us about Valle-Inclán's changing attitude to the cycle. A fragment that appears to be unknown to Boudreau is a 1925 edition of *Cartel de ferias*, closely related to *Viva* V. As the earliest known published fragment of the *Ruedo* (with the possible exception of *Una tertulia de antaño*), it is of special interest since certain features of it suggest that in some ways it may have been the inspiration for the cycle.[5]

Of the later fragments, *El trueno dorado* is the most significant. Valle-Inclán was working on this when he died, and it was published posthumously in *Ahora*

---

[2] Roberta Salper de Tortella points out in 'Don Juan Manuel Montenegro: the Fall of a King', *Ramón del Valle-Inclán: An Appraisal of his Life and Works*, edited by A. N. Zahareas, (New York, 1968), pp. 317-33 (pp. 318-9), that Valle substituted the name of Pablo Iglesias for that of Pedro de Tor in an early article. This type of substitution necessarily undermines theories that Valle may have written *romans à clef*.

[3] José Rubia Barcia, *A Biobibliography and Iconography of Valle Inclán (1866-1936)*, University of California Publications in Modern Philology, LIX, (Berkeley, 1960), p. 21.

[4] Harold L. Boudreau, 'The metamorphosis of the *Ruedo ibérico*', Zahareas *Appraisal . . .*, pp. 758-76.

[5] A. Sinclair, 'The first fragment of *El ruedo ibérico*?', *Bulletin of Hispanic Studies*, XLIX, no. 2, (April, 1972), pp. 165-74. The main critical articles on the fragments of the *Ruedo* are Boudreau, art. cit.; V. A. Smith, '*Fin de un revolucionario* y su conexión con el ciclo ibérico,' *Revista de Literatura*, XXVI, nos. 51-2, (1964), 61-8; five articles in Emma Susana Speratti Piñero, *De 'Sonata de Otoño' al esperpento*, (London, 1968): 'Como nació y creció *El ruedo ibérico*', pp. 243-8, 'Acerca de *La corte de los milagros*', pp. 249-72, 'La aventura final de Fernández Vallín', pp. 295-312, 'Las últimas novelas de Valle-Inclán', pp. 313-27.

between 19 March and 23 April 1936. In his article Boudreau suggests that *Trueno* shows a re-thinking in the orientation of the cycle. In taking up the episode of the policeman who is killed in *Corte* III.xiii (an episode already enlarged in the 1931 *Corte*), and expanding it to give importance to Inda and Sofi, and to introduce Fermín Salvochea, Valle-Inclán was preparing the reader for the characters who were to have most significance in *Baza*, thus strengthening the bonds between the novels of the cycle. The earlier introduction of Salvochea has another effect. He is the one character of the novels obviously admired by the author, and his presence, as an antidote to a view of an otherwise degenerate Spain, is reinforced by this insertion in the first novel.

The other main indication we have of a change of emphasis is the addition of 'Aires nacionales' to *Corte*. This sharpened the focus on revolution and brought the military to the fore. The series of short *cuadros* highlights the activities of the army which co-operates in the control of riots and disturbances right up to the moment of the September *pronunciamiento*. Prim stands out, at this stage leading the forces of control, and not those of revolution. Part of the reason for the concentration upon the army here is to provide a background for the novel : the violent suppression of rioting that it portrays is something that we must assume to continue throughout the duration of the events in the novel. Furthermore, the military, and Prim in particular, are seen as forces to be reckoned with in Spanish politics.

The increased emphasis on the military makes sense in the context of the novels as dealing with a historical period, but this is not all. It is possible that this change in the 1931 edition was intended to make the parallel between Spain of 1868 and modern Spain the more obvious. Primo de Rivera's regime had just bitten the dust, but it was not clear, even in the relative optimism of 1931, that the Spain of the Second Republic would be free of the army as a problematic force. The increasingly jaundiced view in the *Ruedo* of the part played in politics by the army, which reaches a peak in *Baza*, could well have resulted from the author's opinion that history was to repeat itself with another military coup. The events of 1936 were to vindicate such pessimism. Prim is singled out by Valle-Inclán, not so much for his role in 1868 (for which he is admired by most modern historians), but as the epitome of an *espadón* whose presence would bedevil the development of Spain's politics.

The changes in the orientation of the cycle which were taking place towards the end of Valle-Inclán's life show some desire that his readers should grasp modern analogies. The re-working of episodes, and the inclusion of central political discussions in *Baza* 'Alta mar', strongly suggest that between 1931 and 1936 Valle-Inclán became disillusioned with the Second Republic, and foresaw with gloom the political future of Spain, torn by its political factions, and beset with the old problems of corruption and vested interests. The only group possibly outside this closed circle was that of the anarchists : hence the increased emphasis on their role in Spanish life.

In addition to this, Emma Susana Speratti Piñero, a critic responsible for much essential groundwork on Valle-Inclán, has indicated Valle's tendency in this period to see parallels between historical situations and those of his own time. In an article on Manuel Azaña's book, *Mi rebelión en Barcelona*, Valle-

Inclán had established a parallel between the circumstances surrounding the imprisonment of Azaña and those which had caused the fall of Salustiano Olózaga in the preceding century.[6] In another article he had mentioned Cardinal Antonelli, a character who appears briefly in the *Ruedo*, and commented upon his modern equivalents : 'aún anda por el mundo la sombra del cardenal Antonelli. De su política no faltan recientes ejemplos en España. Política inmutable, del más puro egoísmo dogmático, que impone la sumisión de todos los sentimientos y aun de los intereses nacionales a los fines de la Sede Apostólica.'[7] Speratti Piñero concludes that these late articles of Valle-Inclán demonstrate 'que sus ideas o tendencias, con el correr del tiempo, se han agriado profundamente y que el panorama de su época le obliga a predecir horas infinitamente más amargas que las ya vividas por la España de fines del siglo XIX.'[8]

If Valle-Inclán did intend that readers of his novels should grasp contemporary analogies, and it appears that some of the time at least he had this intention, this does not mean necessarily that he indulged in a complex system of closed keys, or that he tampered with the historical material in order to communicate a modern message. There was no need. Spain had remained closely confined to its existential and political *ruedo*. Political revolution had not meant political evolution.

Plot and structure

The assumption that the *Ruedo* is rather like an early shuffle-novel, but totally lacking in guidance to the reader about how he should proceed, is erroneous. Nonetheless one is drawn to initial sympathy with the opinion of Fernández Almagro :

> *La corte de los milagros* y *Viva mi dueño* se pueden leer sin orden o a caprichosos saltos, puesto que no existe un asunto que gradúe sucesivamente sus efectos, espoleando la curiosidad con lo que puede pasar después. Los episodios distribuídos en capítulos muy cortos, viven por sí solos y no los enlaza otra cosa que el vínculo de una común preocupación revolucionaria : el anuncio de que viene la Niña.[9]

It is tempting, but ultimately unsatisfying, to view the *Ruedo* thus, as no more than the kaleidoscopic and distorted re-creation of a historical period, as the artistic portrayal of Spain and her people at a time when the author believed them to have reached an extraordinary level of degradation.

Fernández Almagro rightly pinpoints one element of the structure, however : the growing awareness of the coming revolution. *Corte* is mainly concerned with a general setting of political and social background. It evokes an atmosphere of uncertainty, and shows the realisation on the part of many people of the need for change. The approaching death of Narváez, a reality by the end of *Corte*,

---

[6] Valle-Inclán, '*Mi rebelión en Barcelona:* nota literaria', *Ahora*, (Madrid), 2 October 1935.

[7] 'Sugerencias de un libro (*Amadeo de Saboya*): VI', *Ahora*, (Madrid), 26 July 1935.

[8] *De 'Sonata de Otoño' al esperpento*, p. 338.

[9] Fernández Almagro, *Vida y literatura de Valle-Inclán*, p. 206.

brings to a head the fears of those who rely upon the maintenance of the status quo for their own prosperity, and raises the hopes of those whose prosperity can only come with the disruption of that status quo. The sense of impending revolution is felt most strongly in the books set in Andalucía. Torre-Mellada is made ill at ease by the *mayoral* on the train to Madrid with his notion of money as a social leveller ('el asiento en el tren, como todo en el mundo, es de quien lo paga' (*Corte* 175)) and his news that the date of the revolution is set for September (*Corte* 177). There is question of the sort of politics Spain needs or may have in the future in *Corte* III.iv, VIII.iii, IX.xii, X.xiii, but it is sadly divorced from the *rebaja de caudales* already being brought about by the bandits of *Corte* V.viii. The addition of 'Aires nacionales' to *Corte* in 1931 helped to clarify this progression towards revolutionary awareness by its splintered panorama of minor disturbances, which one must assume to be the background to all the events of the novel. 'Almanaque revolucionario', the opening book of *Viva*, has a similar background function, and focusses attention upon the exiles. A clue that it is background and not the first stage in a chronological progression, lies in a comment upon Vallín : 'Abandonó el halago de una prójima para hacer el gato en los desvanes de las Madres Trinitarias de Córdoba' (*Viva* 10). Vallín's decision to leave Paquita la de los Bufos and to go into hiding occurs in *Viva* II.xvii, and we learn of the suspicions of the governor of Córdoba about disturbances in the convent of the Madres Trinitarias in *Viva* III.ii. *Viva* contains more purely revolutionary material than *Corte*. There is much attention paid to the Vallín story (*Viva* II, III, V, VII), to the plot of the generals (*Viva* II, V, VI, IX) and to the letter Isabel II is persuaded to write to the Pope about the illegitimacy of her son (*Viva* VI, VIII, IX). The question of the next occupant of the throne is uppermost and is stressed not only in the matter of the letter to the Pope, and in that of the Girgenti marriage, but also in *Viva* I and IX, where we see offers made to various candidates, and where the financial involvement in the revolution of the Duque de Montpensier (himself a prospective candidate) is revealed. *Baza* brings us to the very stuff of revolution : plotting, counter-plotting, an attempted coup, and an over-riding preoccupation with those who are to lead Spain to revolution.

The hidden dynamism of the slow, undercover move towards revolution is accompanied by another linear progression in the form of two sub-plots, often difficult to follow through since Valle-Inclán takes no pains to make the way clear for the reader. It is through these plots that we are able to see some of the complex relationships between social groups, and the conflicts of their vested interests.

The first plot hinges upon the meteoric rise to power of Adolfito Bonifaz, who becomes the Queen's favourite, and later loses favour. González Bravo, the man likely to be asked to form the next government after the death of Narváez, has some understanding of Isabel II's capricious approach to politics, and consequently seeks to establish some form of co-operation with the coming favourite, but Adolfito is unwilling. A completely self-centred *señorito farsero*, he is concerned only with his own pleasure, and intends to exploit his favour with the Queen, not to further the political interests of others, but to pay off his gambling debts. He is involved in the killing of a policeman, and in the turbulence at the *feria de Solana*, where he joins in the fray between bandits and gypsies. The Queen's association with this man whose behaviour is so conspicuously scandalous leads to pressure being put upon her to dismiss him. Adolfito himself attributes his downfall to the influence of Sor Patrocinio (*Baza* 17). This may have been one source of pressure, but another almost certainly was the politicians worried by Isabel's reputation as 'otra Mesalina' (*Corte* 233).

That Adolfito is a member of the aristocracy is atypical of the lovers Isabel II had in real life. It may be that the man chosen to be the example of her capricious taking of favourites was made an aristocrat in order to weld together more firmly the complex sections of sub-plots. Adolfito, through his status, is linked to the second sub-plot, that of the 'crimen de Solana', and appears here as the frivolous *señorito* involved in corruption. His fatuous nature lays bare the inability of Isabel II to choose her companions with discrimination, and makes her pathetic striving for comfort and affection the more pitiful.

The second sub-plot, that of the 'crimen de Solana', links the highest and lowest echelons of society by displaying the extent of corruption in Spain. The original crime takes place before the cycle begins. The son of a land-owner has been kidnapped by a group of bandits whose *padrinos* are the Marqués de Torre-Mellada and the Infante don Sebastián. The bandits go into hiding on the estate of the Torre-Mellada family, El Coto de los Carvajales. The central books of *Corte* tell of their problems, and the predicament they are placed in when one of their number is arrested. There is no account of the arrest of the other bandits, but in *Viva* II we find the Niño de Benamejí (Torre-Mellada's steward) trying to obtain help for the *reos de Solana*. It is on this subject that the Vicario de los Verdes approaches Torre-Mellada in *Viva* V.iii. By this time the crime has been immortalised in a *romance de ciego*, and changed out of all recognition with the suggestion of cannibalism on the part of a woman involved.[10] Scraps of the *romance* appear in *Viva* IV.iii and VIII.viii. In *Viva* VIII.ix we learn that Torre-Mellada is pressing for a royal pardon for the criminals, and feels he would be sure of getting it if the monarchy were not constitutional.

The two sub-plots are linked to one another by common participants and by the financial interests they share. The main social groups of the *Ruedo* are those that occupy the extremities of the social scale: the aristocracy, and the

---

[10] It is typical of Valle-Inclán that there is a hidden reference which might support this. The *romance* runs thus:

> La más culpada de todos
> una mujer ha salido;
> a las inocentes víctimas
> sacaba los higadillos,
> y guisados se los daba
> de cena a los asesinos.
>
> *Viva* 219

Earlier we had learnt of a meeting between La Carifancho and La Tía Melonilla with the men bandits at a tavern where 'reunidos en torno de la lumbre, asegurados de que no habría huéspedes ni otro recelo, dándole fin a *una fritada de higadillos*, perfilaba las últimas socaliñas para poner los espartos a la Pareja' (*Corte* 129, italics mine). The recurrence of the diminutive 'higadillos' seems hardly casual.

peasants and bandits. But as Gómez Marín justly asserts, the *Ruedo* shows that by 1868 another important social class had come to the fore : the middle class that had made its money through taking advantage of the weakness of the aristocracy for whom it had acted as steward and banker. Don Segismundo (el Niño de Benamejí) and Salamanca, the banker, belong to this class.[11]

Segis is the vital link between the Madrid aristocrats and the bandits of Andalucía. He asks both Torre-Mellada and Adolfito to help in obtaining a pardon for the bandits who have been arrested, mentioning that the bandits could help them financially in return, an offer that must be tempting. Torre-Mellada, having given over the administration of his estate to Segis, is dependent upon him for the running of his financial affairs, and for the arrangement of loans. In *Corte* VI.x we see how the bandits are aware of his financial straits, and are prepared to use this as a lever for their own ends, providing they have the mediation of Segis. Later the hint made to Adolfito by Segis that 'ese indulto puede ser dinero' (*Viva* 36) shows the former a solution to the problem of his gambling debts. Torre-Mellada himself is further embarrassed by a loan Segis proposes to him to extract him from his difficulties. As it would come from the father-in-law of the revolutionary Vallín, it threatens to compromise severely his position in the Palace.

On a smaller scale, the provision of pleasure, another service rendered by one social group to another, again links the participants in the plots. The decadent nature of the aristocracy is emphasised by its dependence on great numbers of people whose function it is to provide them with entertainment or other services. The relief of tedious burdens is paid for in terms of human dignity, but the characters of the *Ruedo* show a complete lack of dignity and stature in their blindness to this fact.

The general impression that there is a chronological move forward in the *Ruedo* (the presentation of the golden rose in *Corte* takes place in February 1868 and the attempted coup in *Baza* is in August of that year) is undermined by the formal structure of the novels. This might variously be described as circular, pyramidal or even palindromic, in that the outer (i.e. the first and last) books of the novels correspond with one another in setting and subject matter. Such correspondences continue inwards. Thus in the 1927 *Corte* the books correspond as follows :

I 'La rosa de oro' and IX 'Jornada regia' – the Queen in public and private life
II 'Ecos de Asmodeo' and VIII 'Réquiem del Espadón' – the Torre-Mellada family, their life, friends and gossip
III 'El Coto de los Carvajales' and VII 'Malos agüeros' – the Torre-Mellada party arrives at, and departs from, the Andalusian estate
IV 'La jaula del pájaro' and VI 'Para que no cantes' – the bandits and their problems
V 'La soguilla de Caronte', with the bizarre funeral of Dalmaciana, stands as centrepiece and resumes themes of death and degeneration.

[11] José Antonio Gómez Marín, *La idea de sociedad en Valle-Inclán*, (Madrid, 1967), pp. 75-6.

The addition of 'Aires nacionales' to *Corte* stands outside this structure, reinforcing its special position as the opening to the whole cycle.

Viva is similarly organised :

I 'Almanaque revolucionario' and IX 'Periquito gacetillero' – panoramic scene-setting and popular reaction to events

II 'Espejos de Madrid' and VIII 'Capítulo de esponsales' – different aspects of court life, frivolous and serious

III 'El yerno de Gálvez' and VII 'El Vicario de los Verdes' – the convent of los Tres Clavitos, Córdoba : Vallín's escape and its repercussions

IV 'Las reales antecámaras' and VI 'Barato de espadas' – rumours and realities of an uprising of generals

V 'Cartel de ferias', set in Andalucía, establishes the dominant tone of discord and revolution.

Although *Baza* is incomplete, it seems likely that it would have been constructed on a similar pattern.[12]

The formal structure of the novels, which provides an artistically pleasing skeleton, is a strong contributory factor to an impression of timelessness (already partly established by the anticipatory nature of the opening books of *Corte* and *Viva*). The concentric rings of the structure appear to lead nowhere but back to themselves. This static effect is reinforced by a fugal elaboration of mirror patterns, which lead the attentive reader to make absurd comparisons. The mirror patterns are not a series of keys which point to particular historical identities, but simply an aesthetic device to drive home certain absurdities of character and situation in the novels.

Isabel II provokes more mirror patterns than any other character. There are four characters in the *Ruedo* who provide reflections of her in imagery or characterisation. La Tía Melona, who runs an inn, is called 'Reina de España' by La Carifancho (*Corte* 163), but the only obvious connections she has with the monarch are her obesity and the atmosphere of dissimulation and superstition that surrounds her, plus the coincidence that she runs her inn with Paco el Seminarista : this could be a reflection of Isabel's husband Francisco de Asís, whose *neo* leanings were renowned.

Paquita la de los Bufos is another mirror-character who appears in *Viva* II.xvi. Referred to as one of two *palomas* (a possible allusion to the many times Isabel is said to speak with 'bucheos de paloma'), she is described as an 'estrella coreográfica con un lujo que mete miedo : Abono a los toros, peinadora, cenas con toda la goma, una alcoba como la de una reina, cama dorada, armario-espejo' (*Viva* 44). The details of her 'alcoba de una reina' correspond with the 'lecho de columnas con leones dorados' of Isabel (*Corte* 237). It is not surprising that both of them should drink chocolate, but Isabel's 'bigotes de chocolate'

---

[12] For more detail on structure see Jean Franco, 'The concept of time in *El ruedo ibérico*', *Bulletin of Hispanic Studies*, XXXIX, (1962), pp. 177-87; H. L. Boudreau, 'The circular structure of Valle-Inclán's *Ruedo ibérico*', *PMLA*, LXXXII, no. 1, (March, 1967), pp. 128-35; Manuel Bermejo Marcos, *Valle-Inclán: introducción a su obra*, (Madrid, 1971), pp. 324-30.The latter observes how the novels resembles the bull-ring in form as well as in name. To some degree this extends to the social structure of the spectators in a bull-ring.

(*Corte* 238) are exactly reflected in those of Paquita (*Viva* 48). The combined reflection underlines the vulgar characteristics of the Queen. In her tastes and attitudes she is no better than a Madrid *coima*, and there is no difference between her royal suite and the *coima*'s boudoir either in decor or in the events that take place there. In addition, one suspects Valle of having confused, whether deliberately or otherwise, the names of Isabel and her husband, a detail also present in the *Farsa y licencia de la reina castiza*.[13]

Doña Juanita Custodio presents a gentler reflection. A 'jamona de abolengo liberal', she enjoys the social pastime of running a *tertulia*, 'la clásica tertulia con lotería de cartones, noviazgos, juegos de prendas, rigodones y lanceros' (*Baza* 34). Apart from the adjective 'jamona' (often applied to Isabel in the popular press), and her delight in the games and frivolities of the *tertulia* (popular interests shared by Isabel), there is a statement made by her which echoes one of the biggest jokes made about the Queen and her husband in the satirical press. When she is discussing the revolution with López de Ayala, she says that the revolutionaries are being too cautious and declares '¡Como yo llevase calzones, estaba armada la revolución en Cádiz!' (*Baza* 35). This echoes the remark Isabel was reputed to have made at the time of the African campaign of the early 1860s in which Prim made his name. The joke was on her husband, who was said to have murmured 'Yo también', a remark indicative of the fact that he was the underling in the ill-matched couple and that his virility was questionable.

The strongest mirror figure for Isabel however is Doña Baldomera, a real-life character who was the daughter of Larra. We notice in them both a desire to save dubious lame ducks. Isabel is prepared to pawn jewellery to save Adolfito (*Viva* IV.xiii) and we have Torre-Mellada's assurance that she would intercede for the bandits of Solana if she were not bound by the constitution (*Viva* VIII.xi). Doña Baldomera takes the initiative in trying to ease the conditions of captivity of Inda (*Baza* 'Alta mar' xxiii, xxv, xxvii, xxxi). She makes her appeal to the human pity of the other passengers and not to their reason. She shares coquettish tendencies with Isabel, even in exchanges with the prophetic Bakunin : 'A Doña Baldomera no se le iban los azorados arreboles, fluctuaba indecisa y deseosa de iniciar un coqueteo. El apóstol abría sobre ella las flores azules de sus pupilas, y la jamona se inquietaba, deseosa de producir en el grande hombre una impresión inolvidable' (*Baza* 116). She too is described as a 'jamona' (*Baza* 116, 118) and speaks with 'bucheos de paloma' (*Baza* 118). Like Isabel, she shows an enthusiasm for saints, and describes Salvochea as a 'santo laico' (*Baza* 124). What crystallises the connection between the two is a famous *aleluya, Historia de una cualquiera que no es Dª Bal-Domera*. Possibly published before the revolution, the *aleluya* ostensibly relates the financial scandals surrounding Doña Baldomera, but by implication, principally from the title, hints that Isabel II was similarly involved.[14]

[13] See Chapter III, I, note 23.

[14] An *aleluya* is a broadside with a series of woodcuts or engravings, normally forty-eight, each illustration either standing on its own or being accompanied by couplets, tercets etc., or a single line caption. The oldest *aleluyas* have no such verbal comment. Originally *aleluyas* were of a religious nature, recounting, for example, the lives of saints. The individual

Other parallel situations present odd reflections and contrasts. Santiago, the patron saint of Spain, is referred to at several points in the cycle. The celebrations of *Viva* V are motivated by the feast of Santiago el Verde. Prim is given the nickname of 'Santiago Matamoros' or 'Patrón Mata-moros' (*Corte* 11, *Viva* 166, *Baza* 181), but the implication is not that he is the saviour of Spain so much as that he imagines himself to be so, and has a stylised, romantic idea of his own role in the revolution. The illusions and *cursi* nature of his ideals are brought out in *Viva* VI.xii, where there is a description of a statue of Santiago : 'Sobre una consola con perifollos monjiles, mataba moros, entre cirillos verdes, el Patrón de España' (*Viva* 167). Prim, like Santiago, has become a symbol, and this is to lead to the disillusion of many when they see him faced with the political problems of post-revolutionary Spain.

The question of the paternity of Alfonso XII, which is the subject of Isabel's letter to the Pope, is reflected in the insult given to Gonzalón Torre-Mellada by Paúl y Ángulo (*Baza* 201) (the same insult Valle-Inclán is said to have given to the son of Echegaray), and indeed there is a general mirroring of Isabel and her husband in the Torre-Mellada couple. Both the King Consort and Torre-Mellada are shown to be decidedly effeminate, and strong *neos*. Their wives have considerable personal independence, both in their politics and their morality. Both Alfonso and Gonzalón are physically weak and likely to die young. The religious hypocrisy, or religious double thinking, of Torre-Mellada is reflected in both the religious confusions and superstitions of the Queen, for whom he acts as a moral support, and in the religious double-thinking of the King Consort, who adopts motives of moral righteousness to justify actions resulting from wounded pride.

The *Ruedo* is complex in structure and intention. The reader is given an absolute minimum of guidance through the plots, and although close and careful re-readings are capable of rendering many hidden riches of cross-reference and repercussion, the validity of a work of art so intentionally obscure must be questioned. One might want to argue here that, even if the average reader (a concept one suspects Valle-Inclán would have abhorred) cannot follow all the events and implications of the novels, he will at least have gained an impression of the era that is accurate in the following respect : Spain in 1868 was chaotic, its events emanating from the most unlikely sources, its most prominent figures indistinguishable from its criminals in their behaviour. Such an argument does not, however, finally resolve our problem. Without a detailed knowledge of the period, the reader is left with only his instinct to assist him in evaluating where the natural reflection of chaos ends and where art begins. He is impeded in his task of evaluating the novels as art, and the novelist has done himself some disservice in thus restricting both the range of readership and the possibilities of critical assessment.

---

illustrations were cut up and distributed during *Sábado de Gloria* celebrations, and thrown into the crowd at the point where the priest celebrating Mass said 'Aleluya'. Later *aleluyas* extended their subject matter to include folk-lore, stories, plays, moral tales, historical and fabulous material, educational subjects or sheer entertainment of a humorous kind, and contemporary comments on politics and other events. (I am indebted to Mrs. Helen Grant for much of the information in this note.)

III

The Mythical Figures of Reality

Ruede la bola
Caiga el que caiga;
Siga el embuste,
Viva la farsa.

El Papel de Estraza (Valencia), 11 May 1866.

Valle-Inclán's handling of a historical framework is seen at its clearest in the characterisation of central non-fictional figures, since in this area we have a corpus of certain well-defined characteristics attributed by the popular press to men and women prominent in public life, and close comparison and correlation with Valle-Inclán's creations is made possible. There are only a few isolated instances when we can say with some assurance that a particular source was used, and where, as a result, special illumination is given to Valle's intentions and methods. There is, however, overwhelming evidence of a general acquaintance of the author with this type of source, and since myths about the habits and actions of figures in public life were spread through a wide spectrum of the popular press, it is possible to speak of Valle's selection, rejection or modification of a type of material, even when a precise source may not be identifiable. In this chapter, five characters are examined : Isabel II, the King Consort, Sor Patrocinio, Padre Claret and Prim, all of whom were prominent in popular literature and mythology. Within the *Ruedo* itself they dominate in those books set in court circles or, in the case of Prim, in books concentrating on the conspirators. This however is not to the exclusion of the varied background of the petty aristocracy, nor is their importance restricted to those books in which they actually appear, since their actions and attitudes have repercussions throughout the whole of the trilogy. It is because of their central importance in both source and creation that they are concentrated upon here, and not because they are the only instances where Valle-Inclán has drawn upon the popular source for his characterisation. The figures of the Duque de Montpensier, Fernando de Coburgo, Alfonso XII, Nicolás María Rivero, González Bravo, Salustiano Olózaga, Sagasta and Cánovas del Castillo all show a similarly clear awareness of popular characterisation.

When considering popular and journalistic portrayals of public figures in the revolutionary period, we should bear in mind the nature of the press itself, and its approach to comment upon political matters. Even before the revolution of '68, with the scope of comment restrained by tight censorship laws, there had been a general tendency to focus attention upon personalities, personal qualities and defects, rather than to deal with political problems stated in abstract terms.

The historian Bermejo, himself not free of this defect, commented upon the tendency as displayed in the press of 1864 :

La atmósfera política, como ahora se dice, estaba viciada; la prensa española no se ocupaba más que de las personas; los más sagrados intereses nacionales sucumbían, mientras los fundamentos de la sociedad se traían y se llevaban en discusión de cháchara por sueltos y gacetillas; y los vicios, las ridiculeces, los defectos físicos de los hombres de Estado, y hasta los de personas oscuras, a las que se suponían influyentes eran el tema predilecto de los artículos editoriales de los periódicos más reputados. La injuria se hizo tan de nuestras costumbres, que nadie se avergonzaba ni de provocarla ni de inferirla, y las reputaciones y los nombres propios más distinguidos sonaban desde los palacios hasta las plazuelas, sirviendo de blanco por la noche a la calumnia de salón, perfumada y envuelta en seda, y por la mañana a la procaz y tabernaria del más bajo vulgo.[1]

This reference to the press of 1864 can be applied with even greater justice to the post-revolutionary press with which we shall be particularly concerned.

I ISABEL II AND THE KING CONSORT

In the popular revolutionary press, Isabel II is the person most frequently singled out for comment and vilification. She provoked more satirical broadsides than any other figure of authority who lost power with the 1868 revolution.[2] Publications of a serious nature paid her scant attention : while the liberal *Iberia* did relate some anecdotes about her, it maintained its own satire on a relatively harmless level, and sought to deflate the more bombastic comments of others, reserving direct comment for serious criticism.[3] This restraint was not evident in the press of a lower tone, where the Queen was made to bear the brunt of stored-up rancour against the Bourbons, and was made personally responsible for the evils of her reign. The naive assumption made in many violent pieces of this period was that, in ridding itself of Isabel and the multiple immoral practices ascribed to her, Spain was ridding itself of its political problems. In short, Isabel II suffered considerably from the type of personal mud-slinging described above by Bermejo.

[1] Bermejo, *Estafeta*, III, 639.

[2] This follows W. A. Coupe's theory of 'proportional survival of broadsheets' by which it is assumed that there is some correlation between surviving sheets of a certain type in relation to the total number of surviving sheets, and the proportion of the same part to the whole at the time of publication. See *The German Illustrated Broadsheet in the Seventeenth Century*, (Baden-Baden, 1966), I, 83.

[3] Contrast the deflation of 3 January, 1869, 'Isabel y su esposo se marcharon como habían venido, es decir, saliendo por la puerta en lugar de saltar por la ventana', which appeared in the 'Gacetilla' section, with the stronger comment elsewhere in the same number :

Isabel fusilaba por docenas sin dar la menor señal de emoción; cuando venían a contarle que veinticinco sargentos acababan de recibir sus seis balas en el estómago, ella replicaba con una calma heroica

—¿Vamos hoy a almorzar al campo?

Isabel's obesity

In the *Ruedo* (*Corte* II, X, *Viva* IV, VI and VIII), Isabel II dominates, her personal corpulence adding weight to the personal and political power that she wields. Wobbling precariously on the pinnacle of a power structure, she is clearly someone lacking the capacity to exercise that power, or even to maintain her balance. More than human in her moral fragility, she is also inept in the management of difficult personal and political relationships. But, more than in any other way, she dominates the *Ruedo* and the popular press by her all too solid physical presence. Valle concentrates upon this side so that we see her as a woman of 'carne y hueso' and not as any abstract concept, thus highlighting the absurdity of her situation.

The emphasis on her corpulence is such that the Queen appears to enjoy only the life of the flesh, a flesh that is oppressive in its presence, with its quality of 'mantecas' (*Viva* 92), or scarcely more grand, the 'opulentas mantecas' of the official portrait (*Viva* 89). Descriptions of her are predominantly vulgar in tone : she is 'chungona y jamona' (*Corte* 28). Her problem is that she is both 'regia y plebeya' (ibid), a combination which fixes the adjectives 'empechada y matrona' (*Viva* 96) as pejorative rather than neutral comment. For the Queen, her body is an obvious tool of coquetry, so that when she feels a need to manipulate a political situation, her decision is predictable : she tells her lady-in-waiting 'Tengo interés en gustar . . . Ya sabes lo que quiero decir; Me vistes con descote bajo' (*Corte* 238).

Valle-Inclán's portrayal of the Queen uses the main techniques of the caricaturist. Her obesity is singled out for attention, but also we are drawn to concentrate on specific manifestations of it : her hands and lips. Again, it is not just the obesity itself which is revealed to us, it is the incongruous contrast that it presents with the supposed grandeur of the Queen's status. Her hands, 'torpes y feas', do not fit the role of royalty and yet they must : 'tan bastas y grandotas que podían manejar como un abanico el cetro de Dos Mundos' (*Viva* 94). Twice she manages to get inky fingers when signing documents of importance (*Viva* IV.vi; VI.xiv). Her mouth, too, is fixed firmly in contours of traditional caricature. It is 'el belfo borbónico heredado del difunto rey Narizotas' (*Corte* 23),[4] and it emits 'hipos de paloma buchona' (an image repeated in *Corte* 12, 28; *Viva* 10, 207, 209). The primary purpose of making her coo like an over-stuffed dove is to show that she tries to create an aura of gentle regality, but as the cry of the dove is a persistent one, so there is the suggestion that she protests too much, and the constant allusion to the 'buche' (the craw of the dove) reverts our attention to her greed and obesity. Since, moreover, doves are also noted for excessive love-making, criticism on the sexual level is also introduced into the description. In his insistent use of this image, Valle-Inclán perhaps also had in mind the meaning of 'prostitute' occasionally given to the word 'paloma'. (See Besses, *Diccionario de argot español*, (Barcelona, 1906).)

Nonetheless, such moral failings of Isabel II as are highlighted by Valle-Inclán pale in significance when placed alongside the popular vision. Aspects of her person which one could normally assume to be purely circumstantial

[4] i.e. Ferdinand VII.

were seen to be indications of her moral state. Thus, for example, her obesity was taken by many to be a sign of general moral laxity and sensual indulgence. Graphic caricature concentrated above all on her obesity, working on an equation by which her excess weight implied reduced dignity. At their most innocuous, popular graphics make the Queen look like a fat bourgeois matron rather than a regal figure – but others make her seem podgy and stupid into the bargain. In some of the more outrageous caricatures she is presented not just as fat, but in a state of undress. *La Flaca* of 6 June 1869 had a caricature entitled 'Corpus de la Revolución – La procesión que va por dentro' which represented a procession of anti-revolutionary figures bearing a banner on which Isabel II appeared in a topless dress, the implication being that the forces of reaction wanted to support a form of government which was basically vicious and immoral. Again, on 31 July, the paper returned to this theme with a cartoon of 'Los enemigos del alma revolucionaria' in which the figures of the World and the Devil were represented by Olózaga and González Bravo : Isabel predictably appeared as the Flesh.

For Valle-Inclán the cause of the Queen's obesity is obvious : it comes from over-eating, not a vice of infernal standing as in Bosch, but a human peccadillo. It is almost a childish gluttony, in which snacks of *chocolate* predominate (*Corte* 237, 240; *Viva* 99). Similarly, in her world, even slight political rewards come in the shape of sweetmeats : Torre-Mellada is sent away with one like a child (*Viva* 96). Her memory is food-dominated. The central recollection of the time when the Palace was besieged in her childhood is that of the diet : '¡Dos días a galletas y chocolate !' (*Viva* 156) – and here the King Consort is obliquely linked to her by the mention of his 'sonrisa de pastaflora'. The instances in the satirical press where Isabel's obesity is shown to result from such a simple and innocent cause as greed are by contrast rare, although *El Cencerro* (Cencerrada 14, 1869) diverts from the diagnosis of immorality supplied by *La Flaca* by a different and hardly more flattering image :

> Tiene much parecido
> el cerdo con Isabel :
> se ocupan en engordar,
> gruñir, dormir y comer.

Vulgarity of the Queen

In the *Ruedo* the Queen's tendency to greediness is just one facet of a portrait of a person who is essentially vulgar. Adjectives used for her hands, 'bastas y grandotas' (*Viva* 94), 'achorizadas y gigantonas' (*Viva* 208), indicate that she suffers from erysipelas, but also suggest a woman of the *pueblo*. Her joking manner is described as particularly Bourbon ('chungada borbónica' (*Viva* 157)), but it is also low class ('sandunga populachera' (*Viva* 103)), or the two combined ('La Señora amontonaba con sandunga el labio borbónico' (*Viva* 106)). The principal suggestion is not however that the Queen belongs to the *bajo pueblo*, but that she is close to that section of the *pueblo* seeking to better itself. This is revealed above all by her gestures and mannerisms : 'Doña Isabel se abanicaba con reservona suspicacia de alcaldesa' (*Viva* 100). Vulgarity also breaks out in humour and speech. After the strain of the *rosa de oro* ceremony, she relaxes and calls Doña Pepita Rúa 'un badajo cascado', 'pánfila' and 'tarambana' (*Corte* 22–3). For Isabel, the job of monarch requires 'regios disimulos' which are forgotten in the privacy of the Royal apartments (*Viva* 103). She is portrayed as a more than normal, more than human woman, for whom the Spanish throne is uncomfortable in the dignity it requires.

Valle-Inclán's portrait of Isabel II picks up the elements of the popular vision of her, but completely alters the perspective. Whereas for him her tastes are a means of revealing the human creature within the regal casing, a rather base and stupid creature, but nonetheless human, for the press those same tastes were taken as a sign of her lack of concern for the nation's problems, and so just as the legend of Nero fiddling while Rome burned grew, so did the legend of Isabel dancing the can-can while Spain went to rack and ruin. After the revolution, *El Cencerro* (Cencerrada 7, 1869) alleged that she had found new employment as a 'corista de zarzuela', but the previous number of the paper spoke of a more funereal dance :

> Baila Isabel el can-can
> al compás del gori-gori :
> danza Claret; canta Bravo,
> y se lo toca Marfori.

This commentary lacks the bite of another poem whose intent was barely hidden. On 22 April 1865 *Gil Blas* had published a 'Serenata Marrueca' in which Isabel's gaiety was taken to be an affront to the Spanish people whose sufferings she ignored :

> *De todos sabes que eres querida,*
> *por todos sabes que eres hermosa,*
> muchos envidian tu buena vida,
> y te festejan en verso y prosa.
> Bajo la huella de tus zapatos
> gruñen los perros, chillan los gatos,
> buscan su sombra los cigarrones
> y hasta en invierno nacen melones :
> joven y rica, gorda y casada,
> tú lo eres todo, yo no soy nada.

One point on which Valle-Inclán and the popular press coincide here is in ascribing part of the Queen's gaiety to her Bourbon background. The coincidence is, however, minimal since for Valle-Inclán Bourbon associations relate to feature and gesture alone, whereas for *La Saeta* of 25 October 1868, a 'carcajada borbónica' is linked to a history of vice and cruel unconcern, and is emitted by the Queen to hide her anger at the words of Oedipus in a play : 'Huye infeliz, del tálamo y del trono que manchó el crimen.'

The King Consort

If the story of Isabel II had been merely a fictional extravaganza, the King Consort would have been essential as a foil to her in both appearance and character. Reality deemed that he should be effeminate and ridiculous, unable to play out the difficult role of Consort in such a way as to maintain his personal validity and independence without becoming a figure of fun. Moreover, the Royal couple were stock motifs of caricature : the insignificant little husband with a domineering wife is the source of humour of many English sea-side postcards and music-hall gags. In the Spanish context there is an added element in the fun-poking which derives from the concern with *machismo*. Underneath the surface of mockery directed at so-called unequal marriages, there lies a note of real censure.

In the journalistic explosion following on the revolution of 1868, the King Consort features prominently, as a part of an absurd family situation, and as a comic figure in his own right. The more scurrilous sections of the press assumed that because of his reputed impotence he must be a homosexual, and so spread tales about his unnatural vice and perversion. One of the most succinct anecdotes about the King Consort's lack of virility was produced by *El Cohete* on 4 October 1868. It referred to the reactions of Isabel and her husband to dispatches from the war in Africa of the early 1860s, reactions which revealed switched roles in the marriage :

> Tratándose de una guerra
> y estando en pleno senado,
> la reina que han destronado
> esclamó con voz que aterra :
> – De mis vasallos en bien
> si vistiese pantalones,
> mandaría mis legiones. –
> Y el rey dijo : Yo también.

Later, in exile, Isabel was said to have declared that if she were a man she would go to Madrid. *La Saeta* of 25 October 1868 harshly criticised the King Consort for his reaction : '*Si yo fuese hombre, iría a mi capital.* Así decía Isabel y a su lado estaba Paquita. Si no será hombre el compinche de Meneses !' *El Caos* was more graphic in its comment on 20 June 1870. It showed a cartoon with Isabel crowning her son Alfonso and added : 'Panchito, el *menor padre de todos,* apoyado en el brazo de la simpática odalisca Men-á-sés ! murmurará arreglándose los papillotes de vez en cuando, «si yo fuera hombre !»'

Valle-Inclán touches on this anecdote so subtly that only those well steeped in Spanish anecdotic history can catch the full implications. The story itself is renowned, the words have become a catch-phrase, but here it is re-used in a situation to suggest the original characters involved. When the ominous gathering of generals takes place in Madrid, Valle-Inclán strings together the comments of the populace on impending events, including 'A estas horas ya se ha ido por los calzones Paquita' (*Viva* 161). The catch-phrase appears again in *Baza,* this time appropriated by Doña Juanita Custodio, the widow impatient for revolution, who declares '¡Cómo yo llevase calzones, estaba armada la revolución en Cádiz !' (*Baza* 35). The link with the original anecdote is made the closer by the fact that Dona Juanita provides a mirror image for Isabel II.[5]

[5] See Chapter II.

Even better known than this anecdote was the King Consort's nickname which clearly pointed to his effeminacy. Instead of his name Francisco being changed into the familiar Paquito, he was called Paquita. This is reported by Valle-Inclán as a piece of straightforward background information : 'daban el remoquete de Paquita al Rey Consorte' (*Viva* 21). The name Paquita was used so frequently in the popular press to refer to the King Consort that it came to have little critical force, though traces of humour remained. It is worth noting that often the King Consort is the only member of the Royal family and entourage to be called by his nickname, or a variation on it.[6]

The King Consort of the *Ruedo* is not only effeminate, less than a man, but puppet-like, less than a person. All his movements and gestures define him as different from the Queen, more than a person in her over-abundant human presence: 'Se movió discretamente una cortina, y salió entonado el Rey Consorte . . . vino a los medios, doblando con primor el pañuelo, el pasitrote currutaco' (*Viva* 155); 'habló con merengue, sacando la cadera' (*Viva* 98); 'menudo y rosado, tenía un lindo empaque de bailarín de porcelana' (*Corte* 26–7).

The novelist has at his disposal more space and leisure for the creation of a character than is possible in the press, permitting him the addition of extra dimensions and suggestive reinforcement. Valle-Inclán supports characterisation which is principally visual caricature by providing a further linguistic dimension, not only in the selection of words or phrases, but also in the manner of diction of different characters. Hence the sugary, flowery speech of the King Consort contrasts sharply with the vulgar turns of phrase emitted by the Queen, just as his voice itself provides a piping counterpoint.

A further type of contrast is evident within the King Consort himself, since his efforts to assert himself and to give an impression of virility are all belied by his voice and gestures. When, for example, he and Isabel raise the possibility of recognising Luis de Borbón (el Conde Blanc), as their nephew, and meet objections from Narváez, he becomes ridiculous in his attempt to reinforce the request, as it is he who relies on his wife's authority in the State : 'El Rey Don Francisco, como a impulsos de un resorte, sacó del buche los enojados tiples de su voz : ¿Y si te lo exigiese Isabelita?' (*Corte* 27). The recognition of the prince is finally achieved, and the King Consort is clearly bowled over by the imposing *machismo* of the newly acquired relative : '¡Qué fuego tienes! ¡En todito descubres la sangre que circula por tus venas! Los Borbones son todos valientes' (*Viva* 99). The irony is that, in admiring the virility of Blanc, the King Consort displays a sexual interest which belies his statement

---

[6] e.g. *El Cencerro* (Cordoba, Cencerrada 7) 1869 :

> Isabel sigue en París
> con toda su parentela,
> y para vivir se ocupan
> cada cual a su manera
> Isabel es hoy corista
> en teatro de zarzuela :
> Dª Paca comadrón;
> Patrocinio cigarrera;
> Marfori mozo de carga
> y González, saca muelas.

that 'los Borbones son todos valientes' as he too is a Bourbon but lacks the virile attributes. Even in normal conversation, after a bullfight, his weakness and social ineptitude break out, for all he can produce as a comment is '¡Y los toros eran muy grandes!' (*Viva* 216).

Extra-marital relationships of the Queen

A natural consequence of the real or supposed impotence of the King Consort (cited by Palmerston as sufficient grounds for objecting to the marriage of Isabel II to her cousin[7]) was the Queen's reputation for sexual immorality which, linked to her expansive personality, often led to acts of indiscretion. The identity and number of the Queen's lovers must ultimately remain a matter of speculation, but Serrano, 'el general bonito', and Carlos Marfori, who eventually received the Ministerio de Ultramar, seem generally acclaimed as belonging to that number. Speculation in the press about the matter was rife, and inevitably rumour was spread about possible links between the Queen's changing affections and changes which took place in Spain's political life. *El Papagall* of Valencia on 13 October 1868 published some *aleluyas* which alleged that Narváez's toleration of Isabel's affair with Marfori was the result of political bribery : 'El insigne D. Ramón/Le brindó su protección./Porque es suerte nada floja/Llegar a alcalde de Loja.' *El Palitroque* (Barcelona) on 22 November 1868 laid down a series of conditions that a new monarch would have to satisfy, and implied that the incidence of sexual laxity in a monarch was linked to general moral irresponsibility. In March of 1886, *Satanás* again raked up the old history of Isabel's love affairs. It is hard to explain the aim of the paper in so doing except in terms of a general desire to blacken the Bourbon name, since by this time Alfonso XII had reigned and died. It published at least two instalments of 'La Boda de Simplicio (Cuento que parece historia)' in which allusion to the Bourbons was hardly veiled. It began : '1. Allá por los años de mil ochocientos y tantos, ocupaba el trono del reino de Tal (muy lejos de España) doña Filiberta I, señora extremadamente obesa, y muy dada a galanteos y escenas amorosas . . . 5. Doña Filiberta no se cuidaba ni poco ni mucho del porvenir de sus súbditos, cuyos destinos tenía encomendados a varios pajarracos que lo *mangoneaban* todo. 6. Ella gozaba más en sus empresas amorosas, 7. y en las que jugaba el principal papel el [si]mpático Mistori 8. y en las que alguna vez fue sorprendida por su casto esposo.' Even more scurrilous was an *aleluya* which is undated but which seems to have been produced immediately after the revolution, since it comments at the end on Isabel's leaving for exile, and the embarrassment caused to Napoleon III by her stay in France. The eighth illustration shows her in her bedroom, with a canary in a cage by the bed, and a soldier just leaving the room. The comment below is : 'Dicen que en cierto cuartel/un canario penetró/ y todo el cuerpo esclamó :/el canario de Isabel.'[8] The eleventh illustra-

---

[7] Bermejo, *Estafeta*, II, 698, recounts that Palmerston told the Spanish ambassador in London that '*jamás daría su apoyo* al enlace de S. M. con el Infante D. Francisco de Asís, porque este Príncipe *estaba imposibilitado física y moralmente de hacer la felicidad privada de S. M. y de la nación española*'.

[8] *Aleluyas madrileñas*, Museo Municipal, no. 7.713. It is likely that this *aleluya* only had a very small circulation. See Plate I. The detail is picked up neatly by Valle-Inclán

tion suggest that Isabel was as fickle with ministries as she was with lovers, and that changes in the two were not unconnected. It shows her trying on a shift with the name of Narváez on it. Those of Espartero, Miraflores and O'Donnell are hanging up. That of Mendizábal is over a chair, and that of San Luis is being held ready.

It is not my concern here to try to establish just how many lovers the Queen may have had, nor even if the rumours of the press had any basis at all in reality. What does matter is the way the press regarded the private life of this Queen so 'poco castiza' (and who, one suspects, would not have been so severely censured had she been a man), and the link it has with Valle-Inclán's vision of her. The first general statement one can make on this is that, although there is frequently a congruence of 'facts' between the popular source and the literary text, the moral judgments and implications are frequently different. Part of the difference derives from the change in moral attitudes between 1868 and 1928, and part from the desire of the novelist to create a more complex vision of politics and society than was produced by his counterpart in journalism of an earlier age.

The kinder revolutionary papers were charitable enough to attribute the Queen's extra-marital affairs to natural coquetry. *El Cencerro* (Cordoba, Cencerrada 9, 1869) related that 'Isabel de Borbón está muy contenta porque la Emperatriz de los Franceses le ha dicho *amiga mía*. Más contento [sic] estaría si se lo hubiera dicho un sargento de rurales'. The comment indicates vulgarity in the Queen, and a naive desire to please, but nothing more, and as such is closely reflected by Valle-Inclán's vision of a common and overweight coquette.

El Cencerro is, however, fairly well isolated in this indulgent attitude to Isabel's sexual mores. Other sections of the press were not prepared to see her love affairs as a manifestation of personal exuberance and gaiety, and censured her for behaviour which they considered to be directly detrimental to the well-being of the Spanish people. *El Cohete* (Barcelona) of 3 October 1868 labelled her Messallina for her immorality, and it is significant that, while Valle-Inclán includes this detail in the *Ruedo*, and by no means gives the impression that she does not merit it, the nickname is included as reported fact, and not as the author's judgment on her. Firstly Don Lorenzo Arrazola relates that 'se la presenta como otra Mesalina' (*Corte* 233), and then the name is shouted at the gathering of the rebellious generals : '¡Mesalina en el Trono de San Fernando!' (*Viva* 163). This treatment is typical of Valle-Inclán's approach to unsavoury or dubious historical material connected with his non-fictional characters. When dealing with the harshest criticisms that were made of Isabel II he tends to report them as having been made, and nothing more. The inclusion of the nickname in this way in fact shows the epithet up as an exaggeration stimulated by the presence of a new favourite, Adolfito.

It is in broadsides and supplements to regular newspapers that we find the most virulent attacks on Isabel. A sheet called *Disparos, de un marino, a Isabel de Borbón* did not mince matters. It told Isabel to flee :

in his explanation for the affection of Rafael Izquierdo for Isabel II : 'La de los Tristes Destinos fue por muchos años Ninfa de los Cuarteles' (*Baza* 195).

> Tus hechos los más infamos [sic]
> y tu vida depravada,
> te ordenan que desterrada
> salgas ya mujer fatal :
> sal, sal, reina Lucifer;
> sal pues, que te despreciamos
> antes que manchar las manos
> en un cuerpo escomunal.[9]

Another broadside, *A la Caída de los Borbones*, dated Madrid 1868, viewed Isabel's dethronement as a direct consequence and punishment of her immorality :

> Corrida va Isabel como una *mona*
> Ludibrio a ser de pueblos y *edades*;
> Justo castigo de las *liviandades*
> Porque mi noble Patria la destrona.

A supplement to *Las Novedades*, which is difficult to date exactly, but which from its contents appears to have been published in September or October of 1868, continued in like vein. Here the tone of speech is violent and indignant, and attention is centred on the way that Isabel's conduct has alienated Spain from the rest of Europe :

> Ella nos ha divorciado de los grandes pueblos que marchan por el sendero del progreso; nos ha presentado a los ojos de la culta Europa como una Nación envilecida, sobre la cual poder descargarse impunemente el azote del esclavo; nos ha hecho aparecer como la burla y el escarnio de pueblos ilustrados.[10]

From this relatively restrained antecedent of Valle-Inclán's assertion that Spain was 'una deformación grotesca de la civilización europea'[11] the supplement becomes highly insulting :

> Arrojad la podredumbre del trono; limpiad el cieno que ha depositado una dinastía ingrata; barred y sanead lo que ha manchado el contacto de una reina impúdica, un rey cobarde y vicioso y una familia inmunda; romped

---

[9] *Disparos, de un marino, a Isabel de Borbón*. Es propiedad de su autor. A pencil date of 1868 – Oct. 23 on the copy at the Hemeroteca Municipal, Madrid, probably refers to the date of purchase.

[10] This is possibly the supplement to no.25, but this date would not agree with the data in Hartzenbusch, *Apuntes* . . . according to which *Las Novedades* was first published 14 December 1850, publication then being interrupted between 4 May and 1 June 1852 and between 21 June 1866 and 7 January 1868. As he lists the paper as a daily, no. 25 would not fit my estimated date of September, but this is based on the subject matter of the supplement which includes a reference to the desertion of González Bravo, which did not occur until after the Cadiz rising of 19 September 1868, and the confident assertion that the provinces would answer positively to the call to liberty, which we may assume to accompany the arrival of the victorious generals in Madrid. It is most probable then that this copy of *Las Novedadaes* is not the one referred to by Hartzenbusch.

[11] *Luces de bohemia, Obras completas*, I, 939.

ese manto de crímenes y devociones, de impurezas y blasfemos rezos, de adulaciones y hipocresías que ha cubierto a la familia real.

In similar tone, another broadside spoke of Isabel as 'la que fue arrojada de nuestro suelo por su relajada vida y virtudes'. Her vice was the vice of all the Bourbons, a race which 'se ve arrojada y despreciada de todas partes como perros rabiosos' : Isabel was the 'apoteosis de todas las liviandades de su raza'.[12] The most outrageous comment of all came from *El Centinela del Pueblo*. Its attack is the more shocking when we realise that on 23 July 1868, when it was calling Isabel 'la más asquerosa de las prostitutas' and was listing the supposed divers paternities of her children in a piece called 'Dinastías incrustadas por el vientre de Isabel de Borbón, Isabel was still on the throne.

The series of attacks on Isabel outlined above shows the lengths to which the revolutionary press was prepared to go, and gives us some type of yardstick for the evaluation of the vision and criticism of Isabel in the *Ruedo*. Censure and mockery are by no means absent from the *Ruedo*, nor even in short supply. Isabel is shown as a clumsy, vulgar woman, unable to fulfil her role as monarch with either dignity or intelligence. But she is not shown as a monster, not even after the style of Catherine the Great. Instead of portraying her with an endless series of lovers, Valle-Inclán concentrates on the rise and fall of a single fictional favourite, Adolfito Bonifaz. Carlos Marfori, from most accounts Isabel's lover at the time of the revolution, is shown only in passing. The most likely reason for this tampering with accepted fact and chronology is that the creation of a fictional lover gave Valle-Inclán greater freedom to develop his concept of Isabel II, particularly on the human side. Bonifaz, moreover, as we have seen in Chapter II, is an indispensable part of the *Ruedo*'s structure, providing as he does a scandalous link between the Queen and the world of the Andalusian bandits.

The rise and fall of Adolfito, Royal lover, coincides with the course of the existing novels of the *Ruedo*. The stages of his amatory career are not clearly signposted, but emerge regularly as both cause and effect of other events in the novels. Initial success with the Queen at the ball which celebrates the presentation of the golden rose (*Corte* II.xi) is followed by governmental pre-occupation about scandal which may result from Adolfito's part in the killing of a policeman (*Corte* II.xxiv). Political interest of a precise nature (*Corte* IX.iv) and a general nature (*Corte* X.v) is displayed in him. By *Viva* IV.xiv he is enjoying the Queen's full confidence, but by the beginning of *Baza* his career has come to an end. That such a relationship can be damaging politically is shown by the elevation of Adolfito to a Royal office, and the repercussions in diplomatic circles of such folly. At the same time we see that the Queen has genuine need for support and affection. Her plea to Adolfito is both pathetic and, in a political context, horrifying : 'Aconséjame otra cosa. Deseo oírte. Tu no me engañas, y te abro mi corazón. ¡Ay nene, temo el fregado que pueden mover esos revoltosos !' (*Viva* 105–106). Adolfito's rise in the Queen's affections

---

[12] *España pendiente de un hilo*, n.d., n.p. Propiedad de R. Torres. Imprenta a cargo de Diego Valero. This *hoja* pleaded in favour of Serrano as the only man who could lead Spain.

is extremely rapid, and her moves to give him a palace post (supposedly as a token of gratitude for loyal services rendered her by his father) are patently to give him easier access to her as a lover. Her actions here highlight her impulsive nature, and also lead the attentive reader to speculate on the nature of the loyal services originally rendered. Although the concentration on the career of one lover alone reveals Isabel's human needs, there is a strong counterbalance to the softening effect in the cynicism of Adolfito, and the Queen's desperate and wilful blindness to his faults.

Valle-Inclán does extend the amorous interests of the Queen beyond Adolfito, but only in the display of a general tendency to coquetry, manifest even in her political life. When arranging for the placement of Adolfito in the Palace, she has to overcome the opposition of Narváez, and to do so combines a ferocious command with the gesture of the coquette which recalls past favours : this is to impress Narváez with her power, and possibly to do so without alienating him personally :

–¡Me traes la cabeza del que disienta!

La Reina Nuestra Señora, chungona y jamona, regia y plebeya, enderezaba con su abanico el borrego del toisón que llevaba al cuello el adusto Duque de Valencia, Presidente del Real Consejo.

Corte 28[13]

[13]Isabel's coquetry and caprice are shown to even greater effect in the *Farsa y licencia de la reina castiza* (1922), which also gives us an instance of Valle-Inclán's use of sources. In the *farsa* Isabel goes in disguise to a *verbena* and enjoys an anonymous flirtation. Valle appears here to be basing his plot on the record of Antonio Guzmán de León, who relates how Isabel was persuaded to go to a masked ball disguised as a nun. Her escort was a Capitán de Ingenieros she had met at the Teatro del Circo. A scene ensued at the ball which was reported in La «*Esperanza*» 21 February 1848. See Guzmán de León, *El último Borbón*, 2 vols., (Barcelona, 1869), II, 1027 ff.

The closing action of the *farsa*, where the King Consort arrives unexpectedly at Isabel's apartments to demand his conjugal rights and finds his way barred by El Gran Preboste, bears a striking resemblance to the account given by Pedro de Répide of an incident which occurred in April 1857. In both cases, two deaths result from a skirmish which takes place outside the Queen's apartments. In the *farsa* it is Lucero del Alba and El Jorobeta who die (being subsequently revived in the Punch and Judy tradition by a kick in the pants). The participants in the real skirmish were not so fortunate. Répide relates:

Hacía ya un par de meses que su presencia [i.e. Antonio Puig Moltó] era asidua en Palacio, cuando una noche, a fines de abril de 1857, estando la reina encerrada en sus habitaciones, mientras en la antecámara hallábase Narváez, con su ayudante, hijo de un conocido título de Castilla, presentóse de improviso el rey Francisco, acompañado del ministro de la Guerra, Urbiztondo, y dió orden de que se le franquease la entrada al aposento donde la reina se había recogido para los menesteres de su vida privada. Opúsose Narváez a que se quebrantara la consigna de que nadie penetrase en la estancia real, y D. Francisco quiso hacer valer sus derechos de cónyugue, que tan rara vez le preocupaban. Hubo más que palabras, y Urbiztondo, sacando la espada, quiso ser valedor de su regio amigo. Trabóse pendencia, que fue sangrienta, pues Narváez acometió al ministro de la Guerra con una estocada mortal cuando el ayudante del duque de Valencia acababa de recibir otra herida funesta de la espada de Urbiztondo. Madrid supo de una extraña epidemia que se había declarado repentinamente en Palacio, y causó aquellas dos muertes publicadas como naturales. (*Isabel II, reina de España*, (Madrid, 1932), 189.)

Given the date of Répide's work, it seems likely that both he and Valle-Inclán had access to a common source.

The portrayal of Isabel's marital infidelity in the *Ruedo* is not neglected or side-stepped in any way, but it is more moderate than the cumulative vision of the popular press. The fact of her immorality is focussed upon as the indulgence of a weak human being. Unfortunately this has devastating political consequences, but the equation of the press which held royal immorality as directly responsible for all ills in Spain, whether economic or political, is avoided. It is not made out to be a wilful depravity that rots the country to the core, but is clearly inappropriate for the dignity of a monarch. Many features of the characterisation of Isabel, her vulgarity, personal effusiveness, persistent coquetry, are based on the popular vision, but in the *Ruedo* they explain in part the reasons behind her immorality. At the same time the more slanderous suggestions of the broadsides are avoided. To some degree the weighting of material in the *Ruedo* resembles the historical accounts of Bermejo and Guzmán de León, who, at the same time as they recount many anecdotes about Isabel's sexual mores (and report them as anecdote and rumour), also give full accounts of the political problems that faced her. The difference between them lies mainly in the way Valle-Inclán is able to bring some twentieth-century hindsight to questions which were contemporary for Bermejo and Guzmán de León. Such hindsight is never explicit, but implicit in the balance of material.

Extra-marital interests of the King Consort

It would be impossible for the extra-marital relationships of the King Consort to provide an adequate parallel and counterbalance to those of his wayward spouse, since the essential element of his character is its weakness and inadequacy, combined with a general inability to assert himself. Above all, he is much more conscious of the requirements of conventional morality, as we shall see below. Despite these general tendencies, his relationship with Meneses did procure him a certain notoriety.[14] A typical allusion to this is that made by *El Papagall* (Valencia) on 18 October 1868 :

> Dícenme que Paquita
> Se marchó a Roma,
> Allí lucirá el garbo
> De su persona.
> Si acaso vuelve,
> Darle muchos recuerdos
> Para Meneses.

In 1871, *El Cencerro* (Cencerrada 117) stated that the King Consort had taken such a liking to Amadeo de Saboya, now installed on the Spanish throne, that he was prepared to leave both his wife and Meneses.[15]

In contrast with such relatively explicit statements, the *Ruedo*, while unequivocally showing the King Consort with all the features of a homosexual,

---

[14] It seems likely that this was the Sr. Ramos de Meneses whom *La Democracia* of 27 May 1866 reported as receiving the post of 'gentilhombre de cámara'. See Mercedes Agulló y Cobos, *Madrid en sus diarios*, III, 298.

[15] 'Doña Paquita ha simpatizado con D. Amadeo de una manera arrebatadora y volcánica. Dice que está dispuesta a jurarle la más amorosa y delirante fidelidad, y a abandonar por él a su mujer y al mismo Meneses.'

does not include Meneses as a character. We do have the outlines of an amorous relationship between the King Consort and the Conde Blanc, however, again revealing Valle-Inclán's preference for a fictional character within this area of his creation. Here, as on many other occasions, language is the subtle indicator of a warmth of feeling. The King Consort's speech, always refined, becomes quite flowery when he is with his nephew, Blanc, and we glimpse the hopes he has for the future of the relationship : 'Su Majestad Don Francisco le susurró en voz baja : "En la intimidad, puedes llamarme Tío Paco" ' (*Viva* 99). The attractions the Conde Blanc holds for the King Consort do not escape the sharp eye of the Queen, who comments to Adolfito :

> Quizá demasiadas redondeces . . . [sic] Pues yo me sé y tú también, donde ha dado flechazo . . . [sic] ¡Que existan esos vicios por el mundo ! No tengo derecho para ser severa con los pecados del prójimo, sin embargo, se hace de necesidad otra lluvia de fuego . . . [sic]
>
> *Viva* 106

Her judgment that her spouse's homosexuality is more culpable than her own adultery derives from the code of *machismo*, but also shows an interesting reversal of the dual morality assumed by that code. Valle-Inclán goes no further in hinting at the King Consort's homosexuality, and never approaches the extremes reached by some of the press, such as the tardy suggestion on 15 December 1878 of *El Vigía* that Paquita should be kept away from Alfonso XII's sisters in case he should involve them in vice with Meneses, as a reward for the latter's services to him.

Isabel's extra-marital affairs were bound to raise questions about the reaction of the Church to her behaviour, and the legitimacy or otherwise of the Royal offspring. Press comment on the attitude of Rome to Isabel was concentrated in two areas : the *rosa de oro*, and a mysterious papal bull which, it was alleged, Isabel II had received from Pius IX in order to resolve some of her matrimonial difficulties.

La rosa de oro

The golden rose, an official papal gift, was presented to Isabel for her virtue as a Catholic monarch, that is, for having delayed so long in recognising the unification of Italy, a political act which had restricted the power of the Vatican.[16] The popular press predictably took the word 'virtue' in a different sense, and launched a series of attacks on Isabel's 'virtue', linking the gift of the rose with gifts of money that she, for her part, had sent to Rome. Such an expensive rose was moreover considered to be useless. As one broadside lamented :

---

[16] The golden rose (an ornament of wrought gold and set with gems, generally sapphires) was blessed by the Pope on the fourth Sunday in Lent, and sent, as the highest honour he could confer, to some distinguished individual. Of more symbolic than material value, it was usually sent for political reasons. Three were sent to Henry VIII of England, the first in 1510 by Julius II seeking support against Louis XII of France. See Sir Charles Young, *Ornaments and Gifts Consecrated by the Roman Pontiffs*, (London, 1860), pp. 14-15.

La rosita regalada
Bien carita nos costó.
Rosa de oro fue llamada;
Bien en oro la pagó,
Nuestra España desgraciada.[17]

The postscript to another broadside, the *Carta del Diablo al Padre Santo* (dated 'En el Tártaro a 10 de Diciembre de 1868') inferred that Isabel, who had hoped that the golden rose and the papal bull would give her some security as a monarch, was irritated that they had proved to give such poor value for money :

Te hago saber que Isabel de Borbón está muy irritada contra ti, y dice que la has dado un camelo mayúsculo con las bulas y la rosa de oro que le mandaste en cambio de los muchos millones que le habías chupado, y que ella chupó antes a los españoles; que aquellos chirimbolos con que pensaba no había poder humano que la destronase no valen tres cominos, y que le has armado un juego de mala ley.

El Palitroque (Barcelona) was more aware of the political side of the matter. 'Una semana en Roma' of 6 December 1868 described the various stages in the relationship between Isabel II and Pius IX. On Monday, Tuesday and Wednesday, messages from the Queen and papal blessings were affectionately exchanged, including the Pope's pardon of Narváez. Thursday brought a papal request for money, 'que voy acabando los últimos treinta millones'. On Friday the money duly arrived, and the rose was promised (here clearly linked to the question of the unification of Italy). On Saturday the Pope was disturbed to learn of the Queen's flight to the frontier, and on her arrival on Sunday on his doorstep hardened his attitude : 'Dadle un ochavo y que se aleje.' The paper was equally critical of the two sides involved in this dubious relationship.

The approach of *El Palitroque* brings us close to the *Ruedo* in its insistence on the complexity of the golden rose affair. We are always conscious in the *Ruedo* that Spain cannot and does not exist in complete isolation. Before the addition of 'Aires nacionales' to *Corte* in 1931, it was the presentation of the rose which opened the cycle, and this was headed by a background of conjecture about how the rose came to be awarded to Isabel – a background of ecclesiastical intrigue, not without political significance stretching beyond the Pyrenees. The rose is seen from the outset as a symbol at the centre of a complex political web, as a decisive move on the part of the Church to assert its ascendancy over the Queen, and a definite statement on its part to say that the Queen supported and was supported by the forces of law, traditional authority and traditional religion. As a counterbalance lay the anxiety of some religious figures lest the presentation of the rose might make the Queen too independent and confident in her own person and virtues. The description of the presentation and the background to it, with its odd mixture of ecclesiastical and diplomatic manifestations

---

[17] *La Rosa que regaló el Padre Santo a Isabel de Borbón.* Signed R.T.R. The pencilled date of 6 November 1868 on the copy in the Hemeroteca Municipal, Madrid, is probably the date of purchase, but will be close to the date of publication.

of pomp and court celebrations, conveys to us on one artistic level what the complexities of plotting and motivation behind the event may be.

Valle-Inclán does not however limit himself to the evocation of the political side of the event (an evocation which raises his vision above that of the press on artistic and intellectual criteria). At the same time he also conveys the essence of the popular view and judgment. He shows us the rather simple reactions of the Queen, which range from childish 'embobamiento' to a crudely mercantile assessment of her obligations. We see her genuine emotion during the ceremony itself which momentarily makes her forget problems of moral responsibility : 'Sobre su conciencia, turbada de lujurias, milargerías y agüeros, caían plenos de redención los oráculos papales' (*Corte* 22). Immediately afterwards she expresses a long cherished desire to send a gift of money to the Pope, thus turning swiftly from a mood of dreamy exaltation to the practical. Here humour creeps in, since she has no notion of what a suitable amount would be, and settles on the sum her husband used to require for keeping quiet about the paternity of her children. As she rightly reasons, 'Dos millones debe ser una cantidad decente, porque en el pedir nunca se queda corto Pacomio' (*Corte* 25). This reaction, which displays admirably the moral muddle the Queen is irrevocably entangled in, also shows two childlike traits : it resembles the sending of a bread and butter letter, and the pleasure of planning a treat. Valle-Inclán does not make criticism inevitable here. The Queen's project of sending money to the Pope is either the action of one who is so accustomed to using money and honours for bribery or as a token of esteem that the papal honour is automatically regarded as one to be paid for in retrospect, or simply the act of a person for whom the distribution of gifts is a personal pleasure.

Another detail in Valle-Inclán's treatment of the rose suggests that a particular popular source may have been used. On 4 April 1869, *Gil Blas* related a dream of Isabel about her future restoration and subsequent political conduct : she would re-impose and intensify the reactionary conditions which had existed before her downfall. The culmination of the dream was formed by a papal message : 'El Santo Padre, sabedor de que volvéis a España, os da su bendición apostólica y os envía otra rosa, porque supone que la que os dio el año pasado estará mustia.' This bears a close resemblance to the description of Isabel's dream in *Corte* in which her good will and inadequate political understanding are humorously juxtaposed :

> Soñaba con labrar la felicidad de todos los españoles : El Santo Padre, señalándola con nuevas prendas de amor, promulgaba una bula que redimía de las calderas infernales a todos los súbditos de Isabel : Las logias masónicas, en procesiones de penitentes, con capuchas y velillas verdes, se acogían al seno de la Iglesia. La Reina de España sentía el aliento del milagro en el murmullo ardiente con que la bendecía su pueblo. ¡Y en este limbo de nieblas babionas y piadosas imágenes brillaba con halo de indulgencias y felices oráculos la Rosa de Oro !
>
> *Corte* 37–8

Significantly, Valle-Inclán omits from his version the feeling of vengeance in Isabel that was implicit in the *Gil Blas* passage.

The papal bull

The result of supposed financial negotiations between Madrid and Rome, according to the more scurrilous sections of the popular press, was a papal bull which granted Isabel special licence in her personal life. It is hard to ascertain whether such a bull did exist, since ecclesiastical documents of a personal nature in the Vatican archives are not made available for consultation. Correspondence between the Papal Nuncio in Madrid and the Secretariat of State in the Vatican during Isabel's reign is available, however, and the letters of the late 1850s, the period when Isabel was alleged to have received her special enabling bull, reveal great concern on the part of the Nuncio about the impropriety of the Queen's conduct, and the unflinching insistence of the Church that she should return to normal conjugal life with her husband and renounce her lover. In view of this, we are bound to conclude that even if some personal bull did exist, it would be extremely unlikely that it possessed the character attributed to it by the popular press.

That the bull was the creation of History, and not an element of history, seems confirmed by the very uncertainty of the press about its nature, beyond the belief that it somehow permitted Isabel considerable latitude in her sexual conduct. *El Caos* on 4 July 1870 printed a 'manifesto' of Isabel in which she flippantly declared :

> Yo nunca pierdo la chola
> por más que me llamen *chula*,
> para estas *cosas*, yo sola
> tengo del papa la bula
> y dejo correr la bola.

The bull was generally reputed to have been obtained at great expense. Most frequently we find the sum of three million (reales) quoted. *El Relámpago* on 10 February 1867 saw this as a regular financial commitment. It referred to a loan of 350 million reales that had been received by Isabel : out of this was first paid a sum of three millions owing for three months' alms 'que se envía mensualmente a Roma, desde hace diez y seis años, en remuneración de CIERTA BULA que Pío IX ha acordado a Isabel II y QUE SU ESPOSO FRANCISCO HA CREIDO DEBER ACEPTAR'. *El Relámpago* was particularly incensed about the social inequity of the situation : liberating bulls were not within the budget of the *pueblo*.

When Valle-Inclán deals with this topic, we note that, superficially at least, he reports the rumours as rumours, by including them as snatches of song. At the beginning of *Viva* appears part of a *romance* being sold by Don Felipito in Madrid :

> – Pro causa naturae
> el Padre Claret
> una bula obtuvo
> para la Isabel . . . [sic]

Viva 23

Appearing as it does, in the first book 'Almanaque revolucionario', it contributes to the general survey of popular attitudes and rumours in the electric atmosphere of Spain in the summer of 1868. A second snatch is inserted at the beginning of *Viva* IX :

> Si es bula o cartilla,
> no se sabe bien.
> Tres millones dicen
> que costó el papel.
> ¿Serán tres millones,
> o pesetas tres? . . . [sic]

Viva 233

Between the two snatches occurs the main part of Isabel's affair with Adolfito, an example of her sexual laxity. Just as there is a reduction to one man of the Queen's extra-marital wanderings, so too is the example itself marked by the briefest of touches : the popular view of how the Queen was able to enjoy such an affair without offending the Pope, that is, through the enabling clauses of the bull. At the same time as he includes this popular explanation for the Queen's conduct, Valle-Inclán also introduces a counterbalance in his portrayal of ecclesiastical attitudes with the disapproval of Sor Patrocinio, who is finally blamed by Adolfito for his fall from favour. Despite this counterbalance, the Queen's private view of her moral obligations in the *Ruedo* comes close to the popular vision. Though obviously worried about how she stands morally herself, she sees the redemption of Adolfito as a good deed that will gain her pardon for sin committed with him. After this, however, she returns to the convenient notion that public and private morals are separate : 'Yo seré juzgada por los méritos que contraiga en el gobierno de la Nación española. Como Reina Católica, recibiré mi premio o mi castigo, pues no me parece natural que se me juzgue por fragilidades que son propias de la naturaleza humana' (*Viva* 104).

The price of paternity

With or without a bull, the Royal offspring could be a source of embarrassment if their paternity were suspect. *El Relámpago* (see above) had stated the problem clearly. Though the King Consort was officially responsible for Isabel's children, the belief that they were fathered elsewhere was strong. So firmly was it believed that the father of Alfonso XII was Puig Moltó, that the child was nicknamed 'El Puigmoltejo', a name referred to by Valle-Inclán (*Viva* 21). As with other instances of unverifiable but possible fact, it is included as a piece of straight reportage, on the same plane of reality as the report of the words of Fernández de Córdova : '¡El Príncipe arrastra una herencia fatal! Hace diez años el favorito era Puig-Moltó. No hace mucho, le hemos visto morir tísico' (*Viva* 227). If anything, the question of paternity gained more importance after the revolution, because of the possibility that the Bourbons might be restored to the throne in the person of Alfonso XII. *El Caos* on 28 April 1870 treated the matter as a joke, and envisaged a situation where Isabel and Marfori, playing at *mus*, were interrupted by the King Consort :

> Llega Paco y dice ¡copo!
> coge los cuartos y . . . [sic] abur –
> los jugadores se escaman,
> y al ver que Isabela, en un
> pedazo de cinta roja,
> carmesí blanca y azul
> se enreda, Marfori a Paco
> grita poniéndose en cruz :
> ¡Que Isabela se halla en cinta,
> ven, no te escapes, mambrú!

Two weeks later, on 15 May, *Gil Blas* reported a more spirited reaction from the King Consort, who in a farewell letter to his wife referred to the children and stated simply : 'Ya sabes que yo he sido siempre amigo de tu honra. Te he servido de paraguas.'

The financial side of this protection had been spelt out on 21 March of the same year by *El Mono Rey* in a poem called 'Borbonicidio' :

> Isabel odia a su esposo,
> Al complaciente marido
> Que mediante algunos céntimos
> Le reconoce los niños,
> Vengan de donde vinieren :
> El hace de papá *postizo*,
> Antes del parto, en el parto
> Y después si dan conquibus.

The level of scorn expressed here by Isabel is only equalled in the *Ruedo* by the section where she comments upon her husband's homosexuality.

Ridiculed as he was for being a figure of fun alongside his licentious wife, the King Consort was at least credited with the ability to look after his own financial interests. *El Vigía* of 12 January 1879 even credited him with exacting a fee for attending the wedding of Alfonso XII with María de las Mercedes : 'Por de pronto, doña Isabel de Puente parece no conformarse con que don Francisco, metido en el complot, mediante una cantidad crecida, *haga de padre* en las negociaciones y fin de fiesta.' In 1869, *El Cencerro* (Cordoba, Cencerrada 15) had considered that 'la [situación] la entienden como nadie Paquita y el Padre Claret'. *Gil Blas*, commenting on a financial crisis, on 13 May 1865 meted out indulgent praise that condemned by its tone :

> Cuéntase con seguridad que Paquita ha hecho su negocio, – jugando bajo cuerda.
> ¡Ya se ve! ¡Cómo Paquita lo sabe todo!

Similarly condescending was *El Cohete* (Barcelona) on 3 October 1868 :

> Dícese que el célebre Paquita se propone no quedarse con nada de los españoles y trata de devolvernos los hijos de su mujer para que sean distribuídos entre sus verdaderos padres.
> ¡Y decían que no era listo!

The financial astuteness of the King Consort appears in the *Ruedo* not as a dominant character trait, but as a facet only. We see it via his wife's calculations about the amount of money she should send to the Pope (see above in the section on the golden rose). Like the press, the Queen admires her husband's ability with money, but tempers it, as the press does, by the use of a scornful nickname.

The King Consort's affronted dignity

Despite his reputation for weakness and effeminacy, the King Consort was deemed to have a modicum of dignity which was naturally outraged by the conduct of his wife. But in both the *Ruedo* and popular mythology, this very dignity becomes ridiculous in the context of his personal inefficacy. On 15 January 1869, *Jeremías* reported the King Consort in conversation with the Emperor Louis Napoleon, or rather, delivering to him a long, nostalgic lament for the life he had lost :

> Estábamos perfectísimamente. *Cuando uno ha sido rey, no puede ser otra cosa.* ¡Oír a todos los que nos rodean que nos dicen : «¡Qué buen mozo ! ¡Qué piernas tan largas ! ¡qué figura tan varonil ! ¡qué voz de bajo profundo ! ¡qué muslos tan proporcionados ! ¡qué caderas tan recogiditas ! No parecen de mujer. ¡Cuán magnífico estaba con e ! [sic] uniforme de coronel al frente de un regimento ! Sí, porque ha sido coronel, ha ganado todos sus grados con la punta de la espada». Todo eso decían de mí, señor. (italics mine)

Here *Jeremías* lays stress on the type of pleasure that could have been enjoyed by the King Consort : his position gave him importance and attracted superficial adulation by courtiers. His personal weakness is to rejoice in this type of hollow and inapposite praise and, ironically, to imagine that his qualities of virility are the source of genuine admiration.

Such outraged squeaks were reported by Bermejo in his *Estafeta*, but with the added rage of the cuckold. The *Estafeta* text closely resembles *Corte* and it seems indisputable that Valle used Bermejo as a source here. What is interesting about the use is the way it is changed to fit the general characterisation given to the King Consort in the *Ruedo*. An examination of the two texts reveals close verbal correlation :

Corte	*Estafeta*
. . . Se ha omitido consultarme para la provisión de cargos en Palacio. *Se ha querido, sin duda, con esa actitud, ultrajar mi dignidad de esposo, mayormente cuando mis exigencias no son exageradas. Que Isabelita no me ame es muy explicable . . .* [sic] *Yo la disculpo, porque nuestro enlace no dimanó del afecto y ha sido parto de la razón de Estado. Yo soy tanto más tolerante cuanto que yo tampoco he podido tenerla cariño. Nunca he re-*	(Benavides has just said that the separation of the couple can do no good to them) : Lo comprendo, respondía *D. Francisco; pero se ha querido ultrajar mi dignidad de marido, mayormente cuando mis exigencias no son exageradas. Yo sé que Isabelita no me ama, y yo la disculpo, porque nuestro enlace ha sido hijo de la razón de Estado y no de la inclinación; y soy tanto más tolerante en este sentido, cuanto que*

pugnado entrar en la senda del disimulo y siempre actué propicio a sostener las apariencias para evitar un desagradable rompimiento . . . [sic] *Pero Isabelita, o más ingenua o más vehemente, no ha podido cumplir con este deber hipócrita, con este sacrificio que exigía el bien de la Nación. Yo me casé porque debía casarme* . . . [sic] *Porque el oficio de Rey lisonjea* . . . [sic] *Yo entraba ganando en la partida y no debía tirar por la ventana la fortuna con que la ocasión me brindaba, y acepté con el propósito de ser tolerante para que lo fueran igualmente conmigo. ¿Y* qué consideración se me guarda? No hablo sólo por mí. Esos nombramientos van a escandalizar en la Nación. ¡La Nación no puede tolerar dignamente el espectáculo y el escarnio que se hace del tálamo! ¡Godoy ha guardado siempre las mayores deferencias a mi abuelo Carlos IV! En ningún momento ha olvidado que era un vasallo. ¡Cierto que son otros los tiempos! Pero el respeto a las jerarquías debe ser una norma inquebrantable. Es la clave del principio monárquico. Mi abuela María Luisa no sé lo que haya tenido con Godoy. ¡Allá su conciencia! *Lo que todos sabemos es el profundo respeto y amor que siempre mostró a su Soberano el Príncipe de la Paz* [i.e. Godoy]. Pero mi situación es muy otra, y con ser tan bondadoso el abuelo dudo que la hubiera soportado. La Reina, con su conducta, se hace imposible a mi dignidad y a la del pueblo español.

Corte 248–9

yo tampoco he podido tenerla cariño. Yo no he repugnado entrar en el camino del disimulo; siempre me he manifestado propicio á sostener las apariencias para evitar este desagradable rompimiento; pero Isabelita, o más ingenua o más vehemente, no ha podido cumplir con este deber hipócrita, sacrificio que exigía el bien de la nación. Yo me casé porque debía casarme, porque el oficio de Rey lisonjea; yo entraba ganando en la partida, y no debí tirar por la ventana la fortuna con que la ocasión me brindaba, y entré con el propósito de ser tolerante, para que lo fueran igualmente conmigo, para mí no habría sido nunca enojosa la presencia de un privado.* [Benavides asks if it is not Serrano who is the factor preventing the reconciliation.] *No lo niego; ese es el obstáculo principal que me ataja para llegar a la avenencia con Isabelita. Despídase al favorito, y vendrá seguidamente la reconciliación, ya que mi esposa la desea. Yo habría tolerado a Serrano; nada exigiría si no hubiese agraviado mi persona; pero me ha maltratado con calificativos indignos, me ha faltado al respeto, no ha tenido para mí las debidas consideraciones, y por lo tanto le aborrezco. Es un pequeño Godoy, que no ha sabido conducirse; porque aquel, al menos, para obtener la privanza de mi abuela, enamoró primero a Carlos IV.* [He realises that Benavides is shocked by this and corrects himself.] *El bien de quince millones de habitantes exige* éste y otros sacrificios. Yo no he nacido para Isabelita ni Isabelita para mí, pero es necesario que los pueblos entiendan lo contrario. Yo seré tolerante, pero desaparezca la influencia de Serrano, y yo aceptaré la concordia.[18]

---

[18] Bermejo, *Estafeta*, II, 804-5. The same passage is used by Pedro de Répide, *Isabel II, reina de España*, pp.101-2.

It is evident from the above that Valle-Inclán adopts the Bermejo order of words almost verbatim when relating the King Consort's disgust with his situation and his realisation that his marriage could have meant the entry into a life of praise and pleasure. But, while the passages resemble one another and the *Jeremías* text in the King Consort's exaggerated sense of self-importance, and his concentration on the outward trappings of royalty, they give most weight to the concern of the King Consort about the over-riding of his authority, and the ridicule of his position as cuckold. In the *Ruedo* this has been exemplified by the failure to consult him over the appointment of Adolfito. Isabel's habit of appointing her lovers to official posts outrages his dignity. He compares his situation with that of Carlos IV, who was at least mollified by the attention paid him by his wife's lover.

Although this point is made in both texts, we should note that Bermejo is referring to a period about twenty years earlier than the revolutionary context of the *Ruedo*. His King Consort speaks specifically of Serrano, with all the indignation of a man recently married and recently cuckolded. Serrano has been the cause of a rift between the King Consort and his wife, and has made no attempt to get into the King Consort's good favour. The words Bermejo attributes to the King Consort here condemn him by their complaint that Godoy 'al menos, para obtener la privanza de mi abuela, enamoró primero a Carlos IV', suggesting that he would have welcomed similar advances from Serrano.

Valle-Inclán's version is a little more neutral. The King Consort dismisses consideration of what may or may not have gone on between María Luisa and Godoy, and refers only to 'el profundo respeto y amor que siempre mostró a su Soberano el Príncipe de la Paz'. If we take Bermejo's version as an accurate report, then Valle-Inclán, in his use of the source, is obviously toning down the situation to the advantage of the King Consort. Normal chronology has been severely disturbed (the twenty years' slip is a more blatant example of meddling with historical order than is normal in the *Ruedo*) and the reduction of the heat and indignation of the King Consort's statement might well be justified by the need for literary verisimilitude. The King Consort of the *Ruedo* has had to bear infidelities and indignities for twenty years, whereas the wounds of infidelity are still fresh in Bermejo's King Consort. But even taking the chronological disjunction as an initial justification for toning down the language, the fact remains that the King Consort of the *Ruedo* does become, to a limited extent, a man who feels the understandable indignation of a spouse, and is not merely a vain man seeking self-gratification. The King Consort develops in the *Ruedo*, and what dignity there is in this speech in *Corte* is diminished in *Viva* 168–9, when he decides to take a moral stand against his wife's infidelity by joining the conspiracy to persuade her to announce the illegitimacy of Alfonso. Here, although the arguments he uses are moral and religious, it is clear that his reaction is that of a weak man who is prepared to use any weapon to defend himself.

Superstitions and religious beliefs of the Queen

It would be impossible to separate the Queen's moral attitudes from her attitude to her religious advisers, Padre Claret her confessor, and Sor Patrocinio. This aspect of the Queen's life is all the more complex because of apparent ambiguities in the reaction of the Church to her conduct. We have seen one example of this in the distinction made by Isabel (*Viva* 104) between her public and private morals. For her critics, no such distinction could be made. Furthermore, many acts she apparently considered as virtuous, since they were in accord with Church advice, such as, for example, the repression of liberal or revolutionary ideas, were deemed to be vicious by the revolutionary press in so far as they constituted acts of cruelty towards human beings. Because of their superstitious overtones, her religious beliefs also earned her censure from liberal quarters, and many general anti-clerical attacks found in her a useful focus and target.

The most renowned example of the Queen's superstition was the case of the 'camisas de Sor Patrocinio'. In *La Comedia Política*, a satirical supplement to number 65 of *La Independencia Española* published on 31 May 1865, Isabel was given a shift by Sor Patrocinio :

> *Patrocinio* : Bien, toma.
> La camisa me la he puesto
> tres veces seguidas.
> *Isabel* : ¡Hola!
> está bien santificada.

This is a mere parading of popular gossip in comparison with the *Juicio de Isabel de Borbón*, a broadside which, judging by the number and variety of places it was advertised, mentioned or reproduced, received wide circulation in the initial revolutionary period.[19]

The *Juicio* took Isabel to task for her superstition and contrasted her behaviour with what it might have been. It told her that she should have been concerned with the fate of the nation 'en lugar de mandar camisas a un convento, en donde pasan fealdades que escandalizan a los libertinos . . . en lugar de enviar camisas a una monja embustera, que hoy es encubridora porque no puede ser disoluta'. It condemned her for going through the motions of religious observances while remaining fundamentally licentious, using the shifts as moral insurance policies :

> ¿Con qué pensamiento querías que tu camisa fuese santa? ¿Para eso guardas lo santidad? ¿Para tu camisa mujer obcecada? ¿qué ha de hacer un pueblo afrentado y perdido por ti, con la santidad de tu camisa? ¿Camisa santa, y no santificas tu conciencia? ¿Camisa santa y no te acabas de saciar contra los hijos de los que te pusieron en el trono?

---

[19] The earliest certain date of its publication was 25 September 1868 in *La Soberanía Nacional* (Cadiz). Here it was described as a reproduction, so the original date of publication must have been even earlier. *El Despertador* of 14 October 1868 referred to it as having been published on 2 October 1868 by *La Voluntad Nacional* which said it was copied from *La Revolución*, a 'periódico de Jerez'. *La Iberia* printed it on 3 October 1868, as did *El Telégrafo* (Barcelona), the latter taking it from *El Imparcial*, which in its turn had reproduced it with the description that it was a broadside circulating about Cadiz. The pencil note on the *Juicio* at the Hemeroteca Municipal says it appeared in the *Imparcial* on 29 October 1868. This was obviously a later reprint.

It also commented generally on her superstitious practices and suggested that

en lugar de besar estampas, y de alumbrar imágenes, y de llorar, y de arrodillarse ante un fraile estúpido; en vez de tanta abominable y mentecata trapacería ¿por qué no fuiste una reina humana, una madre prudente, una esposa fiel, y una española amante de su pueblo?

Some of the questions posed in the *Juicio* receive a partial answer in the *Ruedo*. Although Isabel is shown to be highly superstitious, and by no means an 'esposa fiel', she has a real affection for her son Alfonso (*Viva* IV.xii) and genuinely wants to retain the love of her people (*Corte* 37–8). The matter of the shifts is treated carefully. Whereas the papal bull is kept strictly in the field of rumour and fertile popular imagination, Valle-Inclán lets our suspicions about the shifts be confirmed. First come Adolfito's suspicions. The future favourite asks Torre-Mellada : '¿Y es verdad lo que cuentan de las camisas? ¿Se las pone primero Sor Patrocinio?' (*Corte* 149). Neither he nor the reader receives a definite reply until *Corte* X where we see the Queen preparing for bed. The facts are reported unequivocally : 'Suspiró los rezos, tomó agua bendita, entró en la cama, santificado el rubio y flamenco desnudo con la camisa que antes había vestido la monja milagrera : Cuarto aspas de sangre en el costado de la preciada reliquia dibujaban una cruz' (*Corte* 234). Here Valle-Inclán makes what has previously been a caricatural feature of the Queen, as she was portrayed in scandalous gossip, into a concrete, visual reality, and the gap between what is real and what is supposed is breached. Before the revelation of the shifts, the reader has had the opportunity of seeing Isabel as a human being. Now the lines of caricature, suggested earlier by rumour, are reinforced, and our perspective is altered from one of believing that we have been reading a caricature of reality to believing that the reality itself is a caricature, a distortion of nature.

Other manifestations of the Queen's superstition occur in the *Ruedo* : her belief in the efficacy of prayer to certain images (*Corte* 36), her guilty exploration of fate through a pack of cards (*Corte* 236–7), her awareness of omens, as when she upsets the inkpot and finds that Patrocinio's letter has escaped damage (*Viva* 170). Valle-Inclán shows such superstitiousness as a desperate reaction to a complex and highly confusing political situation : an answer to her inability to command respect and pick her way safely through the nets of plotting. Her superstitiousness is also shown to be symptomatic of her need for security. Her husband is unable to provide it, and though she trusts Adolfito, he is patently unworthy of it. Pepita Rua too is revealed to the reader as a dubious confidante when she retrieves Adolfito's letter asking for money, viewing it as a weapon for future blackmail (*Viva* 105). Isabel's superstitiousness is as much a part of her childish nature as is her generosity, rendering her more of a credible person, but not more dignified or better fitted for her position. The human element is also what is stressed in her relationship with Sor Patrocinio, since most of the nun's power derives from expert psychological manipulation. Despite muttered insults (*Corte* 241) and a vague sense that the nun may be her enemy (*Viva* 172–3, the Queen never overcomes a superstitious respect for her.

The King Consort's 'camarilla' and correspondence

While in the relationship of the Queen with the Church as shown in the *Ruedo* there is a certain ambiguity (its representatives both support and criticise her), there is a clear alliance between the King Consort and the ultramontane forces of the Church. With Padre Claret and Sor Patrocinio, Francisco de Asís was drawn to form a *camarilla* that would exert influence upon the Queen to make her take such political action as would be acceptable to Catholicism in general and Rome in particular. This relationship is outlined in both the *Ruedo* and the revolutionary press, but with different emphasis and implications.

The revolutionary press was principally concerned to discredit the Church via the form it took in the *camarilla*. 'Indirectas' and direct attacks were made on Spain's monasteries and convents, hinting that vicious practices were rife within their walls. *La Comedia Política* on 31 May 1865 was extremely mild when it referred to the King Consort's plans to go to La Granja with Rafaela[20] saying

> allí Cirilo merienda,
> y Sor Patrocinio baila,
> Orfeo canta un fandango
> y Claret toca la flauta
> y yo me divierto mucho.

The notion of such ecclesiastical indulgence is absent from the *Ruedo*, with the exception of innocuous *meriendas* (*Corte* 240, *Viva* 99).

The King Consort's correspondence is however given considerable weight, although again a divergence from the lines of the popular sources can be perceived. Paquita's letters are part of Spanish popular mythology. This is what is implied by the casual comment in 1869 of *El Cencerro* (Cordoba, Cencerrada 16) : 'Parece que la Asamblea va a pedir algunos espedientes *célebres*. – Pido que pida las cartas de Paquita.' It is possible that the myth was originated by *El Relámpago* on 10 February 1867 in its comments on a manifesto :

> Y en efecto, el objeto del manifiesto del rey consorte era protestar contra el origen de esa prole. Francisco de Borbón, invocando sagrados deberes de conciencia, escrúpulos de santa resignación evangélica, deseos acendrados de paz y religíon para estos reinos, Francisco de Borbón llevaba su caridad cristiana, hasta el punto de aceptar la abdicación de Isabel II y la regencia para sí del príncipe Alfonso.[21]

[20] i.e. Patrocinio, whose secular name had been María Josefa Dolores Anastasia de Quiroga y Cacopardo, and who became Sor María Rafaela de los Dolores y Patrocinio. (Benjamín Jarnés, *Sor Patrocinio, la monja de las llagas*, (Madrid 1929, reprinted 1930), p. 25.)

[21] *El Relámpago*, 10 February 1867.

It appears that the letter to the Pope may have been real. Pí y Margall quotes from an unnamed historian some details about various royal letters :

> Nada más delicado que hablar de estos documentos. Debo sí decir, y me atengo al dicho de la opinión, que según unos, probaban la ilegitimidad de Isabel II; según otros, la del príncipe don Alfonso, luego rey. De ellos se dan tales pormenores, que

El Cohete (Barcelona) of 7 October 1868 was even more explicit, and its comments both stressed the effect of caricature and indicated Patrocinio as the source of plotting, but also suggested that the compromising letter or letters were signed by Isabel :

Isabel, entre otros, tuvo un hijo . . . [sic] natural . . . [sic] y nada más; su marido, hombre muy delicado, no quiso admitir lo que no era suyo, pero le dieron millones y admitió. – En esto Patrocinio, metiéndose a patrocinar al padre convencional, proporcionóle no sé qué cartas en las cuales constaba la verdadera procedencia del chiquillo. – Desde entonces fueron aquellas misteriosas cartas un talismán, pues siempre que al marido se le ocurría algo, como por ejemplo dinero o cambio de ministerio, exclamaba : – Carta canta. –

> Y la carta no cantaba,
> pero el gobierno cambiaba.

The *Ruedo* is explicit about the letters, and seems to follow most closely the myth of *El Cohete*, since it is Sor Patrocinio and Padre Claret who are responsible for the composition of the letter to the Pope. Here the attitude of the King Consort is one of outraged moral righteousness : 'Yo salvaré mi conciencia, sea cual sea la decisión de Isabelita. ¡Es el caso de los Reyes Católicos y la Beltraneja ! . . . [sic] ¡Un heredero que, a bien decir, no es de tálamo ! ¡Pues es el mismo caso !' (*Viva* 169). In spite of the political and moral terminology he uses, he is transparently motivated by a desire for revenge, if only to the extent of acquiring political importance for himself. The wish to have a clear conscience is only a pretext. The ironic Conde Blanc has no illusion : '¡Qué rectitud de conciencia la del Tío Paco !' (*Viva* 169).

Valle-Inclán here then has altered the focus in dealing with the King Consort's letters. The idea of a compromising correspondence remains on the level of reported gossip (see the comments on the literary competition between the Duque de Montpensier and the King Consort, *Corte* 194). We assume that these letters are the ones used by the King Consort to obtain money and favours for services of official paternity. By contrast, the letter sent to the Pope, and which is lost en route, is one requiring the Queen's signature, and which needs the intervention of the King Consort in the conspiracy.[22] In this way, the letter

---

hubiérase dicho, a creerlos, que habían sido patrimonial del público.

Conviene no confundir estos documentos con unas cartas olvidadas por la reina en un bureau de su alojamiento en Oviedo cuando su viaje a Asturias en 1859, que fueron a parar a manos del comité progresista de aquella capital; que las dió a leer a algunos amigos, pero no hizo mal uso de ellos, aun yéndole tanto en aquel juego.

Tampoco parece no debían ser los mismos de que el rey don Francisco se valió, conforme al dicho de las gentes, en tantas ocasiones, para amenazar a su esposa y a los gobiernos; pues aquellos, así se dijo, fueron por él entregados en pago de muchos favores y de no poco dinero. (Francisco Pí y Margall y Francisco Pí y Arsuaga, *Historia de España en el Siglo XIX*, (Barcelona, 1902), IV, 404-5.)

[22] In *Correo diplomático*, a fragment of the *Ruedo* of unknown date of composition, the Conde Blanc is clearly responsible for the 'loss' of the letter to the Pope. Speratti Piñero, in '¿Un nuevo episodio de *El Ruedo Ibérico*?', *De 'Sonata de Otoño' al esperpento*, pp. 311-12, concludes that the fragment is more likely to be an early version than a late one.

is used as a device to explore the characters of both King Consort and Queen in their respective attempts to implement and to resist the counsel of Patrocinio.[23]

The Queen's political views

Many features of Isabel's political ineptitude have already come to light earlier in this section. On the one hand we have seen how the revolutionary press consistently concentrates upon rumour and outward appearances, always making the most scandalous interpretations of possible facts, whereas Valle-Inclán on the other hand, while carefully selecting features from the popular vision, sets them into situations that are psychologically and novelistically credible.

One score on which Isabel was severely criticised by certain sections of the press was her cruelty. Some papers blamed Sor Patrocinio for this. In *La Comedia Política*, for example, Isabel is worried about the state of the *pueblo*, but Patrocinio reminds her of her words to Narváez: '¿Para cuándo guardas la artillería?' The nun, with her enthusiastic recalling of the 'Noche de San Daniel', emerges as the bloodthirsty character in the situation.[24] Other papers regarded Isabel's cruelty as an essentially Bourbon trait. As *La Culebra de Borbón en Pau*, a broadside that appeared on 17 October 1868, summarised it:

> En ellos las diversiones,
> Consisten en ver ahorcar,
> A valientes fusilar,
> Amparar los santurrones.

The harshest condemnation of Isabel on this score came, as always, from the *Juicio de Isabel de Borbón*, which attributed her cruelty to a personal lust for blood:

> Isabel de Borbón, ¿con qué fin nos das el espectáculo de estas mojigangas? ¿Lo haces con el fin de llamar a Narváez, después de las *Matanzas del 10 de Abril*, y gritarle furiosa: ¿*Para cuándo guardas la artillería*? Isabel de Borbón, oye, no satisfecha con los asesinatos cometidos hasta en criaturas de nueve años, muertas por la espalda, (¡parece imposible que seas madre!): no sastifecha [sic] con saber que una joven esposa se había vuelto loca de dolor querías barrer a los estudiantes con la metralla de los canones.

The common factor is that Isabel was assumed to take decisions to inflict cruelty as a deliberate policy, or as acts of self-indulgence, whether on advice or on impulse. This belief about her motivations is supported by an example in

[23] In parenthesis it should be noted that this is not the only occasion on which Valle-Inclán seems to have merged and confused Isabel II and her husband in their epistolary carelessness (a confusion already present, as we have seen, in historical accounts). In the *Farsa y licencia de la reina castiza* it is again the Queen who is responsible for embarrassing the government with a mislaid love-letter, but the letters are signed *Paquita* (*Obras completas*, I, 427), laying the morality of both husband and wife open to question. This is the closest Valle comes to a full attack on the King Consort, beyond the general attack based upon his homosexual tendencies.

[24] On the 'Noche de San Daniel', 10 April 1865, a student demonstration was repressed with excessive violence.

El Cohete of 2 March 1873 which published an imaginary letter : 'Consejos que da Doña Isabel de Borbón a su hijo D. Alfonso para que se despabile y no sea tonto.' In it she counselled :

> Hijo mío : al pueblo, garrotazo y tente tieso; nada de contemplaciones, nada de buenas caras, nada de tolerancia. Si piden libertades, ¡palo! si no las piden ¡palo! y en todas ocasiones ¡palo!

She attributed her own fall to her failure to suppress popular risings harshly enough :

> ¡Ojalá lo hubiera hecho yo así siempre! ¡Otro gallo me cantara! Pero yo fui bobalicona, les dí todo lo que me pidieron, dejé hacer, procuré cobrar (que esto ya es cantar distinto), no me metí en nada y ¡bien que me ha salido a la cara! ¡Ah si las cosas se hicieren dos veces! . . . [sic][25]

Isabel's cruelty appears in the press as a reprehensible and incomprehensible vice. In the *Ruedo* it is certainly there : indeed, it is the first glimpse we have of Isabel : 'La Señora encendida de erisipelas, se inflaba con bucheo de paloma : – ¡Pegar fuerte, a ver si se enmiendan !' (*Corte* 12). If we follow the line of argument pursued earlier in the discussion about the change to the perspective of the *Ruedo* effected by the addition of 'Aires nacionales' to the 1931 *Corte*, we must conclude that Valle-Inclán intended to give special emphasis to this aspect of the Queen, a vision of a woman in a rage coming to supersede the incompetent matron of the golden rose section. Valle-Inclán's portrayal of this aspect of the Queen is, however, more complex. First, even in the initial glimpse of her anger, we see one possible cause, the skin disease which inflames her. Then we move on to a detailed exposition of her mental and emotional confusion. Popular myth is followed in that Patrocinio is shown as the force operating most strongly on the Queen. Although at times she rebels against the nun, as in *Viva* 172–3, the Queen knows that the alternative to taking her advice is to become more entangled in the complex net of Court politics. Though confused by the muddle of plotting, bribery, tact and diplomacy of Court circles, the Queen nonetheless retains the desire to make her wishes known and to assert herself in no uncertain manner, regardless of what the situation or the possible outcome may be. *Viva* IV.vi shows her in a mood of authority. The names of Concha and Novaliches are to be sent to the *Gaceta* as holders of the *Tercer entorchado* even though she knows this will upset the Unionist generals. Valle-Inclán outlines delicately her feelings at the presentation, including weird arrière-pensées and intentions of unloading responsibility for the act on to other shoulders : 'La Señora . . . al firmar aquellas mercedes no era ajena al propósito de aplicar con guiños gatusones el resquemor de los Generales Unionistas. En reserva, con fe borbónica, maduraba cargar la culpa sobre los Consejeros de la Corona' (*Viva* 94). In another decision, to recognise the Conde Blanc, she emphasises her authority by the offhand tone in her announcement : 'Me

---

[25] *El Padre Cobos*, 15 April 1856, had attributed Isabel's cruelty to natural inclination. This contrasts with the attitude of *La Iberia* on 3 January 1869 (see note 3), which regarded it as a lack of sensitivity. See also Fernando Garrido, III, 1093, who lays part of the blame on Isabel's ministers, and Pí y Margall, IV, 370.

olvidaba deciros . . . [sic] La Real familia ha tomado el acuerdo de reconocer como a uno de sus miembros al Príncipe Luis María César de Borbón' (*Viva* 92).

In the *Ruedo*, the Queen is frequently seen to be moved to decision on impulse, or to satisfy a whim, or to make some final desperate clarification of a confused situation, with the result that it is easier to understand, though not to condone, acts of cruelty authorised by her. There is perhaps something even more horrifying in the way that her political decisions are taken in so undeliberate and capricious a fashion. Her reply to her small son's suggestions that the problems of Spain might be solved by the creation of a 'cuerpo de zuavos' ('¡Pobre tontín, si piensas hacer la felicidad de los españoles con la creación de un cuerpo de zuavos!' (*Viva* 102)) reveals some normal maternal affection, and some understanding of her own inability to cope with the political situation. The final impression left by her is of a bewildered and unintelligent woman, eminently not suited to her position, but who does retain vestigial human qualities and emotions. The popular caricature of a vengeful, vicious and wilful monarch has been softened but not reversed.

II PADRE CLARET AND SOR PATROCINIO

As the two people generally designated by the revolutionary press as ultimately responsible for those of Isabel's decisions which caused political disruption, Padre Claret and Sor Patrocinio, her confessor and her personal friend, merit special attention. They became targets for criticism in their time, not only for the influence they were alleged to exercise at Court, but also for the narrow-minded type of Catholicism they represented. In a situation where belief was polarised into the extremes of heresy/freemasonry/atheism or neo-catholicism/ultramontanism/superstition they formed useful focal points. They play an appropriately important part in the *Ruedo*, where Valle-Inclán, particularly when dealing with things miraculous, displays to the maximum his ability to present pieces of evidence in such a way as to admit a variety of interpretations. Although the names of Claret and Patrocinio were often coupled together in anticlerical comment, they had clearly separate roles and characteristics, and as such will be dealt with separately here.

Claret: the man and the theology

There is no immediate gap of credibility between the Queen's confessor in the *Ruedo*, simple, almost superstitious, of obvious piety and lacking in worldliness, and the Antonio Claret y Clará of history, beatified in 1934 and canonised in 1950, a zealous missionary and the author of numerous religious books. A more serious gap exists between these two views and contemporary accounts of his activities as a shady mediator between Isabel and her conscience, or Isabel and the Pope.

All accounts seem to be agreed on the matter of his home-spun simplicity, his flamboyant humility, and lack of care for social polish or niceties of speech. Added to this was the fact that he was Catalan, which drew childish scorn from Madrid journalists, who seized the opportunity of criticising that 'barbarous' region by ridiculing the type of pedestrian religion exemplified by Claret. *Gil Blas*, for example, on 29 July 1865 sniped :

Ya ha llegado a Vich, su país natal el reverendo y reborondo padre Claret.

Parece que para festejar su feliz arribo, la población puso salchichón en vez de colgaduras.

El Palitroque (Barcelona) on 22 November 1868 followed in the sausage tradition :

¿A cuántos estamos del Padre Claret?

Las longanizas de Vich han sufrido una gran baja. ¿Si será porque no anda por allí su paternidad trajanópoli-borbónica panzuda?

Gil Blas did not emancipate itself from this childish level of attack after the revolution, and on 25 Ferbuary 1869, commenting on a report that Claret, now in France, had preached in Spanish, queried : 'En efecto, ¿No es más fácil la restauración de los Borbones de primera y segunda rama que predicar en español el P. Claret?'

It was furthermore convenient for those intent on ridiculing Claret to suggest the existence of an affinity between the linguistic infelicities of a Catalan speaking Castilian, and the pedestrian unpolished content of what the man said, thus finding expression for both regional and religious prejudices. *Los Neos sin Careta* on 14 May 1870 printed a sermon, 'Estomagus apretatus discurrit que rabiat', said to have come from Claret's *Consejos a un sacerdote* (presumably a 'mistaken' reference to his *Avisos a un sacerdote*). Claret in this was appealing for money for masses for the dead :

¡Amados oyentes! Tal vez os chocará esta función de ánimas y sermón en día que no es de *tabla* : pero sabed que viene de *cajón* porque esta noche me ha sucedido una cosa *estupefacta*. Tres o cuatro veces me he despertado *estando dormido* quedándome todo *tremendo* y relijando porque me parecía que tiraban de la ropa. Esto nos suele suceder amados oyentes, a los sacerdotes cuando hay en el Purgatorio muchas almas de la feligresia, las cuales nos tiran de la ropa quedándonos algunas veces *hastas en cueros* con lo cual nos avisan que están padeciendo y se lo digamos a su familia . . . Encargádselas [las misas] al sacerdote que *os dé la gana*, si bien es de suponer que las benditas ánimas de vuestros padres y abuelos desearán que yo se las diga. Y sino, ¿para qué tirarme tan fuerte de la ropa *a pique de arrecirme de frío*? Por bien empleadas doy yo todas las misas del mundo con tal que las ánimas benditas no se metan conmigo.

The attack here was, superficially, on a linguistic level, but was ultimately more concerned at the blundering religion of the speaker. Claret formed a useful target for a publication which aimed in general at ridiculing the *neo-católicos* as a group.[26]

The well-meaning reader may consider the above attack as rather unfair. The mock sermon is obviously intended to deride and debase. Our perspective

---

[26] The neo-católicos were a party formed in the 1860s. An extreme conservative group, they based their politics on a renewed interest in Catholicism, and in many ways resembled the French ultramontane party.

may be corrected by looking briefly at Claret's own writings. In *La llave de oro*, his most renowned work, he discusses the Commandments, with examples to show the necessity of adhering to them. Under 'Honour thy father and mother' come two strange accounts. The first relates :

Una madre dicen, tenía dos hijos : el mayor andaba de noche, y por más que le amonestaba su madre, eran inútiles los avisos que le daba. Una noche, después de haberse recogido de rondar, se estaba tendido en la cama, al lado de su hermano mayor [sic], cuando *hé aquí que Dios le mandó* cinco demonios, y el principal de aquellos infernales ministros cogió por los pies a aquel mal hijo, le arrastró fuera de la cama, y tendido en el suelo, con una grande cuchilla le abrió de arriba abajo y le partió por medio. Tomando al momento los otro cuatro demonios un cuarto cada uno de aquel infeliz se le llevaron en cuerpo y alma a los infiernos.

The second example, briefer, but still horrifying, gave out its lesson like a threat :

Se lee en la sagrada Escritura que Absalón faltó al respeto a su padre : le quiso quitar el reino y le levantó guerra, pero Dios le castigó de tal manera que murió colgado en una encina por sus cabellos, y traspasado por tres lanzadas del general Joab. ¿No ve V. cómo castiga Dios los malos hijos?[27]

In the *Ruedo* the main impression of Claret is much as we might expect to find it from his own writing, and from the not too divergent mockery of *Los Neos sin Careta*. His strong Catalan accent is also 'payés', thus differentiating him from others by dint of both regionalism and rusticity. His voice virtually forms his personality, acts instead of him : 'El Padre Claret . . . acogía con crasas vocales payesas la inteligencia con la rama sálica' (*Viva* 168); 'Dilataron sus odres las anchas vocales catalanas del Padre Claret' (*Viva* 172). His vowels act as an unfortunate Homeric epithet, announcing an unwelcome presence : 'entró orquestando con crasas vocales payesas el frailuno latinajo' (*Viva* 291), and spreading aesthetic discord : 'El Reverendo Padre derramó el bálsamo frailuno de sus consuelos embastecida la boca por crasos dejos catalanes' (*Viva* 208). Typically, when recommending a remedy for the Queen's headache, instead of the 'sales inglesas' extolled by Franchi, he swears by 'sanguijuelas en salvo sea la parte para bajar la sangre' (*Viva* 207).

In the counterpoint of musical imagery used by Valle-Inclán for the three ecclesiastical presences of Padre Claret, Sor Patrocinio and Monseñor Franchi, Claret is always the droning bass.[28] Contrast is also predictably present in the selection and rhythm of words as well as in the tone of voice, so that Patrocinio's measured statement 'La Reina de España es un dulce muy regalado para los festines de Lucifer. Las Legiones Infernales no descansan para poder ofrecérselo' is followed by Claret's jolly and emphatic '¡Naturalmente! Patillas apetece siempre el piperete preferido del Rey de Reyes. La Reina de España,

[27] P. Antonio Claret y Clará, *La llave de oro*, (Barcelona, 1860) pp. 40-2.
[28] See J. M. García de la Torre, *Análisis temático de 'El ruedo ibérico'*, (Madrid, 1972), pp. 210-12.

ante todo, debe mostrarse madre cristiana y resguardar de la pestilencia la flor tiernísima del Augusto Niño' (*Viva* 100).

For Claret of the *Ruedo*, as for the Claret of *La llave de oro*, God intervenes personally in the lives of his creatures. Whereas Patrocinio attributes Isabel's awkward political position to her compromise with 'jacobinos', Claret envisages God in a personal struggle against them, a struggle in which Isabel must participate : '¡Que España no vuelva a caer en los errores del liberalismo es la obligación primera de Su Majestad Católica! *Dios Nuestro Señor, en sus altos designios dispuso* que en una guerra sangrienta fuese vencida la rama sálica y que las sienes de la augusta huérfana recibieran la corona de San Fernando. ¡Ahí es nada! *Dios Nuestro Señor ha coronado vuestras sienes para su servicio en la tierra*, no para el fin execrable de entregar al influjo de las logias el Gobierno de la Católica España' (*Viva* 101, italics mine). The Devil too intervenes : '¡Las asechanzas del maligno han enredado esta madeja!' (*Viva* 106). In his religious examination of Alfonso he warmly congratulates the child for rattling off the summaries of some of his works, and wildly mixes metaphors in his praise, in a manner close to the *Llave* : 'Vuestra Alteza me ha hecho recordar al Gran Rey David, que en edad párvula venció la soberbia filistea aplastando con la piedra de su honda la dura frente del Gigante Goliat. Mis felicitaciones también para el modesto jardinero que mantiene lozano el tierno arbolillo, limpiándole de malas yerbas' (*Viva* 213).

Claret as Royal confessor

Even if we are critical of the simplistic theology Claret puts forward in the *Ruedo*, there is no suggestion in his actual words that he is anything but the down to earth country priest, once missionary, now Royal confessor. Other touches are introduced by Valle-Inclán, however, which undermine the façade of homely sincerity. His recitation of the events of his crowded ecclesiastic day to a crowd of gushing ladies of the court is doubtless intended to draw praise, which ostensibly he avoids : 'El Reverendo Arzobispo de Trajanópolis acabó la cuenta tapándose las orejas, negándose a oír el laudoso murmullo del bando palatino' (*Viva* 210). As his gesture of avoidance precedes the description of the chorus of praise, it appears premature, and the image of his bluff unambitious nature is deflated. His subsequent distribution of 'hojas de oraciones, medallas, estampas, ramitas de espliego, todo con la bendición del Santo Padre' (*Viva* 211) is conclusive proof of his preparedness.

This last detail of the holy images was often mentioned in unfavourable accounts of Claret's life. An anonymous biography of Claret in Valle-Inclán's library at Pontevedra, written not from the standpoint of Church history, but from that of a commentator on Claret's role in politics, recalls that his sermons were habitually accompanied by handouts of rosaries and religious pictures.[29]

[29] *Biografía del Padre Claret por O * * *, Colaborador de *La Iberia* de Calvo Asensio (Madrid, 1869), p. 21. The date of the work is early enough to place it in the wave of fierce reaction against all that Isabel's reign had represented, including the intervention of members of the clergy in politics through their capacity as religious advisers. The 'liberal' origins and attitudes of the book are confirmed by the association of the author with *La Iberia*, a *progresista* paper founded in 1854.

An *aleluya* of 1869, *El Padre Clarinete*, was concerned to show that nothing in Claret's life was above suspicion. The relatively innocuous couplets 13 and 14 :

A las *pollas* confesando
Se iba el *padre* entusiasmado.

A las que eran más bonitas
Las regalaba estampitas

were accompanied by unequivocal illustrations of Claret embracing the woman confessing to him, and admiring the ankle of the one he presented with an *estampita*.[30] It is perhaps significant that Claret's habit of distributing religious objects was not mentioned by Villarasa and Gatell's *Historia de la revolución de Setiembre*, which rejected the image of Claret as a fanatic trying to sway the will of the Queen in favour of the portrayal of a man who, albeit uneducated and inept in choice of imagery as shown by his critics, had no desire to involve himself in politics.[31]

As Isabel's confessor, Claret was obviously in a position to influence her. Concern was caused by the belief that he might either be going beyond his brief as her spiritual adviser in influencing her political actions, or that he might be not going far enough in censuring her for her activities as a private individual. After the revolution, the first notion was often used as a means of diminishing Isabel's culpability for the reactionary politics of her reign. The biography of Claret in Valle-Inclán's library attributes political importance to the Royal confessor in 1868 : 'En febrero del año de 1868, trataron en efecto los neos de escalar el poder, para lo que contaron con que el Padre Claret aconsejara a la reina su abdicación en el príncipe Carlos de Borbón y Este, o sea Carlos VII.'[32] While *El Cascabel* on 22 October 1868 criticised Claret for failing to influence the Queen in politics ('El Señor Claret ha podido hacer mucho bien y no lo ha hecho, ha podido aconsejar bien a los que fueron reyes de España y les ha aconsejado mal') it was also uneasy about the possible closeness of the confessorial relationship :

El autor de la *Llave de oro*, comenzaba así un oficio, dirigido a un señor sacerdote :
'Yo y la reina hemos determinado . . . [sic]'
¿Tendría literatura el Señor Claret? . . . [sic].

Similarly *El Guirigay* on 19 August 1865 had supposed Claret to be a likely candidate for the regency. Such doubts were not entirely without foundation. In a letter written by Claret to Isabel in 1859, he asked her to support the Religiosas Terciarias del Carmen who were in financial difficulties as their teaching duties were being taken over by the schoolmistresses appointed by the

[30] *El Padre Clarinete*, (Madrid, 1869), an *aleluya* with 30 illustrations, Museo Municipal, Madrid, no. 4961. See Plate II.
[31] E. M. Villarasa and J. I. Gatell, *Historia de la revolución de Setiembre*, (Barcelona, 1875), pp. 49-50. The conservative tone of this account may also have been contributed to by the fact that Alfonso XII was by this time on the throne, and excessive comment on the evils of his mother's reign would have been indecorous.
[32] *Biografía del Padre Claret*, p. 71.

government. The conclusion of his letter gave a straight directive : 'Por tanto, señora, el exponente no sólo suplica, sino que además, como director espiritual de V.M., le prescribe que en conciencia debe mandar al Gobierno que enmiende este error, que quizá inadvertidamente comete.'[33]

Inevitably Claret's name was linked with that of Sor Patrocinio. Bermejo reported such suspicions : 'Las suposiciones llegaron al extremo de creer que el padre Claret y Sor Patrocinio estaban en reservado concierto para disponer a su antojo del ánimo de los Reyes, lo cual era una grosera calumnia.' In matters of historical accuracy and propriety Bermejo frequently tries to have his cake and eat it, and here, having stated that Claret tried to avoid Sor Patrocinio as much as was possible, given that his duties often brought him to places where she was present, he returned to the scandals spread about them : 'Pero la maledicencia y el ardor de las pasiones políticas han estado durante cinco o seis años asegurando que el padre Claret y Sor Patrocinio ataban las manos a los ministros y dominaban a los Reyes, pintándolos, no sólo en íntimo acuerdo político, sino en otra intimidad no menos calumniosa e indecorosa'.[34] Such statement of scandal, and the subsequent mention of, though refusal to describe, an obscene caricature, neatly reported a series of popular beliefs about Claret, while maintaining the respectability of the author.

In contrast with Bermejo, Valle-Inclán is rather more careful about the way he reports rumour. On the political level, Claret is seen mainly as the homely confessor, who in *Viva* IV.xi joins with Patrocinio in counselling the Queen to a line of action which is unfavourable to liberalism. Even more care is exercised in the treatment of the rumour that Claret had negotiated a special papal bull for the Queen.

To gauge this caution we can see first the extremes reached by the press. The *aleluya El Padre Clarinete* had explicit graphic comment on Claret's relationship with Isabel. Couplets 18 and 19 ran :

> Le hace confesor *Paquita*
> de la reina Isabelita.
>
> Para el perdón de esta chula
> contrata en Roma una Bula.

The illustration to number 18 shows Claret seated on Isabel's bed, holding her hand : Isabel is obviously naked beneath the sheets. Number 19 shows Claret going to see the Pope with a huge sack of money over his shoulder : that the bull should be a financial transaction reflects upon the morality of both Pius IX and Claret.

It was supposed that Claret, as confessor, had been particularly flexible with his Queen. *Gil Blas* on 25 February 1869 had an article on a 'concurso de confesores' which included letters from would-be replacements for Claret who was reported as leaving for Rome. The first applicant reassured Isabel that 'los

---

[33] Letter to Isabel II dated 12 January 1859 (Archiv. Claret, Roma, Ms. Ep. 5 Orig. minuta), quoted in *San Antonio María Claret: Escritos autobiográficos y espirituales*, Col. *Biblioteca de Autores Cristianos*, Vol. 188, (Madrid, 1859), pp. 856-8.

[34] *Estafeta*, III, 661.

pecados de Vuestra Real Majestad (que Dios guarde) son muy gordos, pero como esos me las [sic] trago yo todos los días antes de almorzar'. He ended with a bargain : 'Dígame V.M. si puedo contar con esa placita, y yo le aseguro el perdón anticipado de los pecados que ha de cometer en la próxima temporada.' The second applicant produced the reassurance that he had a parishioner who

Es una señora muy ardiente. Eso lo trae consigo la sangre. Todos los días me trae el mismo pecado, la impongo la misma penitencia, arrepiente y hasta otra.

Ni la penitencia, ni el pecado, ni el arrepentimiento varían de una confesión a otra : lo único que varía es el amante.

With this situation, the applicant said, he was well used to certain duties, implying that Isabel needed a confessor to absolve her daily of acts of immorality. The third pleaded his case on financial grounds : 'Esto de echar todos los días diez o doce absoluciones por un miserable jornal, me parece algo *climatérico* para un hombre que hace el papel de Dios, que siempre es papel de primer barba', hinting that Claret received princely sums for the absolutions he gave to the Queen. The fourth applicant offered an inclusive service : 'a toda la compañía de V.M. confieso yo en un periquete y los dejo más limpios que una patena.' He added as a footnote : 'También ayudo a bien morir.'

It seemed then that the post of confessor to the Queen was a convenience to be provided for a monarch who could not be prevented from sinning. Bermejo avoids such comment, but the anonymous biographer is detailed about Claret's dilemma and solutions, although we should note that much is offered as supposition and not as fact :

En sus continuadas visitas, en sus conferencias y en sus confesiones con la reina Isabel, debió hallarse muy embarazado y perplejo el Padre Claret; porque no siéndole posible, y acaso él lo conocía mejor que nadie, separar a la regia penitente de sus aficiones y ardientes deseos, y no siéndolo tampoco el sancionar ciertos escesos y pecados, limitábase a los principios a absolver con frecuencia, dand [sic] aquellos consejos suaves que a todos se nos alcanzan; y como, por una parte venía reemplazando a la afición la necesidad y al ardimiento la pasión, y por otra Sor Patrocinio había llegado a infundir una ciega y exagerada beatitud, que el reverendo confesor acabó de fijar y remachar, tuvo éste que buscar un arbitrio que salvando los dos escollos le abriese paso franco por aquel piélago peligroso.

Y le hallaron en efecto, haciéndole entender a Isabel que mientras llevaba su ropa interior y sobre todo la camisa beatificada, todo pecado se borraría, que el pecado está simpre más en la intención que en los hechos.[35]

Again, the biography is detailed and scathing when dealing with the papal bull :

Por lo tanto, principiaron las delicadas negociaciones de obtención de indulgencias, primeramente para los pecados que la regia penitente había cometido, con algunas más para aquellos que era una necesidad cometer; y mientras los favoritos cruzaban ante el país asombrado por las escaleras del

---

[35] *Biografía del Padre Claret*, p. 46.

alcázar, los ríos de oro iban a Roma a buscar las recetas para regularizar las conciencias y alcanzar el milagro permanente de que lo que es pecado en sí mismo y para todos, deje de serlo para los que pueden ribetearlos de doblones.

De todas estas negociaciones con la corte romana debió hacer lógicamente el subirse a mayores y pretender una bula, es decir un *permiso* para acudir sin escrúpulo a la satisfacción de las exigencias corporales. Mas como esto era pedir el capital para no pagar los réditos, dicen los investigadores que la *bula costó* doce millones, y añaden que principia con estas solemnes y estudiadas palabras : *Pro causa naturae, etc.* Que si tal razón es válida ante Dios para pecar en una cosa, no es fácil adivinar cual otra sería la que quedase vedada a la naturaleza humana.[36]

The papal bull, as we have seen in the section on Isabel II, is kept strictly in the realm of reported rumour by Valle-Inclán. There is no indication that Claret was party to that particular type of underhand negotiation. Indeed, in view of the fact that Valle-Inclán possessed this biography of Claret and presumably consulted it, it seems that he deliberately chose to avoid implicating the confessor in condoning the immorality of his spiritual daughter. The description of Isabel wearing Patrocinio's shifts is more damning of her superstition than of her confessor's integrity, whereas the biography clearly lays blame on Claret. There is a point in the *Ruedo* where we have a hint that Claret has adapted his advice to suit the Queen where Doña Pepita Rua reminds Isabel that she does not have to seek her salvation 'como mujer, sino como Reina de España' (*Viva* 104). The Queen's elaboration of this condemns her advisers :

En ese respeto me hallo perfectamente tranquila. Mis flaquezas de mujer son independientes de mis actos como Reina : Teólogos muy doctos me han dado las mayores seguridades sobre este particular. Como Reina Católica he de ser juzgada, y por eso quiero seguir escrupulosamente los consejos de la Santa Sede. Patillas habrá de chincharse, si tengo por abogado en la Corte Celestial a su santidad Pío IX.

Viva 104–5

It is difficult not to see a reference to Claret under 'teólogos muy doctos' and one to the papal bull in the Queen's reliance upon Pius IX to plead for her in the heavenly courts.

It would be misleading if, in view of Valle-Inclán's avoidance of the more scandalous assertions contained in a source he possessed, we were to conclude that Claret escaped his criticism. Some care has been exercised in the selection of material, and the subtle preferred to the sensational. It is enough, more than enough, that he should be portrayed as a clumsy, superstitious provincial priest whose advice is always expressed in ill-chosen and unbalanced combinations of metaphor, and whose feet are of clay, although not always firmly on the ground. The obvious alliance with Sor Patrocinio, and his willingness to involve himself in backing her more sinister political machinations does him as little credit as connivance over personal immorality would have done.

[36] ibid., p. 57.

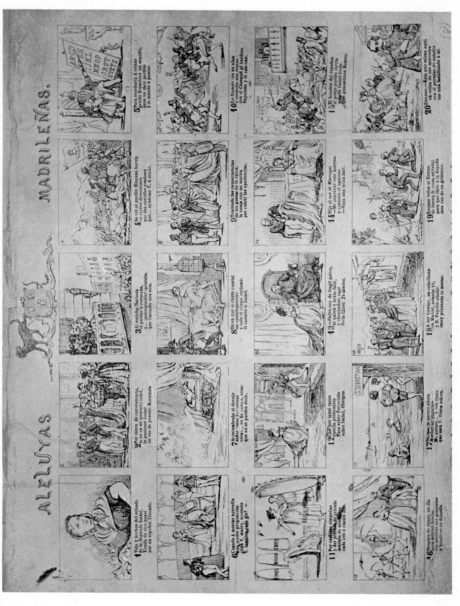

1. *Aleluyas Madrileñas*, n.p., n.d. Museo Municipal, Madrid.

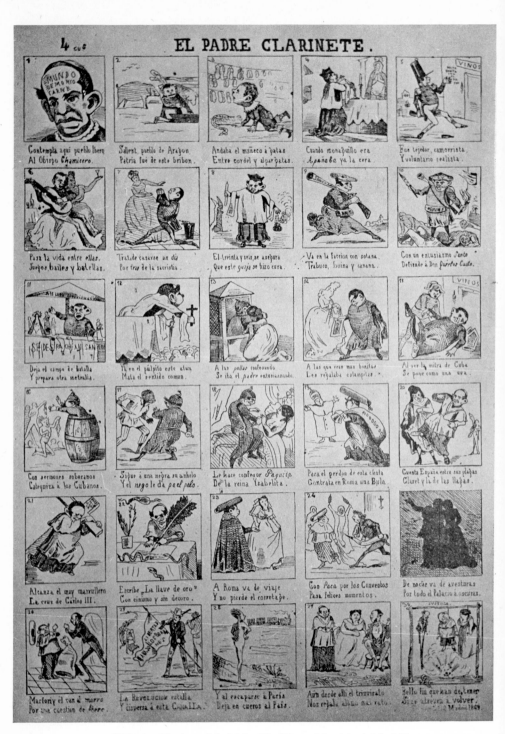

11. *El Padre Clarinete*, Madrid, 1869. Museo Municipal, Madrid.

111. *Vida de Guzmancito*, Madrid, 1869. Museo Municipal, Madrid.

NOS AVTEM GLORIARI
OPORTET,

IN CRVCE DOMINI NOSTRI
IESV CHRISTI.

iv. Frontispiece from *Copilación de las leyes capitulares de la Orden de la Cavallería de Santiago del Espada*, Valladolid, 1605.

v. 'Las nuevas cruzadas', *La Flaca*, (Barcelona), 18 September 1870.

VI. 'La cabeza conspirante', *El Caos*, (Madrid), 4 July 1870.

—Pero Paco, ¿qué estás haciendo para no prestar atencion á este jóven tan estirado y tan *terso*, que se nos presenta solicitando la *fusion?*

—Que hable por mi Gonzalez-Regato; pues yo estoy haciendo pajaritas de papel para que se divierta nuestra bendita madre la de las *llagas*.

VII. Cartoon by Ortego, *Jeremías*, (Madrid), 31 January 1869.

viii. *D. N. M. Rivero*, Madrid, 1869. Museo Municipal, Madrid.

La monja milagrera

It is not altogether surprising that Sor Patrocinio should occupy a more prominent role in the *Ruedo* than her male counterpart, nor that more rumour and
suspicion be circulated about her. Sor María de los Dolores y Patrocinio, known
generally as 'la monja de las llagas' after her trial in 1835 for faking the stigmata
and other miraculous manifestations and occurrences, was regarded with widespread suspicion, not the least for her close relationship with Isabel II. Both
during and after the end of Isabel's reign, popular papers considered that
Patrocinio was in a position to exert influence over the Queen, which caused
concern in two main ways. Any close friend belonging to a religious order might
be supposed to recommend anti-liberal political action. Furthermore, there were
strong grounds for believing that Patrocinio was not a true religious, but an
'embustera'.

Central to her reputation as an 'embustera' were the faked stigmata for
which she was brought to trial. As a result, the 'llagas' were bandied about as a
cheap means of obtaining a smile or a snigger. They were introduced in incidental fashion by *El Cascabel* on 24 December 1868 in a piece about a gathering
in Madrid for a public demonstration. The mere mention of 'llagas' drew one
speaker in the dialogue to believe that it was a question of 'las llagas esas de que
tanto se ocupa todo el mundo', although he was unable to define them except by
saying 'ello es que en España ha debido haber alguien con ellas, porque yo
siempre he estado oyendo decir : "la de las llagas" '. Two months earlier, on 22
October, this paper had made its scorn for the nun clear : 'La monja no merece
consideración alguna, porque no podemos guardarla a una monja, castigada por
los tribunales, y que salía y entraba y viajaba y en todo se ocupaba menos en sus
deberes de religiosa'. *El Cencerro* (Cordoba, Cencerrada 12) in 1869 jocularly
suggested that those who had retreated to exile in France after the revolution
needed the following :

> Una peinadora para que arregle la cabeza a Paquita,
> Una niñera para le niño *terso*
> Un practicante para Sor Patrocinio, y
> Un pinche para Marfori.

El Cencerro was to move from believing in 1869 that Patrocinio's stigmata
merely required medical attention to suggesting in 1870 that the 'llagas' had
some magical powers. Liberto (originally a character from *El Padre Cobos*, a
conservative paper of the 1850s) and his master discussed which of four possible
candidates was likely to gain the throne of Spain. Liberto used a combination
of cards to predict the future, and a little magic :

Aquí tiene su mercé los cuatro reyes : todos quieren la corona de España.
¿Quién cree su merced que se la llevará?
  – El rey de oros.[37]
  – Pues diga su mercé conmigo :

[37] i.e. Montpensier.

Tu velis coroni
dabo tibi miqui
convertitur in moni.

Le echo los polvos de las llagas de Sor Patrocinio : Una dos y tres : y a que no me acierta su mercé cuál es el rey de España.

– Éste.

– Cabalito : el rey de oros.[38]

It was the decided opinion of the liberal and revolutionary press, and historians such as Bermejo, that the stigmata were false, and the 'case' of Sor Patrocinio was referred to repeatedly in the 1860s, even though the trial had taken place thirty years earlier. Advertisements offering extracts from the trial appeared in 1864, a time of relative freedom for the press, and consequently a time when many attacks on Patrocinio and Claret were made in both word and drawing.[39] A series of advertisements came out in *La Nueva Iberia* in February 1868, almost identical to those in *La Democracia*, with the same agent for sale. Their appearance was almost certainly linked to the presentation of the golden rose to Isabel on 12 February 1868. On 2 February the advertisement had appeared in the normal position in the paper, the back page, but by 5 February had moved to the front page. This coincided with the build-up towards the ceremony of the presentation of the rose which was occurring in other sections of the press,[40] and was no doubt intended to draw attention to the negotiations supposed to have preceded the presentation.

A similar revival of interest in Patrocinio's trial as a means of prompting doubts about her integrity was intended by an article called 'Misterios' published by Señor Lorenzana in the *Diario Español*, probably in 1865. It began by discussing in general terms the nature of mystical experience which led to complete union with God, and which could produce certain phenomena visible to the outside world such as the appearance of the stigmata. Then it turned from the general to the particular :

[38] *El Cencerro* (Cencerrada 87) 1870. The reason for the reference to the 'polvos de las llagas de Sor Patrocinio' was in the connection often made between the nun and Celestina. *Los polvos de la Madre Celestina*, a play by Hartzenbusch, was popular in the 1840s. See Félix Herrero Salgado, *Cartelera Teatral Madrileño II: años 1840-1849, Cuadernos bibliográficos*, no. 9, (Madrid, 1963).

For other passing references, see *Jeremías* of 25 April 1869, *Gil Blas* 'Sin nombrarla' of 11 February 1865 : 'el éxtasis llagó sus manos, y se las curó un trozo de papel sellado,' and 'Cantares', of 1 July 1865 :

A la reja del convento
no me vengas a silbar;
ya que no me quitas llagas
no me las vengas a dar.

[39] e.g. *La Democracia*, 30 December 1864 :

ESTRACTO
DE LA CAUSA SEGUIDA
A LA MONJA SOR PATROCINIO
POR EL JUZGADO DEL BARQUILLO DE ESTA CORTE

Véndese a Dos Reales en la administración de *La Iberia*, Calle de Valverde, número 16.

[40] *La Época*, for example, carried items related to the ceremony on 9 January and 6, 10, 11, 12, 14, and 21 February.

Mas hé aquí que entre nosotros se declara un caso de estigmatización cuya celebridad viene en *crescendo* desde 1835. No necesitamos describir puntualmente ni individualmente este *caso*, porque basta aludirle para que sea de todos conocido. Este *caso*, lejos de edificar, escandaliza; lejos de consolar, aflige; lejos de regocijar, entristece. Con motivos de este *caso*, unos se ríen, otros se lamentan, éstos insultan, aquéllos compadecen, algunos lo explotan, no pocos le consideran como un plagio diabólico, y nadie, absolutamente nadie, le concede un origen divinamente místico. Entre este *caso* y los siniestros que con tanta frecuencia conmueven hondamente los cimientos del edificio político, media, según el común sentir del vulgo, un lazo indisoluble y pavoroso. Si los ministerios se forman, se modifican, se disuelven o se levantan, resucitando al cuarto día de entre los muertos, de una manera insólita y chocante, tiene el *caso* la culpa, dice el vulgo.[41]

It argued then that the 'caso' threatened the whole system of representative government in Spain, since it appeared that the superstitious monarch of the country was under the power of a nun of doubtful integrity. Such a use of Patrocinio's 'caso' was absurd in its extremism, and some insight into other aspects of the matter can be gained from the pro-Patrocinio biography by Benjamín Jarnés which includes as an appendix the *causa y sentencia* relating to the faking of the stigmata.[42]

Valle-Inclán's line on this aspect of Patrocinio is based on her reaction to the statements made about her. This is more complex than the simple expression of resentment at the exaggerated attacks of anti-clerical groups : it is inserted into the text so as to show Patrocinio's skill at playing on the Queen's sense of guilt :

– ¡Señora, los consejos de una monja nada valen!
– ¡A ti te visita el Epíritu Santo!
– ¡Mis cinco llagas, escarnecidas por la impiedad, no son favores celestiales! ¡Los falsos libros de la ciencia masónica lo declaran!
– ¡No me aflijas, Patrocinio!
– ¡En Francia hubo una epidemia de beatas con las cinco llagas!
– ¡Me matas!
– ¡Señora, ya una vez fui desterrada, y mis trabajos y persecuciones no acabaron!

Corte 244

As for the 'llagas' themselves, some doubt is thrown on their validity by the Queen's petulant outburst : '¡Patrocinio es una santa insoportable! Suponiendo que sea santa, porque hay quien se ríe de sus llagas' (*Corte* 241). A categorical statement is thus avoided, although Valle-Inclán weights the evidence psycho-

---

[41] Quoted by E. M. Villarasa and J. I. Gatell, op. cit., 45. As conservative historians they point out how exaggerated a view of Patrocinio this was, and add that it was natural that such a talented woman should captivate Isabel.

[42] Benjamin Jarnés, *Sor Patrocinio, la monja de las llagas*. Published in 1929, this work was too late to have been a source for Valle-Inclán.

logically towards the possibility that they were faked.[43] It does not matter ultimately whether they are real or false : what matters is that they were believed to be false.

The charisma of Patrocinio

In general, the reputation of being either miraculous or miracle-working is not derived solely from amazing feats accomplished to the wonder or satisfaction of onlookers : the charisma of the person deemed miraculous often induces onlookers to a miraculous rather than a rational interpretation of events. In the case of Patrocinio, both those who were for her and those against felt the strength of her personality, the aura of saintliness or assumed saintliness. Baldomera Martínez, a schoolgirl under Patrocinio, recalls : 'Entraba en el colegio y era como si entrase la Virgen. Las niñas cruzaban los brazos, quedábamos mudas, como mármoles.'[44]

More detail about her physical appearance is given by Guzmán de León, who adds reservations about whether she possessed a moral beauty equal to her physical charms :

No podríamos llamarla hermosa porque sus facciones no eran perfectas, pero tenía un cutis sumamente fino y sonrosado, pequeña y bien formada la mano, lustroso el cabello, y la frente sobre todo, tan tersa y limpia que no parecía sino que en ella se hubiesen de transparentar las más leves ideas, las menores sensaciones de alma.

Un mediano observador hubiera notado sin embargo, que sus labios eran harto delgados para expresar la dulzura y sencillez del corazón, y su mirada demasiado penetrante, a pesar de elevarse rara vez del suelo, para ser la de un espíritu tímido como a primera vista parecía.[45]

'Sin nombrarla', a piece published by Roberto Robert in *Gil Blas* on 11 February 1865, moved similarly, but more dramatically, from an evocation of the traditional odour of sanctity, to a tone of increasing attack :

Esparce alrededor suyo suave fragancia . . . [sic] es lirio en capullo, es azucena blanca, es violeta escondida; su aroma es regalo de magnates . . . Es bella como las vírgenes del Señor; sombra su labio el bozo y la noche sus acciones; es incombustible como el amianto; sobrenada como el corcho; rasa el agua sin mojarse como la blanca pluma del cisne; atrae el hierro como el imán; levanta edificios como las hadas . . . [sic]

More lighthearted were the deflating comments of *El Cascabel* on 23 July 1865, where a writer told of how his desires to meet the nun had been tempered by the report of an interview another person had with her : 'una persona, que la ha visto y hablado, dice que en los diferentes diálogos que ha tenido con ella, no ha hecho nunca más que *"responder concisamente y arrojarle miradas, que*

---

[43] Galdós, by contrast, is quite unequivocal on this matter. Domiciana tells Lucila of how she helped Patrocinio to induce the wounds : all that was needed was '*la clemátide vitalba*, que el vulgo llama *hierba pordiosera'*. *Los duendes de la camarilla. Episodios Nacionales Cuarta serie, no. 3*, (1903, reprinted in *Obras completas*, Madrid, 1968), II, 1651.

[44] Jarnés, op.cit., p. 168.

[45] Guzmán de León, *El último Borbón*, I, 95.

dicha persona las sentía a veces como si algo de aire tocase en su pulmón". Digo a VV. que es una ganga una conversacioncita con la reverenda madre. No tengo yo el pulmón para esos tratos.'

In the *Ruedo* Patrocinio's charisma provides an admirable means for measuring the gullibility of the characters. In *Corte* IV.i there is a reference to a miraculous appearance of the nun in El Coto de los Carvajales at the same time as she was in the convent of the Trinità dei Monti. Here the fervent credulity of the Marqués de Torre-Mellada is challenged by the disbelief of his wife and Feliche. The example he adduces to reinforce his argument does nothing but bring the original miracle into disrepute through association : '¿Vas a negar los milagros? Ahí tienes el Cristo de Medinaceli. ¡Pues ése todos los viernes guiña un ojo y tuerce la boca !' (*Corte* 92).

Yet despite the scepticism aroused in the mind of the reader by the enthusiasm of a fool like Torre-Mellada, Sor Patrocinio does emerge as a woman of imposing presence, who by sheer force of personality alone would have been able to exert considerable influence at Court. Her honeyed speaking tones and gliding movements are evoked in the *Ruedo* by recourse to the imagery of music and dramatic theatre. Furthermore, the odour she emits appears an authentic proof of sanctity. After the 'miracle' in which the inkwell is suddenly filled (causing the Queen immediately to sink to her knees) Patrocinio's presence gives the full impression of the saint : 'Sor Patrocinio extasiaba los ojos con musicales quejas, rendida a los dones del Espíritu Santo. La envolvía el aliento de aquellos celestes mensajes. Exudaba una suave fragancia de rosas y nardos, un divino bálsamo, que hacía traslucido el rostro de la seráfica' (*Viva* 173). There is a suggestion that the odour of lilies Patrocinio habitually leaves in her wake makes the Queen dizzy for natural reasons, although the dizziness becomes a transport of relief when it appears that attached to the lilies that produce the overpowering perfume is a note of suggested ministerial changes (*Corte* 245).[46]

It appears also from Valle-Inclán's version that the impressiveness of Patrocinio is not entirely involuntary. In the dramatic encounter between Isabel and Patrocinio in *Corte* X.vi at the convent of the Madres de Jesús, the nun appears in full glory : 'La Seráfica Madre quedó en pie, los brazos abiertos en cruz, mostrando la palma sangrienta de las manos, sobre las dos novicias arrodilladas, alumbrantes con sus velillas verdes : La figura de la monja tenía un acento de pavor milagrero y dramático' (*Corte* 239).

Patrocinio the political intriguer

Patrocinio as a public figure was complex. The biography of her by Jarnés supplies ample information about her desire to remain a poor, humble nun, and yet this was coupled with a close relationship with Isabel which inevitably brought her into contact with a more sumptuous and more worldly existence. Roberto Robert in 'Sin nombrarla' outlined the contradiction:

Su vida es el escondido retiro, y *La Correspondencia* publica por donde desliza su lijera planta; su voto es la pobreza, y suntuosos gabinetes, llevados en alas del mágico vapor, la trasladan instantáneamente de un estremo a otro de la

[46] The possible interpretations of this incident receive sensitive treatment in Emma Susana Speratti-Piñero, *El ocultismo en Valle-Inclán*, (London, 1974), pp. 160-1.

Península; se consagró al cielo, y la imbécil tierra gime hipócritamente a pretesto de que abre su seno a cada paso con zanjas y cimientos.

Such discrepancies are not over-stressed in the *Ruedo*, although some liking for the pleasures of life is hinted at in the 'secreta merendona de compota y chocolate' that she enjoys with the Queen and Claret before the saying of the rosary (*Viva* 99). There is, moreover, a marked discrepancy between the series of clichés produced by the prioress ('La Madre Patrocinio, fuera de su convento, no es más que una pobre monjita ignorante, como todas nosotras' (*Corte* 241)) and Patrocinio's evident interventions in the Queen's decisions (*Corte* 245, *Viva* 171–3, *Baza* 16–17).

Most of what was said about Patrocinio's interventions in political life could inevitably only be conjecture, with the result that one of the most salient features of her public self was her mystery. We have seen already how Valle-Inclán shows the relationship of Queen and nun to be psychologically credible and the belief in miraculous appearances and manifestations to be an optional extra. The Queen's belief in the nun's miraculous nature, though fluctuating, is part and parcel of a personal submission to a stronger personality, which deals out deft deflation to the monarch's floundering attempts to regain self-confidence. Thus, when Isabel maintains that it will be possible to crush the revolt of the generals since they must ultimately be loyal to her out of gratitude for positions they owe to her, she is rapidly and neatly rebuffed : 'La Señora se encendía con despechado desgaire y buches de paloma real. Clavaba su alfiler la monja con musicales mieles' (*Viva* 172).

Another light is shed on the nature of Patrocinio's power immediately after the supposed miracle of the inkwell when she undertakes a journey of great secrecy to deliver the signed and compromising letter to the Pope :

Se aleja entre los sollozos de la Señora. Por el postigo del Moro *voló, alechuzada,* a meterse en un coche con tiro de mulas *que tenía apagados los faroles.* Rodó el coche : *Una mano presurosa, saliendo entre lutos, bajó las cortinillas.* La Seráfica Madre, al trote de las mulas bernardas, *huía* por las callejuelas del viejo Madrid. *Penetró el coche en un zaguán palaceño,* y detrás, *con lento sigilo, fueron entornadas las hojas del portón.* La seráfica, *sin ruido, toda velada, desaparece* por una galería con los cuadros del Vía Crucis. *De trecho en trecho, un brasero de cobre. El fámulo* de sotanilla y vericú corre el sahumerio, inflados los carrillos sobre la chufleta. Al final de la galería los espejos de un estrado multiplican las luces.

Viva 173 (italics mine)

The effect of this passage, and in particular of the italicised sections, is to suggest a cloak and dagger atmosphere of conspiracy, secrecy and danger worthy of a poor pot-boiler. Elements 'typical' of Valle-Inclán and others closer to popular sources are mingled. The adjective 'alechuzada' and the twinkling lights multiplied by mirrors are features we find in the *esperpentos* and earlier works, while the coach with its lamps out, the stealthy hand lowering the blinds, the cautious entry through the gateway, the muffled and veiled nun disappearing down the gallery lit only by the glow from the *brasero* are all details which could have come straight from a novel by Eugène Sue or one of

68

his imitators. They represent the type of action common in the literature most liked by the characters of the *Ruedo* and undermine by association the integrity and dignity of Patrocinio. Valle-Inclán does more than emulate the atmosphere of this sub-standard literary genre. The subtle changes of tense add to the confusion and excitement of the moment, and are evocative of possible changes in the order of time. Thus the idea of existential chaos is created, chaos that is the echo of the disturbed state of affairs in Spain when religious advisers resort to subterfuge and immerse themselves in melodramatic action worthy of a film by Eisenstein. This new depth of suggestion enriches what would otherwise be a mere parody of the melodramatic novel, and combines real, apparent and possible distortions in reality and the portrayal of it.

Patrocinio's private life

As a part of general press attacks which hinted or declared that Patrocinio was not the poor or obedient nun she professed herself to be, inevitably doubts were cast on the vow of chastity also. At its most innocent such comment merely included Patrocinio with other religious figures in scenes of indecorous behaviour. *El Caos*, for example, on 20 June 1870 added the following details to its creation of the scene of Isabel's abdication of her right to the throne in favour of her son Alfonso :

> El tío *infalible*,[47] tocará un solo de violón a cuatro manos, acompañándose con los pies del Concilio.
> Claret y la *llagada* amenizarán el espectáculo con un can-cán.

In the *aleluya El Padre Clarinete*, illustration number 24, accompanied by the couplet which says of Claret 'con *Paca* por los Conventos/Pasa felices momentos', Patrocinio in the background appears to be brandishing *banderillas* for a mock bullfight between the King Consort and the Queen's confessor. On 21 April 1869 she appeared in a cartoon in *La Flaca* as providing gay accompaniment to Isabel's imagined arrival in Spain from France.

More serious were the suggestions made by the revolutionary *Jeremías* on 11 April 1869. It had been reported that Patrocinio was to found a convent in France into which some Spanish nuns would be admitted. *Jeremías* raised a 'practical' question about the buildings :

> Nada se dice del ingeniero de minas que debe acompañar a Sor Patrocinio para hacer la vía subterránea que ha de poner en comunicación el convento de monjas con alguna corporación de padres de almas tan fornidos como buenos creyentes; pero la obra se hará, porque las monjas, como son tan medrosas, necesitan fuerte compañía.
> Y pregunto yo : ¿No sería más económico fundar conventos que fuesen a la vez de monjas y de frailes?

Bermejo, anxious to repeat gossip, and yet remain respectable, reported rumours of an unnatural relationship between the King Consort and the nun : 'Se murmuraba que D. Francisco, por las frecuentes visitas y a horas desusadas, que hacía a Sor Patrocinio, hubo de tener con ella apegamientos fuera de modo

---

[47] i.e. Pius IX, who in 1870 had promulgated the doctrine of papal infallibility.

que debilitaban en mucho la santidad de la monja y la fe del adorador.' Although this was then tempered by an evasive 'pero éstas son cosas muy hondas, de las cuales no puedo dar testimonio', his conclusion, admittedly qualified, still damned Patrocinio : 'aun cuando soy dado a presumir que Sor Patrocinio no ha de haber sido digna compañera entre las verdaderas vírgenes del Señor. Esta es presunción mía, que no obligo a nadie a que la respete, ni me enojaré contra aquel que me la contradiga.'[48]

Of all this we find very little in the *Ruedo*, perhaps a sign of better taste in Valle-Inclán, perhaps omitted in order that more weight should be given to the indecorous behaviour of the Queen. Furthermore, this side of Patrocinio is on the extremes of the suppositions of the press, and as such must be strictly relegated to the category of rumour. No hint is given of a cavorting or immoral Patrocinio, except by association, in the reported coplas

> – ¡Isabel y Marfori!
> ¡Patrocinio y Claret!
> ¡Para formar un banco,
> vaya unos cuatro pies!
>
> *Corte* 219

There is also the moment in *Viva* VI.xv when Isabel pleads human frailty and her love as a mother as excuses for her actions : '¡Patrocinio, no te enojes, pero es una lástima que no hayas parido ! ¡Ya veríamos lo que tú eras puesta en mi caso!' Patrocinio's immediate and unusually long and spirited reply puts the reader on guard :

> ¡Jamás he quebrantado mis votos! ¡Jamás he abjurado de mis promesas! Casada en el mundo, hubiera implorado la divina ayuda para guardarle fidelidad al tálamo. ¡Esposo mío celestial, tú sabes cómo tu sierva te ama ! ... [sic] ¡Sin duda, puede mucho el maligno! ¡Pueden mucho sus tentaciones! ¡Las concupiscencias y los malos ejemplos pueden mucho! *¿Pero qué estado se ve libre de asechanzas y ocasiones de pecar? ¡El ser monja profesa no excusa las tentaciones, y el más santo, más tentado!*
>
> *Viva* 172 (italics mine)

The compromising end of the outburst is not lost in the spate of general lamentation about the world and its temptations. Patrocinio's ready protestations about her virtue and innocence, followed by the statements on temptation, quietly condemn her out of her own mouth. But Valle-Inclán goes no further in following this aspect of the popular image, retaining as his main target the 'monja embustera' who held the gullible Queen of Spain under her sway.

III PRIM

In the *Ruedo*, General Prim stands out as the probable leader of the coming revolution. Even in the brief glimpses we have of him in the first book of *Corte*, he is singled out for our attention, although at at this point he is at the head of those repressing the rebellious masses, and not the rebel general that he will

[48] Bermejo, *Estafeta*, III, 238.

become later. From the very outset then, the military, and Prim above all, reveal themselves as an essential element in Spanish politics. The presence of a soldier at the heart of political power in Spain is nothing out of the ordinary, but both historians of the time and those of the present day look on Prim as something more than a good general who happened to have become involved in politics.[49] Before he reached the height of his power in 1868 and 1869, Prim was already a man to be reckoned with, and enjoyed considerable national prestige. His military exploits in Morocco and Mexico in the 1860s and his involvement in the minor risings of the pre-revolutionary period marked him out as the natural focal point of revolutionary plotting.

Nonetheless, Prim's national prestige has its paradoxical side. The popular image of him before the revolution seems to be that of a man of attractive temperament, with an imposing personality, who had demonstrated his patriotic loyalty to Spain by his feats as a soldier. His victory in battle and his personal charisma won him the warm feeling and respect of the *pueblo*, so that when the time for the successful revolutionary coup came in September 1868, his participation in the rising was absolutely necessary as the man who would command the support of the *pueblo*, thus ensuring the success of the coup. But for Prim himself, revolution was a political act better carried out without the intervention of the *pueblo*, and this attitude was to arouse the anger, not so much of the maligned populace, as of the politicians of a radical persuasion who envisaged the revolution of September 1868 as something which might be different from the traditional *pronunciamiento*. Standing in opposition to this apocalyptic and radical vision of revolution was the fact that a revolution modelled on the French example of some eighty years earlier would not have found favour with the majority of those seeking change in Spanish politics, since they ranged from Carlists to Socialists, with a broad band of liberals in the middle whose vested interests made their enthusiastic support for radical reform unlikely. A major part of Prim's importance was that he was able to bind these disparate elements together better than any other one man at the time. This was despite other factors besides his limited revolutionary intentions which could alienate groups whose support he needed. His attempts to negotiate with the Carlists, for example, were doomed to failure because of their suspicions about his reputed freemasonry. For other groups, the mere fact of being a Catalan counted against him.[50]

[49] The role of Prim in the pre-revolutionary period was followed closely by Fernando Garrido, *Historia del reinado del último Borbón de España*, 3 vols, (Madrid, 1868-9), and by Francisco Pí y Margall, op. cit., IV. Raymond Carr, op.cit., p. 310 summarised Prim thus:

El más capaz de los conspiradores era un hombre de orden; militar, habiéndose quedado con la cartera de Guerra, sabía pensar como un político civil; progresista, podía recurrir a los radicales, pero creía que debía conservarse la coalición revolucionaria con los unionistas, única esperanza de que el régimen llegase a ser aceptado por los más. Aunque duro – sus adversarios le consideraban un dictador –, era capaz de las sutilezas y los compromisos de la política parlamentaria. Más fuerte que el ambicioso Serrano o que el orgulloso Topete, fue indiscutiblemente el hombre de Estado más grande de la revolución. Prueba de ello es que su muerte significó el fin de la coalición de 1868.

[50] Cf. the anti-Catalan criticism of Claret.

Two main sides of Prim are outlined in the *Ruedo* : the popular image of a national hero, and speculation about his possible post-revolutionary politics. This double vision acquires a certain unity from its sources, since the two contradictory aspects are linked to criticism made of Prim in the popular press of 1868 onwards : criticism by extreme revolutionaries for displaying, so they thought, personal aspirations to wield absolute power in Spain, and by conservative sections of the press for the same supposed ambitions, and for realising all their worst fears about the revolutionary movement.

Prim the national hero

It is hardly surprising that the satirical press should have compared Prim as a national hero to other figures of the same stature. He himself suggested one such point of comparison in a speech made as Minister of War in the first session of the Cortes to be held after the revolution. He declared vehemently that he was opposed to any restoration of the Bourbons. Any intended restoration of this type would have supposed personal ambitions in him, as the Bourbon heir was Alfonso, only eleven at the outbreak of revolution. A regent would have been necessary, the best qualified candidate being Prim. In his speech he stressed his political altruism, and praised his own virtue and humility :

> Nunca he tenido ambición ni he envidiado nada a nadie. Y si no he tenido antes ambición, menos lo tendré ahora, que por mi posición en todos sentidos no tengo nada que desear. Sí, sólo una cosa con toda la vehemencia de mi alma : ver constituído el país y asegurada la libertad. Para esto no repararé en hacer todo género de sacrificios : soy de la raza de los Guzmanes, he dicho más de una vez a la condesa de Reus [his wife], haciéndola estremecer.
>
> ¡Restaurar en el trono a D. Alfonso de Borbón! ¡Qué delirio! ¡Qué imposibilidad! Y esto no necesita más demostración de la que toda España dice como yo : restaurar la dinastía caída imposible, imposible, imposible.[51]

Prim's reference to his being 'de la raza de los Guzmanes' was no doubt intended to recall the legendary case of the loyalty of a soldier to his state as found in Alonso Pérez de Guzmán el Bueno (1256–1309), who refused to surrender the besieged town of Tarifa where he had been sent as *alcalde* by Sancho IV and which was under attack by the king's rebellious son, Juan. Even when the infante threatened to cut the throat of his eldest son, Guzmán refused to surrender : some accounts say that he even offered his own dagger for the killing.[52]

[51] Prim's speech of 22 February 1869, as reported in the *Gaceta de Madrid* 23 February 1869. The speech was given on the day on which the members of the provisional government renounced their powers and agreed on one person, Nicolás María Rivero, to form a ministry. *La Iberia* reported on this on its front page 23 February 1869, and singled out the section where Prim declared that 'ha sido echada la dinastía al extranjero por la fuerza de la opinión del país; por eso mi convicción de que no volverá jamás, jamás, jamás !'.

[52] See the 'Crónica de don Sancho el bravo', *Crónicas de los reyes de Castilla, I, Biblioteca de Autores Espanoles*, no. 66 (Madrid, 1875), p. 89.

There was an almost immediate reaction to these words by the popular press. On 25 February 1869, just three days later, *El Padre Cobos* commented that 'aun admitiendo la hipótesis de que Prim fuera descendiente por línea recta del gran Alfonso Pérez Guzmán, tanto ha podido cambiar su naturaleza que por más que me restrego los ojos, no veo entre uno y otro paralelismo'.[53] After this, Prim was characterised frequently as Guzmán, particularly in the conservative press. *La Mano Oculta* was the first to seize the idea, which it elaborated in a series of playlets ironically entitled the 'Teatro de los bufos revolucionarios' published between 10 January and 9 June 1869.[54] On 10 March the setting of the playlet 'Un conjuro misterioso' was 'Época – la de los Guzmanes'. The playlet dealt with the triumvirate of Serrano, Prim and Topete (here appearing as El papá, Juanillo el Moreno and Neptunete) and its pledges to the *pueblo*. At the suggestion of a monarchy, Prim's reaction was drawn almost verbatim from his speech in the Cortes :

> Imposible . . . imposible . . . imposible . . . [sic]
> lo juro por la cruz de aquesta espada.
> Yo de la raza soy de los Guzmanes.

He continued as Guzmán in the next number of the series, when he drew on his claims of illustrious ancestry to justify his political actions. Here he showed regal ambitions, and at the question of General Bum-Bum, '¿Buscas un rey?' replied 'Te equivocas, pienso en mí, y esto me basta'.

Another conservative paper, *Las Ánimas*, had made a passing reference to Prim as Guzmán on 22 March 1869, and on 19 March launched into more direct attack with an article called 'Las Ánimas'. In this, the souls or spectres of various characters were conjured up, among them that of Prim, whose words revealed the uncertain nature of his claim to belong to a race of heroes : 'Yo me figuro que soy Guzmán : Yo me figuro que soy valiente : Yo creo que hago temblar a mi mujer.' His pretensions were crushed by a reaction that might have been more appropriate to a disillusioned liberal than to a last-ditch conservative paper, and which smacks of Dante in the choice of appropriate castigation :

> Calla menguado : ésa es la pena que te se ha [sic] impuesto, por todo lo contrario de lo que tú crees. Tendrás miedo de las mujeres : te atormentará la idea de la lealtad, por lo mismo que no supiste lo que era en vida : todos

---

[53] This was the first number of the third series of *El Padre Cobos*, a paper whose conservative nature had been defined when it appeared during the Bienio Liberal 1854-6.

[54] The playlets in the series were as follows :

10 January 1869 : 'Fragmento de una comedia que lo mismo puede parar en tragedia que en sainete'
28 January 1869 : 'Duelo entre un infante y un duque'
7 February 1869 : 'La Gloriosa. Comedia de magia en varios actos'
10 March 1869 : 'Tragi-Comedia. El Conjuro misterioso'
15 April 1869 : 'Desde Toledo a Madrid'
23 April 1869 : 'El rigor de las desdichas'
11 May 1869 : '¿Quién quiere esto? Comedia burlesco-sentimental en varios actos'
9 June 1869 : 'Sainete titulado la espada de Pompampie'

se reirán de tu valor; porque saben que te ocultaste cada vez que hubo peligro, y sacrificaste a tus amigos.[55]

The contribution of *Don Quijote* on 5 May 1869 was yet more refined in its satire : it published a sonnet supposedly dedicated to Prim by the illustrious ancestor he had claimed. Mockery is gently present even in the title 'Alonso Pérez de Guzmán el Bueno a su deudo D. Juan Prim y Prats', throwing into wry contrast the unmistakably Catalan name of the general and the fully *castizo* name of Guzmán. Tongue-in-cheek satire and hidden barbs appear throughout the poem, which is the most sophisticated of all the popular criticism of Prim :

Tú que imitaste la feroz porfía
Con que supe vencer a raza impura;
Que sabes parodiar con tu bravura
Mi valor, mi lealtad y mi hidalguía.

Vástago ilustre de la raza mía
Que a España presta paz, dicha y ventura;
Que cumple el juramento cuando jura,
Que nunca la ambición sus pasos guía.

Yo te saludo Juan, con la esperanza
De que no asustes nunca a tu chiquillo,
Ni al clamor de tu esposa te hagas sordo.

Que al largar los *jamases* de ordenanza,
Y al escupir también por el colmillo,
Te acuerdas que está encima el trueno gordo.

The reason why the characterisation of Prim as Guzmán should interest us is a negative one. The only paper to give detailed development to the Guzmán theme was *La Mano Oculta*,[56] and yet, although all the relevant numbers of the paper are in Valle-Inclán's library at Pontevedra, he appears to have chosen deliberately to develop instead the image of Prim as a new Santiago.[57] The choice is odd, since it is obvious immediately that the two heroes are not equivalent in their implications : whereas Santiago suggests valour, apocalyptic military zeal and overpowering charisma, Guzmán, albeit also known for valour too, is noted more particularly for his loyalty and for complete submission to the monarch of the time.

[55] Other more serious writers had directed the same type of criticism at Prim. Fernando Garrido, for example, criticised him for failing to appear at the rising of 22 June 1866 :
El jefe de un movimiento no puede contar con la eventualidad de llegar a tiempo presentándose en la hora precisa que va a estallar, sino que debe hallarse en el centro de la acción para que todos los actores se presenten oportunamente y no se omita ninguna de las circunstancias precisas al buen éxito. Así fue horrible en esas circunstancias el abandono en que se encontraron los instrumentos dóciles de la ambición de los aventureros, y, lastimoso el cuadro que presentaba el pueblo después de la derrota.
op. cit., III, 1055.
[56] Besides the examples already cited, Prim was mentioned in passing as Guzmán in the revolutionary *La Flaca* (Barcelona) on 31 December 1869, and appeared as such in the same paper in 'La Casa de Poco Trigo' 9 January 1870. He was also mentioned as Guzmán by the conservative *Jeremías* on 13 April 1869.
[57] See Chapter II.

In his hypercritical vision of Prim, Valle-Inclán may have wished to avoid any suggestion of loyalty, except as broken loyalty. Even the parallel with Santiago is presented in such a way as to cast Prim in a bad light. He first appears in the *Ruedo* as a type of Santiago, but already stereotyped by popular imagery. While allusions to Santiago Matamoros evoke some echoes of his valour and patriotism, he is seen essentially, with the wisdom of hind-sight, as a puffed-up actor who relied on past prestige and the momentum of popularity to carry him into future victory. Valle-Inclán's tone here expresses the strong disappointment felt by republicans at the behaviour of Prim after the revolution. In this he differs from the other Spanish novelist turned chronicler of the revolution, Pérez Galdós, who, while telling us of Prim's shortcomings, always presented him in an optimistic light. Valle's Prim is always a caricature, and set as such from the start :

El General Prim caracoleaba su caballo de naipes en todos los baratillos de estampas litográficas : Teatral Santiago Matamoros, atropella infieles tremolando la jaleada enseña de los Castillejos : – ¡Soldados, viva la Reina!

Corte 11

This first glimpse brings an early reminder from Valle-Inclán that Prim had sworn fidelity to the Queen, and is therefore placed in an incongruous position through his plotting. In *Baza* the parallel between Prim and the patron saint of Spain is taken up again, this time with more explicit censure, since, instead of the report of the popular vision which appeared in *Corte*, we find the author's direct description of Prim which emphasises his blind faith in himself as the saviour of Spain :

Soldado de aventura, con una fe mesiánica en su estrella, no dejaba de mirarse sobre un bélico corcel de tiovivo, bordando los campos hispánicos, como otro patrón Matamoros. Con albures de cuartel y arrogancias de matante, presumía que, puesto el ros sobre una ceja, tosiendo fuerte y echando roncas, podía ser el salvador de España.

Baza 181

Here Prim is stripped of all pretension to being a person, the merry-go-round horse provoking ideas of superficial attractiveness, mechanical action and a circular motion which prevents any escape or real development and the whole implying that Prim believes he can qualify as the saviour of Spain if only he strikes the correct attitude.

Galdós also writes of a parallelism between Prim and Santiago, but his perspective and intention are quite different. In his description of the general at the battle of Los Castillejos which was to win him fame, Galdós suggests why Prim appeared to act in the miraculous way Santiago was reputed to have done at the battle of Clavijo in the ninth century. At the same time he gives us a liberal and rational explanation of how the legend of Santiago at Clavijo may have come into being. One of the main legends was that Santiago came to the aid of the Spaniards in their battle to reconquer Spain from the Moors. Early versions of the legend say that he was there at Clavijo, but only as a source of inspiration. Later accounts magnified the extent of his participation, and say that he appeared armed and mounted, and killed many infidels.[58] The idea put forward by Galdós about the origin of this legend and its parallel in Prim, was that the figure of the general in battle, bearing the standard and brandishing his sword, must have had considerable effect on both Spaniards and Moors, encouraging the former to victory, and disheartening the latter. Any impression that Prim had increased in stature, concludes Galdós, must have been due to the subjective perceptions of those present, and suggests that the appearance of Santiago at Clavijo would have been a similar case :

> Sin duda, en el ejército del rey de León hubo un Prim, que en un momento propicio a las alucinaciones produjo en todos, moros y cristianos, la ilusión perfecta de lo sobrenatural, terror para unos, enardecimiento para los otros . . . [sic] El furor del combate ciega y enloquece a los hombres . . . [sic] Los hombres que creen firmemente en los milagros, los hacen . . . [sic][59]

The different perspectives of Galdós and Valle-Inclán reflect the general differences in their attitudes as novelists. For Galdós, Prim embodies a mythical and magical power for the Spanish people, and is a means of making them respond in the best way possible. Valle-Inclán has eyes only for Prim's blind confidence in himself, in himself as a second Santiago, that is, for his own belief

---

[58] See T. D. Kendrick, *St James in Spain*, (London, 1960), pp. 19-20.

[59] Benito Pérez Galdós, *Aita Tettauen, Episodios Nacionales, Cuarta Serie* (1904-5, reprinted in *Obras Completas*, Madrid, 1968), III, 277.

Prim appears in no less than sixteen of the *Episodios nacionales* : *Montes de Oca* (1900), *Los Ayacuchos* (1900), *Bodas reales* (1900), *Los duendes de la camarilla* (1903), *La revolución de Julio* (1903-4), *O'Donnell* (1904), *Aita Tettauen* (1904-5), *Carlos IV en la Rápita* (1905), *Prim* (1906), *La de los tristes destinos* (1907), *España sin rey* (1907-8), *España trágica* (1909), *Amadeo I* (1910), *La primera República* (1911), *De Cartago a Sagunto* (1911), *Cánovas* (1912).

Galdós certainly does not neglect problematic aspects of Prim, such as his open scorn of the *pueblo*, and on this score poses a difficult question through Gervasio :

> Su amigo de usted profesa ideas que casi, casi tocan en el republicanismo y, no obstante, se junta con retrogrados, y sus principales amigotes son lo más granado de la *moderación* . . . No le sorprende a usted esta contradicción entre las ideas políticas y los gustos sociales?

All implicit censure here is dispelled by the reply of Ibero, a sympathetic character who is intended to communicate his admiration for Prim to the reader, praising qualities which others would regard as reason for criticism :

> Antes que ese contraste veo yo otro más fundamental en ese bravo chico, y es que siendo de origen muy humilde no le gusta tratarse más que con aristócratas. Ya ve usted qué bien viste : no hay otro que lleve mejor la ropa, ni quien le iguale en el refinamiento de los gustos; su rumbo, su esplendidez, nos harían creer que es noble de nacimiento; sus ideas dicen que es hijo de la plebe. Yo le quiero y le admiro.
> *Montes de Oca, Obras Completas*, II, 1162.

Likewise in *España trágica* criticism of Prim by Paúl y Ángulo is invalidated by the favourable portrait of Prim given directly by Galdós, which concludes with a comment on the criticism : 'Nadie hacía caso de estas groseras bravatas'. (*España trágica, Obras Completas*, III 998.)

A similar invalidating technique is used by Valle-Inclán in the case of Bakunin. He places the only criticism of the anarchist in the mouth of the decidedly unlikeable Boy (*Baza* 64-5).

in the puffed-up public image that has been created out of him. In terms of historical verisimilitude, it is arguable that Prim's belief in himself as a Santiago expressed the climate of opinion in Spain when war was declared against Morocco on 22 October 1859, but it seems inconsistent with a notion of his political astuteness.[60]

Valle-Inclán's Prim, created with constant reference back to the image of Santiago, is made by the constant matching to a stereo-type, into a man who is politically simplistic. The simple popular view (albeit one that is presented with irony and criticism) is counterbalanced by the demonstration of Prim's political awareness in *Baza*. Despite this counterbalancing which makes Prim as a character more credible in the terms of the novel, the dominant impression of him is close to the caricature produced by the disillusion and scepticism of the conservative press after 1868. Valle-Inclán reminds us relentlessly that the similarity between Prim and Santiago is not only a figment of the imagination of the populace, but also an integral part of Prim's concept of himself (as in *Baza* 181) All this stands in strong contrast with Galdós' recreation of the excitement engendered by the mere name of Prim in his novel of that name, where the chant '¡Prim . . . [sic] Libertad!' appears as a recurrent motif and underlying driving force.[61]

It is possible that Valle's choice not to adopt the figure of Guzmán as the source for his caricature of Prim derived from a wish to elaborate a figure better known than the one used in such a particular way by the satirical press. It is perhaps more likely that he wanted to combine certain facets of these two giants of Spanish legend and history. They had already been merged by one popular publication : an *aleluya* of 1869, the *Vida de Guzmancito*, which recounted the life of Prim in heavily satirical terms. Couplet number 16 referred to the African campaign : 'Imita a Guzmán el Bueno/ Derrotando al Saraceno' and the illustration showed Prim on a charger in battle in a position habitually given to St.

---

[60] Pí y Margall (op. cit., IV, 218) reports that a sense of missionary zeal was felt about the Moroccan campaign. Commenting on the warm reception given by the Cortes to O'Donnell's request of 22 October 1859 that war be declared, he explains :

España, país imaginativo por excelencia y cuya historia, más o menos gloriosa, cuenta como principal episodio la epopeya de la independencia, acogía con verdadero entusiasmo una guerra contra el moro. La lucha contra el supuesto eterno enemigo, la revancha de ocho siglos de dominación morisca (beneficiosa en grado sumo) era, en todos los ámbitos de la Península, popularísima. Constituía aquel entusiasmo guerrero un caso de atavismo. Por esto los diputados, haciéndose eco del sentimiento poco reflexivo, pero al menos bien definido, de la masa popular, no vacilaron en acoger con frenético entusiasmo la declaración de guerra pedida por el Gobierno de O'Donnell.

[61] Prim himself may have originally suggested the parallel with Santiago. He is said to have encouraged Spaniards in the African campaign of 1860 by the song :

A l'Africa minyons
a matar moros, a matar moros.
A l'Africa minyons
a matar moros amb canons.

See J. M. Miquel i Vergés, *El General Prim, en España y en México*, (México 1949), p. 137, and R. Olivar Bertrand, *El Caballero Prim: vida íntima, amorosa y militar*, 2 vols., (Barcelona 1952), II, 195. In the latter it is reported that Prim was greeted in September 1865 in Perales, Chinchón and Colmenar by the cry '¡Viva Prim, el Matamoros!'.

James as Santiago Matamoros in traditional iconography.[62] At all events, even if Valle did not adopt the same national hero as the conservative press did, he used the model in the same way : to suggest Prim's inflated vision of himself, not without foundation in some aspects (his courage proved in Morocco and Mexico) but with decided dangers (his ambition to wield power, perhaps to become King).

Prim the actor

The imagery which shows Prim deliberately assuming the characteristics of a well-known national hero, whether Guzmán or Santiago, is naturally related to a whole range of evocations of gestures, expressions and other features of the histrionic art. In the case of Prim, more than in any other, we see how the imagery of the *Ruedo* goes beyond a mere extension of the language of the *esperpentos*, since Prim's theatrical ways are based on the popular vision of him, and not on the aesthetic ideas of Don Estrafalario or Max Estrella.

The Prim of Valle-Inclán is totally ostentatious :

> Don Juan Prim, verdoso, cosméticas la barba y la guedeja, levita de fuelles y botas de charol con falsos tacones, que le aumentaban la estatura, sacaba el tórax. Pisando fuerte y abriendo vocales catalanas, hacía temblar el Trono de Isabel II. Decoraba sus jaquetones propósitos con la retórica progresista que resplandece en los himnos nacionales. Si juraba, era por su espada; si prometía, era por la gloria de sus laureles. – César, en las tragedias de los corrales, no declama con más pompa endecasílaba sus hechos de Farsalia.
>
> *Baza* 164

Here Valle-Inclán leads us through the levels of Prim's pretence, from the strikingly false additions, the dyed beard and high heels, intended to make him look younger and stronger than he really is,[63] then to his gesture and speech, not even in the well-modulated tones of the good actor, but in the ranting of the ham actor, with the automatic use of showy gesture and phrase.

Prim's theatrical nature is presented from a variety of perspectives. For many of the characters in the *Ruedo* he is a person of high importance in the immediately pre-revolutionary situation, an importance derived from the legend of valour and military prowess which has grown up about him. The first time we see him in *Viva*, in the opening survey of the intensification of political activity, he is a mythical figure on the horizon, swathed in the mists of exile :

> El Soldado de África, como escribían los retóricos del progresismo, conspiraba emigrado en Londres. Don Juan Prim y Prats, Teniente General, Marqués de los Castillejos, Conde de Reus y Vizconde de Bruch, era el más señalado caudillo de la revolución liberal, que prometía convertir a la patria española en feliz Arcadia. El Soldado de África, enfermo del hígado, amarillo de bilis

[62] See plates III & IV. Although it is true that Guzmán fought against the Moors on several occasions, he had also fought on their behalf. The confusion displayed in the *aleluya* suggests that Guzmán was better remembered for his battles against the Moors than for his patriotism and loyalty to his overlord.

[63] Prim's vanity was such that he refused to accept a portrait painted of him by Regnault, since it included the *pueblo* and showed him with his hair dishevelled. See Olivar Bertrand, op. cit., II, 274-6.

regicidas, aborrascaba el horizonte político con los metafóricos relámpagos de su matona, aquella que en los albores isabelinos habían feriado las camarillas apostólicas, revolucionadas frente a la Regencia Baldomera. Al General Prim las ratas palaciegas se lo figuraban siempre a caballo.

Viva 13–14

Here Valle shows the extent to which Prim's stature has become magnified by his absence. For some he is the 'Soldado de África', a figure already accepted and acceptable. For others he is a Catalan and definitely not acceptable. Valle-Inclán's language here must be treated with care. The clause 'que prometía convertir a la patria española en feliz Arcadia', expresses the exaggerated hopes held of him by liberals and revolutionaries, rather than any concrete promise on the part of Prim to bring about a political miracle in Spain. The next sentence views him from a more openly critical distance, with the perspective of a twentieth-century man contemplating the antics of the century that preceded him. Finally, the description comes full circle with an indication of the distorted way in which Prim was seen by palace inhabitants. They see him in a position of power and strength, and are afraid. There is a suggestion of them cowering in corners in order to avoid this creature that threatens to destroy them. This final vision incidentally helps to fix more firmly the Queen's perspective of Prim. Her childhood memory in *Viva* 156 is 'Al General Prim, desde los balcones le veíamos caracolear en torno a Palacio'. Now the picture is more direct and threatening, with the ugliness of possible proximity : 'La cara verde de bilis, lleno de salpicaduras el pantalón.'

This variety of perspective is continued throughout the course of the *Ruedo*. At first Prim is above all a person of imposing presence, his stature and valour increased by the imagination of the *pueblo*. He appears little in *Viva*, and on relatively formal occasions : in council with *émigrés* (*Viva* I.xii) and in council with Cabrera (*Viva* IX.v). On these occasions there is no breakthrough to what lies behind the public image. If anything, that public image becomes more rigid and fixed. When, in *Baza*, he is finally seen in more informal surroundings, the falsity of the public image and gesture is made more apparent. Captain Estévanez goes to see him in England and is non-plussed by the sight of Prim pruning roses, 'ajeno a recuerdos clásicos', but the General immediately assumes his better-known image : 'El General sacó el pecho con animosa arrogancia' (*Baza* 160); 'El Conde de Reus le abrazó, siempre con exceso de comediante en tablas' (*Baza* 161).

In the popular press, Prim's theatrical tendencies are almost invariably related to the 'género ínfimo' of the theatre. On 10 May, *La Gorda* (often wrongly taken at face value under its title of 'periódica [*sic*] liberal') suggested unkindly that 'el ilustre Conde de Reus debe en conciencia una indemnización a los empresarios del Circo de Madrid' since the spectacles at the theatre were unable to compete with the performances he was giving : the can-can was an *auto sacramental* compared with

la cabriola bufonesca que el General Prim da en la Asamblea en esta frase, digna de ser pronunciada con el estrangulado acento de una actriz bufa : 'Yo, puesta la mano sobre mi corazón honrado, respondo que no.'

79

La Gorda was inventive when it seized on an idea. Frequently its elaborations of a comparison became tedious, but in this case it took the idea of Prim's gestures with his hand and cleverly introduced the idea of subterfuge :

> Pero éste es el secreto de las zarzuelas bufas; una acción aparente encubre una acción real, y bien examinado el caso, si la mano de Prim, sube desde el puño de su espada a su pecho, baja desde su pecho a su espada y en continuo tejemaneje trae distraídos a los espectadores, éstos no acaban de comprender que la gracia de este manipuleo consiste, en que el Presidente del Consejo y su *digno compañero* el de Hacienda se dan cariñosamente la mano.

By this description of sleight of hand, a secret agreement between Prim and Figuerola, then Minister of Finance, was hinted at, and discredit was thrown upon Prim as a loyal and honourable leader of the revolution.

The press gave considerable attention to the oaths of Prim as an extension of the caricature of his claim to belong to the family of the Guzmanes. The conservative section of the press was particularly scathing about the way he had sworn loyalty and subsequently broken faith. Their point was that, since Prim had already broken his oath of loyalty to the Queen, little trust could be placed in his more recent oaths about his political intentions.

Prim's most famous oath, referred to above, was one made in 1861 at the ceremony in which he was made a Grandee of Spain. In his speech of thanks to the Queen, Prim declared that one who had been ennobled by his monarch for services to the country should fight all the harder on her behalf, because of the debt of gratitude incurred. He ended with an elaborate oath :

> Deberá hacer señora lo que, puesta la mano en el puño de su limpia espada, promete hacer el Marqués de los Castillejos : defender vuestros derechos al Trono de las Españas contra los que osaran atacarlos, y defender también vuestra persona siempre, en todas ocasiones y cualesquiera que fuesen las vicisitudes de los tiempos, hasta derramar la última gota de mi sangre, hasta exhalar mi último suspiro.[64]

La Gorda was more interested than any of the other papers in Prim's sword and the way he swore on it. On 15 July 1869 it mocked Prim's repeated references to his sword, saying that he spoke of it so often, it must be in his body, 'puesto que se le sale por la boca'. As a result, one only had to pull Prim's tongue to make him unsheath the sword. *La Gorda* returned to the same theme on 20 April 1870, reminding readers how Prim had sworn fidelity, hand on sword, to Isabel II, and was now swearing, hand on sword, in congress. The lesson of experience should be clear. Although the mockery of Prim's oaths is an extension of the Guzmán caricature which is rejected by Valle-Inclán, the oaths themselves are included by him. In *Baza* the detail of the sword is included in a welter of other details : 'Decoraba sus jaquetones propósitos con la retórica progresista que resplandece en los himnos nacionales. Si juraba, era por su espada; si prometía, era por la gloria de sus laureles' (*Baza* 164). This detail shows a knowledge of the popular image, but no eagerness to over-exploit it.

[64] Reported in *La Época*, 21 January 1861.

Prim's oaths had called public attention even in their original serious context. The day after the speech of 22 February 1869, *La Iberia*, a paper concerned principally with the serious reporting of political news, published in isolation the section where Prim had declared 'ha sido echada la dinastía al extranjero por la fuerza de la opinión del país; por eso mi convicción de que no volverá jamás, jamás, jamás'. Three months later, on 30 May 1869, *Don Quijote*, continuing its campaign against Prim, and disillusioned by the discrepancies between Prim's declarations and what it suspected to be his real intentions, quoted a series of statements made by Prim and commented upon them. The two of most interest for us come from the speeches of 22 February and 8 May 1869. The first selected the most extravagant bits from the 'Guzmán' speech : '¡Yo restaurar la dinastía caída! ¡Imposible! ¡imposible! ¡imposible! ¡Jamás! ¡Jamás! ¡Jamás!'[65] The second, also made in a session of congress, showed clearly how Prim was carried away in a frenzy of self-importance :

> *¿Cómo acusarme de felonía, cuando en el escudo de mis armas tengo las palabras honor y lealtad?* ... [sic] *Yo no deseo nada que no sea digno, que no sea noble y honrado* ... [sic]
> ... [sic] COMO YO NO TENGO UN HECHO EN MI VIDA QUE SE PUEDA CREER DESLEAL, irán viendo en los acontecimientos que hemos de ver, que no soy ambicioso, que no soy codicioso, y QUE NI EN SOMBRA PUEDO SER DESLEAL (italics and capitals as in text).[66]

In this extract, the phrases related to honour and loyalty were singled out, giving a false impression of Prim's speech. Nonetheless, the statements about honour and loyalty had been made by Prim, and *Don Quijote*'s final words had a

[65] The relevant sections of Prim's speech of 22 February were :

La historia presenta casos de Reyes que cayeron de tal o cual manera; pero no como ahora, que ha sido echada la dinastía al extranjero por la fuerza de la opinión del país; por eso mi convicción de que no volverá jamás, jamás, jamás ... Restaurar en el trono a D. Alfonso de Borbón! Qué delirio! Qué imposibilidad! Y esto no necesita más demostración que la de que toda España dice como yo : restaurar la dinastía caída imposible, imposible, imposible.

Although *Don Quijote*'s version is contracted, it does not distort.

[66] The speech from which these statements were selected by *Don Quijote* was made in defence of hints that Prim had high ambitions, reaching perhaps to the throne. His reply was addressed to Sr. Balaguer, and the relevant sections of the original were :

Hay una intención en esto; yo no puedo conocer cuál sea. ¿Cómo se me había de hacer una acusación semejante? ¿Cómo acusarme de felonía cuando en el escudo de mis armas tengo las palabras *honor y lealtad*?

Sí, lo he dicho una vez y otra vez señores diputados, y la Cámara me ha de permitir que lo repita : yo no ambiciono nada; yo no quiero nada; yo no deseo nada que no sea digno, que no sea noble y levantado, y los que dicen lo contrario, si lo creen, yo tengo el honor de decirles que se equivocan; y si no lo creen y sin embargo de todo dicen eso, los abandono a los remordimientos de su conciencia, que ya lo voy dudando.

Por fortuna, el tiempo y lo que vaya sucediendo convencerán más y más, no a la gran mayoría de los señores diputados, que no lo necesitan sino convencerán más al país, a ese país que me puede a mí creer con intenciones maquiavélicas, y yo no pienso tal cosa, porque los hechos valen más que las palabras, y como yo no tengo un hecho en mi vida que se pueda creer desleal, irán viendo en los acontecimientos que hemos de ver, que yo no soy ambicioso, que yo ni en sombra puedo ser desleal.

vicious sting : '*La posteridad y la historia apreciarán la lealtad y el honor* POR EL SISTEMA PRIM' (italics and capitals as in text).

Prim's other much-used rhetorical device, repetition of such key words as 'jamás' and 'imposible', was noted by papers of all political opinions. It came to be a motif by which one could identify him in any satirical sketch. The very short-lived anti-Amadeo paper *El Mono Rey* had as its subtitle '¡¡¡Jamar . . . jamar . . . y . . . jamar!!![sic]', a dig both at Prim's emphatic verbiage, and at the fact that he had finally restored the monarchy, although it was not the hated Bourbon monarchy. Again, Valle-Inclán's use of this device is brief, and relatively well-hidden. In Prim's reaction to the news that Fernando de Coburgo has rejected the offer of the Spanish throne, Prim deflects attention from his own rhetoric by paying attention to that of Olózaga :

> Don Salustiano Olózaga, gloria del progresismo, nos abrió el horizonte de una elocuente promesa. Todos los mitos son bellos, y a mi corazón de soldado, ninguno como la Unión Iberica. Pero yo pregunto : Ese hermoso mito, ¿puede conciliarse con las realidades? La revolución debe alejarse de toda política de aventuras. ¡No soñemos! ¡No soñemos! ¡No soñemos!
>
> *Viva* 17[67]

Valle-Inclán's creation of Prim vacillates between the portrait of a man who is a bad actor and knows it, and the portrait of a man who actually believes in the rather extravagant image he has created for himself. When talking to fellow conspirators for instance, Prim's intention is to create an impression of invincible immortality. Pául y Angulo refers to the case of the plot on the *Omega* to kill Prim, and the general's reaction is unrealistic and over-confident, but true to his public image. He relies on the art of the theatre to give weight to his words : 'El Soldado de África respiró el aura de sus grandes horas. Arranque teatral, gesto fogoso de farsa mediterránea', and declares melodramatically :

> ¡Mi vida, señores, la respetan las balas! Soy providencialista, y creo que la respetan para abrir una nueva senda en los destinos de España. En Castillejos, el plomo que rasgaba la gloriosa enseña, que hería a mi caballo, que mataba a mis ayudantes, a mí me respetaba.
>
> *Baza* 163

This claim of immortality is no invention on the part of Valle-Inclán. We learn from Pí y Margall that at the battle of Wad-Ras in the Moroccan campaign (23 March 1860), a friend advised Prim to be careful of the bullets flying about

---

[67] Galdós supplies us with two references to the 'jamases' of Prim in *España trágica*. There is at first a hint of irony, since at the moment when 'comenzó Vicente a expresar su opinión recordando los tres jamases de Prim', children's laughter is heard outside. Later in the novel, as he comments on the death of Prim, Galdós seems to take the subject more seriously : 'Su figura histórica era la puerta de los famosos *jamases*, la cual tapaba el hueco por donde habían salido seres e institutos condenados a no entrar mientras el viviera. Muerto Prim, quedó abierto el boquete, y por él se veían sombras lejanas que miraban medrosas, sin atreverse a dar un paso acá.' (*España trágica, Obras Completas*, III, pp. 903 and 1008.)

him. Prim replied : 'No hay cuidado. Las balas vienen todas con sobre y ningún sobre va dirigido a mí.'[68]

In short, Prim's theatrical performances are nearly always linked to a sense of and concern for his own prestige. This is made abundantly clear in the case of the rising of 9 August 1868. Prim at first is made to say 'Jamás arriesgaré el triunfo de nuestros ideales en una aventura romántica', a piece of impeccable reasoning, but this is subsequently undermined by the concern for his own prestige which emerges as the most important factor in his decision not to support the rising : '*Por mi prestigio y la grandeza de nuestros ideales*, no puedo echarme al monte con cuatro gatos, exponiéndome a ser deshecho por la primera partida que me salga al camino' (*Baza* 200, italics mine). Here we see Prim's order of priorities, and the whole of the sentence expresses his desire to withdraw in personal terms. He alludes to himself in the singular, and not in the 'we' of himself and his revolutionary comrades : a sign of his self-centredness.

Prim's politics

Both conservative and liberal sections of the popular press drew on the same aspects of Prim for their satire : his theatrical manner, his oaths, his rhetoric. His histrionic public manner must have clouded his real intentions for all political groups, and the resulting antagonisms make it difficult for us to ascertain the real nature of his politics. The solution adopted initially by Valle-Inclán is to give us a complete range of subjective views of Prim, each with its own degree of distortion. The views range from the cynicism of Dolorcitas Chamorro, who says of Prim's attitude to the candidature of Montpensier : '¡Ya sabes que pone el veto a su candidatura para rey el trasto de Pringue!' (*Corte* 41), that is, that he is a spanner in the political works, to the cynicism of Adolfito Bonifaz : 'De Prim a Narváez, son todos ellos más absolutistas y menos constitucionales que Calomarde. Prim es Narváez, con acento catalán y sin gracia gitana' (*Corte* 189). By contrast, Torre-Mellada takes Prim seriously, but is equally simplistic in his judgment. He discounts the possibility of Prim's rising to power because he is 'grado treinta y tres de la masonería' and therefore cannot be 'consejero de la Reina Católica de España' (*Corte* 187), his innocence revealed first by his belief that the two are mutually exclusive, and second by his belief that a rise to power can only be within the monarchy. A very different perspective of Prim is given in the meeting at which he learns of Fernando de Coburgo's rejection of the Spanish throne. For one follower, the problem with Prim is his lack of illusion ('le faltan las alas. ¡No sueña!' (*Viva* 18)) but this same realism of Prim is praised as a virtue by Vallín when he speaks to the *habitués* of the Casino in the hope that these conservative elements will support him. He stresses, for example, Prim's distaste for popular participation in revolution (*Viva* 40), and reassures his audience on Prim's attitude to slavery. (Prim's moderate and cautious approach to slavery was in fact revealed in 1869 by his support for Becerra's policy of *coartación*, a scheme by which slaves could gradually buy their liberty.[69]) From early on, then, it is made clear not only that Prim needs conservative support,

[68] Pí y Margall, op. cit., IV, 235.
[69] J. Maluquer de Motes Bernet, 'El problema de la esclavitud y la revolución de 1868', *Hispania* (Madrid), no. 117, (1971), pp. 55-75 (p. 61).

but also that the qualities which might win it for him are precisely those which will alienate more radical revolutionaries.

The section of the *Ruedo* which sheds most light on Valle-Inclán's view of Prim's politics is *Baza* 'Tratos púnicos' x–xi. Here the author comes close to fixing the angle of the reader's vision. The survey is devastatingly slanted. Prim's astute grasp of the political situation is outlined fully, but the indirect speech and thought show how he relates everything to his personal ambitions and possible gains, with the result that the final impression is of a man who is an empty shell, a fake, a gaudy figure of no depth :

> El glorioso hijo de Reus se emocionaba con romanticismo de tenor menestral que canta solos en el orfeón de su pueblo : *Pero la falsía de sus tratos perduraba sobre aquellos sentimientos.* Solicitado por la conjura alfonsina, *fluctuaba en medias palabras, encapotado con la suspicacia de verse pospuesto* si la minoría del Príncipe de Asturias aparejada [sic] la política personal de un regente. ¿Acaso el naranjero de San Telmo? Acaso, por segunda vez, el tresillista de Logroño.[70] España no escarmentaba. El Emigrado de Londres, *oportunista y capcioso, sin doctrina y sin credo, cabildeaba, con segundas miras,* el abrazo de todas las fracciones revolucionarias, bajo el señuelo rojo y gualda de la voluntad nacional. Hecha la revolución, que sería un alegre juego de pólvora, *juzgaba inmediata la desavenencia de los bandos extremos. Comprometiendo pactos con las sesudas calvas moderantistas y las desmelenadas democracias, buscaba centrarse en un justo medio, que presentía propicio al logro de sus grandes ambiciones.*
>
> *Baza* 180–1 (italics mine)

The devastating condemnation of Prim in this passage is based upon the overwhelming importance of his personal ambitions. He is essentially 'oportunista y capcioso, sin doctrina y sin credo', a man consistently guilty of duplicity. He is intelligent, but ambitious, above all aware of the personal risks he runs. The description above is as much a condemnation of nineteenth-century Spanish politics as it is indulgence in the expression of a personal dislike of Prim. There is ironic force, for example, in the statement that Prim made the Spanish throne shake with his ranting (*Baza* 164). It seems barely possible for a bad actor to have had such far-reaching effects. Nonetheless, as the very fact of Prim's existence, popularity and conspiracy did shake the throne, such touches underline the unsafe nature of the throne and of the monarchy itself.

But Valle-Inclán's creation of Prim is far from being a crude mosaic of motifs culled from the popular press. The main features of the satirical characterisation of him in both sides of the press are to be found in Valle-Inclán's portrait, although the final impression is probably closest to a disillusioned republican view. This clarification of Valle's political perspective on Prim distinguishes him from the other non-fictional characters, as does the fact that he is completely devoid of the small humanising touches which soften other characters such as Isabel II and even Sor Patrocinio.

As a background to this exceptionally harsh treatment of Prim, it is helpful

[70] i.e. Montpensier and Espartero.

to look at a series of articles in which Valle-Inclán was even more outspoken in his criticism of the general. The articles were published in *Ahora* between 18 June and 20 September 1935.[71] They were written in a period when the *Ruedo* appears to have been undergoing considerable revision, and thus constitute evidence of prime importance as indications of the possible future re-working of the novels and as a gauge of Valle-Inclán's political attitudes at the end of his life.

The series of articles began with a review of *Amadeo de Saboya* by the Conde de Romanones,[72] which developed into a general commentary on Prim and other political figures of the period. Even in the first articles it is clear that Valle-Inclán has a special axe to grind. His intention seems to be to provoke a critical re-appraisal of Prim's role in post-revolutionary politics. He expresses amazement at the Conde de Romanones' apparently naive judgment of Prim, when 'hay tantas cosas que inducen a la sospecha de que estuviese representando una comedia y que su secreto designio fuese el fracaso de todas aquellas negociaciones en busca de rey'. Such intentions are not mentioned directly in the *Ruedo*, but it is quite clear that Prim is capable of envisaging more complex future political possibilities than are his fellow conspirators. In a later article, Valle-Inclán was more emphatic in his criticism of Prim, and spoke of his essentially reactionary nature, and the degree of unease he felt at the thought of popular participation in the revolutionary movement. According to Valle, Prim 'hubiera querido que fuese únicamente baza de espadas y milagro de los cuarteles', that is, that he viewed the 1868 revolution as a traditional military *pronunciamiento*. Here Valle-Inclán's criticism runs along aesthetic and ethical lines. It is inevitable that he should be at loggerheads with Prim's political pragmatism, when what he values above all else in revolution is not success but human dignity. A traditional coup is unacceptable because it lacks the dignity of 'las explosiones populares, cuando las demagogias, en sus grandes horas, abren los brazos y sacan el pecho frente a las bocas de los fusiles'. This clear reflection of Goya's painting, 'El 3 de Mayo, 1808', attractive though it is, is suicidal in its political idealism.

Prim's repugnance for popular intervention in politics was singled out (with critical intent) by Republican historians of the period. Pí y Margall, for example, recalls Prim's attitude to the Villarejo rising of January 1866. In reply to Muñíz, who asked him about his plans for the rising, Prim stated that he wanted a simple change of government. The *pueblo* should be excluded from the rising because its intervention would have a detrimental effect on political stability :

---

[71] 'Un libro sugeridor', 18 June; 'Sugestiones de un libro (*Amadeo de Saboya*) II', 26 June; 'Sugestiones de un libro (*Amadeo de Saboya*) III', 2 July; 'Sugestiones de un libro (*Amadeo de Saboya*) IV', 11 July; 'Sugerencias de un libro (*Amadeo de Saboya*) V', 19 July; 'Sugerencias de un libro (*Amadeo de Saboya*) VI', 26 July; 'Paúl y Ángulo y los Asesinos del General Prim I', 2 August; 'Paúl y Ángulo y los Asesinos del General Prim II', 13 August; 'Paúl y Ángulo y los Asesinos del General Prim III', 16 August; 'Paúl y Ángulo y los Asesinos del General Prim IV', 28 August; 'Paúl y Ángulo y los Asesinos del General Prim V', 20 September.

[72] *Amadeo de Saboya, el rey efímero. España y los orígenes de la guerra franco-prusiana de 1870*, (Madrid, 1935).

Si dejo que se mezclen en el asunto los paisanos a los soldados, pierden éstos su disciplina, se apresuran aquéllos a formar Juntas y me tiran el Trono por el balcón; mientras que así obrando independientemente, me pongo a las puertas de la capital con fuerzas superiores a su guarnición, la Corte se me rinde, y cuando el País se aperciba del pronunciamiento, ya tiene un Gobierno vigoroso que sin sangre ni disturbios ha verificado el cambio político.[73]

Prim did not in the end participate in this rising, which in turn earned him the censure of Fernando Garrido, who upbraided him for his 'falsedad revolucionaria'. He relates with scorn Prim's reasons for withdrawal :

El Conde de Reus decía haberse levantado para evitar una revolución social; declaraba que al tomar la iniciativa revolucionaria era su propósito encausar y dominar los elementos revolucionarios. Y después de esto todavía hubo quien siguió paso a paso las órdenes, los consejos, las advertencias del dictador revolucionario, que debía llegar a consumar su propósito, presentándose como dique a la marcha del progreso.[74]

But even if Valle-Inclán's criticisms of Prim have some backing in these Republican historians, they are made the more harsh by his insistence on Prim's total falsity and theatricality. It is the combination of different types of criticism which is so striking. The *Ahora* article of 26 July 1935, for example, describes Prim as 'falso y teatral' and this undermines all that follows. Prim's efforts to balance factors in the power struggle, for which he is generally praised by the modern historian, are portrayed as insidious efforts to guarantee his own position : 'Fue su política en aquella hora avivar y recordar las diferencias entre unionistas y demócratas, a fin de situarse entre uno y otro bando como mediador y garantía.' The article develops into a crescendo of insults, a personal tirade directed by the author to his subject :

Orquestaba con sus crasas vocales catalanas las más huecas y retumbantes frases del almanaque revolucionario. Ocultaba, ladino, sus sentimientos e intenciones, y a la clara significación de las otras banderías sumadas a la conjura revolucionaria oponía el futuro enigmático de la voluntad nacional. Descubría una genial astucia para ocultar sus propósitos en la vaciedad metafórica y truculenta de una retórica sin ideas. El general Prim, después de correr la pólvora, fiaba la última decisión revolucionaria a la taumaturgía de las urnas electoreras. Como se sabía falto de la asistencia de unionistas y demócratas, no descubría su intención por el príncipe Alfonso.[75]

The tone of this extract is important for other reasons. What strikes one immediately is the style of the article, very close to that of the *Ruedo*, so much

[73] Pí y Margall, op. cit., IV, 351-2. Pí's final comment on Prim is crushing : 'Seguía Prim las vulgares huellas de los Narváez y los O'Donnell.'
[74] Fernando Garrido, op. cit., III, 1038.
[75] There were other complications besides the problem of balancing Unionists, monarchists and democrats. Iris Zavala's article, 'Historia y literatura en *El Ruedo Ibérico*', *La revolución de 1868: Historia, pensamiento, literatura*, edited by Clara E. Lida and Iris M. Zavala, (New York, 1970), pp. 425-49, discusses the essential dichotomy between Prim's aims and those of the bandits and the anarchists.

so that it could easily be considered as a first version of something to be inserted into a later novel of the cycle. But it is not a novel. It is Valle-Inclán apparently talking not qua novelist, but qua historian. Valle-Inclán, historian, however, is far from being an objective assessor of history : his view is always dominated by thoughts of the ideal, of ethics and aesthetics. His judgment of Prim is a personal one, symptomatic of a relationship as intense as his relationships with contemporary writers. He seems to have come to believe entirely in the myth or bogey of Prim as presented by those who found him too reactionary. The disillusion of Republican historians is echoed by his own disillusion, not just at the mechanics of nineteenth-century politics, but at the way they foreshadowed twentieth-century politics. Such disillusion is natural, given Valle-Inclán's general political inclinations. Since his sympathies always lie in the end with the extremists in politics, whether Carlists or anarchists, because of the idealistic elements in their political credos, then middle-of-the-road men who try to cope with existing political situations, as Prim did, cannot prove attractive to him.

Furthermore, the tone of the *Ahora* articles suggests that Valle-Inclán's criticism of Prim became more intense towards the end of his life. This is borne out by the development of the portrayal of Prim in the *Ruedo*. The Prim of *Corte* and *Viva* is certainly showy and imposing, but always seen at a distance. In *Baza*, he is viewed at closer range, and impressive showiness degenerates into sham. There is also much more discussion, particularly in 'Alta Mar', of what revolution means to the various groups involved in the conspiracy, and it is made clear that Prim will be unable to satisfy the desires of all. The blame for this is laid on Prim, rather than on the complex political situation.

The novelistic Prim of the *Ruedo* is not exactly the same as the Prim of the *Ahora* articles. The composite vision presented by the novels is more varied and admits of more subtleties than the condemnatory and stylised description of him in the articles. Although the latter clarify Valle-Inclán's attitude to some extent, problems of intention still remain. It is clear that Valle-Inclán knew and used the criticisms that were made of Prim in the press, both conservative and republican, achieving the effect of a garish composite caricature on a piece of tattered paper. This caricature is given breadth and depth by the way his attitudes are set in a complex context, but remains essentially as caricature and criticism. When balancing factors are introduced, such as comments from characters about his political ability and importance, they in turn are met by counterbalance of comments about his personal ambitions, his pride and failings. The whole is set in the system of official politics in which the revolution occurred, with the result that the personal rancour against Prim becomes a more general condemnation of the system. The *Ruedo* is cyclical. Things happened the way they did because the system ordained such a pattern. This serves as a warning to contemporary Spain that there can be no escape from the meaningless revolutions of the *ruedo ibérico* unless a totally new system of politics, akin to the secular saintliness of the anarchists, is attempted.

IV

The Language of the *Ruedo*:
An Indicator of Social Relationships

> La mengua de nuestra raza se advierte con dolor y rubor al
> escuchar la plática de aquellos que rigen el carro y pasan
> coronados al son de los himnos . . . Y de la baja sustancia de las
> palabras están hechas las acciones.
>
> Valle-Inclán, *La lámpara maravillosa.*

Valle-Inclán's linguistic virtuosity has become a commonplace in modern Spanish literature. Few authors (Miró being an obvious and immediate exception)
demand of the reader such a range of vocabulary and sensitivity to nuance. Few
authors are still capable of producing shock tremors in a theatre audience by the
linguistic extremes they resort to in the artistic stylisation of the language of
the Madrid gutter or the Galician pig-sty. It would be repetitive and unneces-
sary to embark here on a full study of Valle-Inclán's linguistic range. What
I propose to concentrate on, therefore, are those aspects of Valle-Inclán's
language which support and enrich most directly his view of the social turbulence of the *Ruedo*, partly in the language of the narrative, but most particularly in the language of dialogue.

The social world of the *Ruedo* is mixed: it is also insecure and therefore
given to pretence, occasionally to clumsy revelation. The creation of a façade
is achieved partially by dress, gesture or manner, but equally by the choice of
word or phrase. Frequently Valle-Inclán fuses the two sides together by substi-
tuting for a verb of diction one of gesture. Thus we have in one exchange the
following indications that diction is occurring:

El Marqués de Redín, se incrustaba el monóculo, con engalle de británica
elegancia:

. . . .

Torre-Mellada se compungía con asustados pianillos:

. . . .

Tenía la voz una celeridad confitada. El Marqués de Redín, con el reflejo
del monóculo, temblante en el arco de la ceja, adoptaba un docto y almido-
nado empaque académico:

. . . .

Insinuó con embozada zumba el diplomático:

. . . .

88

Sentenció Redín con sorna petulante :

. . . .

Sonaba con hoja de moneda fullera el remilgado cacareo del palatino.
Redín le miraba incrédulo, con remotos dejos de lástima :

. . . .

Chifló con ladina quejumbre el palaciego :

. . . .

El diplomático, burlón y risueño, se ajustaba el monóculo :

. . . .

Admiróse Redín con irónica sorna :

. . . .

Adoptaba un aire de fatua suficiencia el Marqués de Torre-Mellada :

. . . .

Redín le clavó los ojos con aguda malicia :

Viva 157-9

Verbs indicating speech, or even sound, are not of course absent. What occurs is
merely an indication of the speaker, and, as we shall see further in Chapter V, a
sense of decrease in pace as the speakers involved are repeatedly fixed into static
and stylised gesture. This process, whether we label it fusion, or whether we
label it the creation of a heightened dichotomy between speaker and word, since
word becomes just another social gesture, another layer of camouflaging make-
up, instead of the expression of emotional or intellectual activity, is the necessary preliminary to the revelation of role-playing or falsity within the character's
speech. The characters move within this static gesture, a limited flexibility in
their attitude deriving from the fluctuation between the imperfect and preterite
tenses.

Once we reach the words of dialogue, of uttered speech, we find that flexibility
is very little increased. Some movement and range is to be found, but contrast is
mainly between the different linguistic registers employed between characters,
or the registers between which one character may move, voluntarily or involun-
tarily. The self-consciousness with which a register is chosen is underlined partly
by the type of imagery employed in dialogue, the imagery itself performing two
functions : that of showing the imaginative boundaries of the characters, and
that of adding a further depth of contemporary documentation to the novels. It
is also underlined by self-consciousness indicated by the author in the narration
in a way which resembles the visualisation of language in the major novels of
Miró. Thus Toñete reveals an unexpectedly sharp appreciation for his master's
choice of phrase :

— ¡Con todos sus defectos, la patria es la patria, y tenemos el deber de
amarla!

Toñete asintió pasando la navaja por el cordobán. Eran palabras mayores,
palabras escandidas con una claridad tipográfica de libro escolar, redondeadas,
pulimentadas en un fluir de conceptos y deberes, intuídas con la palmeta del
dómine. El ayuda de cámara sentía la retórica como un papanatas.

Corte 143[1]

Admiration for manifestly rhetorical or grandiose forms of speech is especially pervasive among the lower echelons of society, and such forms are employed by them when they deem the occasion worthy, as does Coronel Merelo, offering his aid in a revolutionary rising :

El Coronel Merelo, con caprichosa ortografía y mucho rasgueo, aseguraba el triunfo de los ideales revolucionarios. El pueblo, el noble pueblo gaditano, sólo esperaba una orden para oponerse al embarque de los ilustres veteranos presos en el castillo. El Coronel Merelo se ofrecía con heroicas gárgaras.

Baza 32

Moving up the social scale, we still encounter self-consciousness in speech, and see both differences of taste, and a political sophistication which can call for a higher level of circumspect phraseology. Don Félix Cascajares, who visits Don Carlos on behalf of the revolutionaries, reveals Valle's scorn for this group by his ill-chosen verbiage :

– Aceptad el ofrecimiento de quienes antes fueron leales enemigos y ahora acuden a vos intérpretes del sentimiento monárquico, consustancial con la Nación Española.

Don Félix Cascajares copiaba el estilo de trenos lacrimosos que había pasado de moda con el corbatín del Divino Argüelles. Por la rocalla de tópicos progresistas, apuntaba la buena intención del viejo Cascajares. Entre el acento de la ribera, por veces sacaba notas de chirimía, subiendo la voz a la cabeza como los vascos de la montaña.

Viva 248

By contrast Canofari, a member of the retinue of the Conde de Girgenti, is more polished in his assumption of a linguistic register, but it is nonetheless obvious that he is assuming a register rather than speaking naturally within one :

– ¿Puede dudarlo Su Alteza? Pero admitamos la posibilidad de un complot urdido contra vuestra augusta prima. Procedamos a cerciorarnos, sin incurrir en la ligereza de dar crédito a las murmuraciones . . . [sic] Otra cosa sería una ofensa a los leales sentimientos de la Católica Majestad.

El Caballero Canofari hablaba con premioso atildamiento, rebuscando las expresiones como si dictase una nota diplomática. Se advertía que sus reparos y salvedades eran fórmulas de protocolo, maneras de viejo cortesano que en todo momento elude la censura de las regias flaquezas.

Viva 229

More flowery still is the type of speech habitually employed in the immediate vicinity of Isabel II. Torre-Mellada is one of the chief exponents of the art of muddling matters political and theological in measured and meaningless phrases :

Torre-Mellada se adornó con un ramillete de sentencias florecidas en la Real Antecámara :

---

[1] c.f. Miró, *El Obispo leproso, Obras completas*, (Madrid, 1953), p. 987 : 'Dobló el húsar su codo izquierdo; adelantó la diestra, como si prorrumpiese del manto de la diplomacia, y fue refiriendo su misión con tan bellas palabras, que el señor deán las veía pronunciadas con letra redondilla'.

– La Constitución está en pugna con el Derecho Divino. Ninguna vieja monarquía puede hallarse conforme con recibir el poder del pueblo, cuando lo tiene recibido de Dios. Bien mirado, es una aberración pretender que haya Reyes Constitucionales.

Viva 220

The use of phrases such as 'está en pugna', 'puede hallarse conforme', 'es una aberración', apparently indicate a line of argument, but remain as empty and disconnected assertions.

Given that for Valle-Inclán politics is as much a masquerade as is social life, the language used for political opinion or statement of intention is the main indicator for the degree of pretence, crudeness or pretentiousness involved. Music is the predominant image used to differentiate between the different types or levels of political propaganda and rhetoric, and just as in the reflection of the contemporary theatre there is differentiation between the Romantic drama, the copy of the French *théâtre utile,* and the less respectable genres of the Bufos and the *zarzuela,* so too in musical images used for politics there is distinction between the popular muse of the streets, the *costumbrista* return to flamenco music, and a more classical idiom. Part of the initial stage-setting of *Corte* is given to a musical expression of politics :

Al dramatismo libertario y anárquico de las peonadas andaluzas, romántica falseta de cante jondo, respondían bromas de vinazo, bermejas de pimentón, las ribereñas cabilas del Ebro. Los bonetes de aldea predicaban la cruzada carlista, el jaque valentón rasgueaba el guitarrín patriótico, cantando la jota. La musa popular coronada de ajos y guindillas romanceaba en el laureado umbral de los ventorros : El rejo temerón y selvático de aquellas métricas, era punteado por todos los guitarros del Ebro.

Corte 16

In the corresponding closing book of *Viva* the theme is resumed, with emphasis on the music of the streets, rather than on imitations of the *cante jondo* :

A la Historia de España, en sus grandes horas, nunca le ha faltado acompañamiento de romances. Y la epopeya de los amenes isabelinos hay que buscarla en las coplas que se cantaron entonces por el Ruedo Ibérico. Tomaba Apolo su laurel a la puerta de las tabernas, como en la guerra con los franceses, cuando la musa populachera de donados y sopistas, tunos y rapabarbas, era el mejor guerrillero contra Bonaparte. Toda España, en aquellos isabelinos amenes, gargarizaba para un Dos de Mayo.

Viva 233

The confrontation then outlined between the popular muse and the high-flown attempts of republicans who, like López de Ayala, saw the literary accompaniment to Spain's political future in the Golden Age classics, shows the popular muse to win hands down on grounds of vitality :

Rijos y toros, temas de la charla castiza, alternaba con el cante de los regios devaneos. El escándalo chulapón de coplas y guitarrones reverdecía glorias beltranejas por tascas y por cuarteles, de mar a mar y de frontera a frontera.

En vano los morriones progresistas se ponían plumas calderonianas; los corrillos populares tomaban a chunga las regias lozanías, y, sin propósito moralista, las sacaban en coplas, sólo por gustar el puro goce maldiciente.

Viva 233-4

The third alternative is the complete absence of music in the heavy-footed pedantry of Cánovas del Castillo, politician of the future. The identifying feature of Cánovas is his 'pedante gramática' (*Baza* 19). In ordinary speech, Cánovas deals in short, clipped sentences, defying contradiction or even modification. There is the element of the machine-gun in this, although the parallel of the tank might be more appropriate to the pace and inevitability of his assertions :

Córdoba . . . ha sido un militar estudioso. Ninguno tan bien dotado. Siempre he creído que su muerte prematura constituyó una desgracia para España . . . Zumalacárregui está más en nuestra tradición. Un gran instintivo, pero con muchos menos estudios militares que Córdoba. Probablemente, en otro tablero militar hubiese fracasado.

Baza 20

When delivering a formal speech, he is no less formidable, just more taxing syntactically :

No pertenezco, no he pertenecido jamas, al moderantismo histórico, y mi asistencia a esta reunión no supone, no puede suponer, mudanza en el ideario que durante toda mi actuación política he sustentado. Los grandes sucesos de la hora presente, la zozobra en que nos une a todos los hombres de orden la preocupación por los patrios destinos, que, a cuantos con nuestra actuación hemos contraído una responsabilidad histórica, no puede menos de inquietarnos, explica, razona, y aun hacía inevitable que preopinantes de distintos credos nos juntásemos en evitación de males que hacen peligrar a las Instituciones.

Baza 21

That this style is no imposition of Valle-Inclán on the person of Cánovas, but reflects in a masterly fashion his tedious pedantry, may be seen by selecting at random any passage from his *Discursos*. Here, for example, is an extract from the first speech made by Cánovas in the Ateneo in 1884 :

Tal es, senores, la convicción que me ha traído a meditar en voz alta delante de vosotros, y a solicitar sobre este inmenso asunto vuestras propias meditaciones. Para estos singularísimos casos, mucho más que para los ordinarios, es útil la libre institución del Ateneo. Discutiendo los unos, los otros enseñando, o más bien exponiendo sus noticias y opiniones; oyendo, comparando, estudiando los demás, podemos, entre todos, ilustrar los sucesos actuales, y conocerlos y juzgarlos con completa exactitud, no bajo su aspecto externo únicamente, sino también en su sentido íntimo y trascendental.[2]

Of the three alternatives given, musically speaking, the classical return of the *progresistas* may be the most harmonious, although the popular stamping and shrieking muse has ultimately most vigour and charm. The dull, solid political

---

[2] A. Cánovas del Castillo, 'Discurso primero del Ateneo', *Problemas contemporáneos*, 3 vols., (Madrid 1884-90), I, 5-52 (p. 42).

speech-making of Cánovas could not be further from the racy *coplas* of the *pueblo*. Ironically, the reader realises the extent to which the latter will prevail. With many characters, speech is relatively constant and recognisable, a strait-jacket of habit. Torre-Mellada we can normally expect to be sugary : Adolfito can normally be relied upon for outrageous cynicism. But, as shown by the practice of Canofari and Cascajares above, many characters strive to produce a particular linguistic register for a particular occasion. Thus Don Lope Calderete, confronted by the shambles created in his cafe by the group of high-born Madrid hooligans, recognises the need for measured, undramatic speech. The words themselves have evident dignity and control :

> Este desavío supongo que me será abonado. No querrán ustedes, que representan lo mejor de la juventud y de la nobleza, mejor no cabe, arruinar a un pobre industrial, siempre deferente con el público y el progreso. Recomiendo a ustedes que sean benévolos con las faltas. Si tienen alguna queja, les agradeceré que me la manifiesten para ponerle correctivo. Este desavío ya se incluirá en la cuenta. Ustedes, caballeros, no pierdan la formalidad, que están ocupadas todas las camas.

Unfortunately, the whole of this has already deflated by the original 'setting' of the speech : 'Cacareó Don Lope, sacando el gallo de la voz entre el aspa de los brazos.' Even if one had forgotten this, a reminder not to regard the man as a dignified representative of humanity follows directly on his speech :

> Don Lope Calderete remató la faena del trasteo, saludando a lo payaso con el acordeón de la chistera, entre la algazara y la burla de los perdis madrileños. Gonzalón Torre-Mellada, enternecido y baboso, con rosetas de fiebre, le abrazó y besó la calva.
>
> *Viva* 116

Occasionally the linguistic impoverishment of the characters is so extreme that their speech is reduced to cliché and the repetition of a fashionable phrase. This is particularly so in the case of the Torre-Melladas and their acquaintance. It is thus automatic to classify the sickly Alfonso XII by reference to a contemporary sentimental novel, 'Flor de un día' (*Viva* 166). When the range of bourgeois comment on Spain ('¡aquí todo es bufo ! – ¡Bufo y trágico ! – ¡Pobre España ! Dolora de Campoamor' (*Viva* 24)) is exhausted, the Torre-Mellada stratum of Spain goes about mindlessly repeating the words of the latest bufo production : '¡Me gustan todas ! ¡Me gustan todas ! . . . ¡Pero la rubia ! ¡Pero la rubia !' (*Viva* 24).[3]

---

[3] We have here an instance of Valle-Inclán's unobtrusive insertion of a completely topical and authentic detail. The song '¡Me gustan todas !' came from *El joven Telémaco*, a production of the Bufos de Arderíus which opened on 22 September 1866 at the Teatro de Variedades. The song was absurdly simple :

> Me gustan todas
> me gustan todas
> me gustan todas
> en general.
> Pero esa rubia,
> pero esa rubia,
> pero esa rubia,
> me gusta más.
>
> Act I. sc. vii

93

The King Consort, never inventive, habitually resorts to oblique phrase incorporating a cliché which stamps him firmly in his role of *marica*, as with 'Mi cuñado es el único para descubrir estos genios que se ocultan como modestas violetas' (*Viva* 97).

In *Viva* II.vi-x, Gonzalón's 'vómito de sangre' provides the society of the Torre-Melladas and their friends with the opportunity of living out the pathos of a tear-jerking novel. The stock types and situation of this genre of literature have come to supplant genuine experience among those who devour them eagerly and with monotonous regularity. Valle-Inclán underscores this by repeating in the narrative the vapid phrases used by the onlookers of Gonzalón's drama to make some show of emotion, or at least some reaction. Valle-Inclán prepares the reader for a romantic novel treatment of the situation by the opening words of *Viva* II.vii ('Las malas noticias tienen alas, vuelan desaforadas en lenguas') but then the first hint that this is to expose the masks of the society of the Torre-Melladas follows on : 'Hay como un placer en divulgarlas, y así ocurrió con el accidente de Gonzalón Torre-Mellada : Al Palacio de Medinaceli, que ardía en fiestas, se metió el notición de una vez por cien ventanas iluminadas.' At this point our vision is focussed on one of the onlookers-to-be who predictably can only work out her reaction by its appearance in the mirror. Reaction does not arrive naturally, but must be arrived at : 'La Duquesa Ángela, de rosa y crema, en el primer espejo que halló ante los ojos, ensayó un bello mohín, de condolencia, indispensable en aquellas circunstancias. – ¡Qué contrariedad !' This, however, is not the phrase deemed by her to be most appropriate, even though as a reaction it is more genuine than '¡Qué dolorosa nueva !' which she puts in its place. The source of the phrase is not left in doubt : 'Las damas del gran mundo suelen tomar su lección de retórica en las revistas de salones. La dolorosa nueva, dinámica y sombrona, llevó un ligero trastorno a la fiesta de Medinaceli' (*Viva* 29-30). The Marqués de Torre-Mellada, himself a devotee of the romantic novel ('Me he aburrido toda la mañana leyendo una entrega tonta de *La Mujer Coqueta*' (*Corte* 142)) puts on an act as patently false as the make-up with which he habitually daubs himself :

> Se detenía en la puerta de los billares, falso y lacrimoso como si le arrestase la zozobra de una fulminante desgracia. Al cabo, pisando de puntas, con un gesto de aparatosa consternación, acudió al lado de su hijo :
> – ¡Qué disgusto ! ¡No has pensado en tu pobre madre !
>
> *Viva* 31

His wife is a more accomplished actress than either her husband or the Duquesa

---

El joven Telémaco was also the source of another 'in' word, 'suripanta'. In *Corte* 29 we learn that Torre-Mellada 'a la hora del rosario acudía secretamente al reclamo de una suripanta y ponía fin a la jornada en un palco de los Bufos'. The word occurred in a chorus song in mock-Greek in Act. I sc. viii, as a result of which 'suripanta' came to mean chorus-girl. According to Sr. Fernando Delgado, Secretary of the Museo Municipal, Madrid, in the case of this song the author had been obliged to fit his words to the 'monstruo' written by Maestro Rogel. *El joven Telémaco* was not forgotten with the rapidity of most theatrical productions in this period in Spain. According to *Los Sucesos* of 7 October 1868 it was with this work that the Bufos had re-opened, now embellished with more up-to-date comment.

Ángela. Taking up Torre-Mellada's final selection of appropriate phrase, Valle-Inclán puts her gently in her chosen setting : 'La pobre madre, ya instalada en su nido de cojines y faralaes, en la luz rosa del gabinete malva, olía un pomo de sales y susurraba mimosos cumplimientos a los buenos amigos que dejaban la fiesta por acompañarla.' As the author comments, 'La Marquesa jugaba muy discretamente la comedia de madre afligida', but her practice and preparedness are more of an indictment of her social pretence than the clumsier reactions of those who surround her. Lest this should be lost on the reader, a third phrase, '¡Tan fuerte que parecía !' is uttered as an 'hipo rotundo' by Pepín Río-Hermoso who at least has a genuine reaction of fear in the face of possible death. His friends condemn him for coming so close to the realities of the situation (one may think of sad news, and disconsolate mothers, but never of death), but his comment, repeated at the end of *Viva* II.viii, throws into relief the inanities that have surrounded it. Significantly this is a phrase left in dialogue, and not re-inserted into the narration for purposes of irony. (When Río-Hermoso tries his hand at elegant wit in *Corte* 47, speaking of his krausist father as 'el autor de mis días', the effect is that of the schoolboy who believes that the soul of wit lies in elaborate circumlocution. Río-Hermoso is condemned to failure in his social milieu.)

The linguistic register of this social group is not, however, one-faceted. Political divisions exist, even though there is little substance in the different attitudes assumed. An essential division exists between the Marqués de Torre-Mellada and his wife, he being all that is *carca*, traditional and pro-Isabel II, she leaning consistently to liberalism of both politics and morals. Carolina, in her liberal role, moves between the new puritanism derived from a political credo that despises Isabel II, and rejects with her, among other things, her immorality, and a vacillating disregard for the niceties of courtly language with which her foppish husband tiptoes around the manifestations of lust of his monarch. A spectacular session of nineteenth-century newspeak is provoked by the arrival of a telegram at Los Carvajales. The meaning of the message, 'Ven con el quiquiriquí, Luis', is finally realised by Carolina despite the initial parry offered by her husband of 'Carolina, tendría que darte explicaciones muy enojosas para que pudieses comprender toda la trascendencia de este telegrama. ¡Son secretos de Estado !' She is quick to signal the moral level of what the telegram refers to (that Adolfito, the new favourite of the Queen, should return to Madrid), and her own disapproval of the 'papelucho' by the violence of her language : 'trae tal olorcillo de faldas . . . ¡Qué asco ! ¡Apesta a mujerzuela !' (*Corte* 125). For his part, Torre-Mellada rejects the lowest linguistic register, for one that is absurd in its pretence of delicacy, in what should be a 'delicate' matter, but in fact can no longer be so because of public notoriety : 'Perdóname que no sea mas diáfano . . . esa aberración es incompatible con tu talento . . . Voy a levantar una punta del velo. No quiero que existan nubes entre nosotros, querida Carola . . . ¡Carolinita, no me pongas en el trance de serte desagradable !' More striking than the contrast between Carolina's flashes of gutter vocabulary and Torre-Mellada's attempts to tip-toe daintily around the subject is the contrast within Carolina herself, produced by the two trends of her liberalism. She envisages herself continually in the role of a wronged but virtuous heroine of the French *théâtre utile*, and combines the refined euphemisms imposed by that role with her 'liberated' woman's urge to call a spade a spade and to name both the Queen's philandering and her husband's assistance in it for what they are. Not only is she capable of switching registers mid-speech : she accomplishes it in mid-sentence :

> Escucha Jerónimo. Si tus deberes de hombre importante te imponen silencio, nada te pregunto, supuesto que ese telegrama sea de González Bravo . . . [sic] Pero trae tal olorcillo de faldas, que pudiera no serlo, y en este caso tendría derecho a una explicación. Cuando menos, a reprocharte que no hubieses sido un poco más discreto reservándome el contenido de ese papelucho !
>
> *Corte* 125

Carolina's outspokenness is outstripped by that of Adolfito who takes even more delight than she does in shocking Torre-Mellada. When Adolfito complains that his position in the Palace has been shaken by pressures from the Church (something which injures his pocket more than his pride), he becomes the flamboyant Madrid *chulo* :

> ¡Me haces demasiado panoli ! He pinchado en hueso, después de una faena que ¡ríete tú de Frascuelo ! Cuando ya tocaba la guita, se ha puesto otro más chulo por medio, y cargó con el santo y la limosna.
>
> *Viva* 222

In this exchange, Torre-Mellada clearly feels more responsibility for Adolfito's indelicacy than he did for that of his wife, since he has to some extent been his protector and backer in the Palace. Hence the rapid parries of indecency :

> – ¿Hay moros en la costa ?
> – El Vicario de Cristo. ¡Ese pollo ha copado !
> – ¡Adolfo, que es el Padre de los Fieles !
> – ¡A mí me han jorobado !
> – ¡No blasfemes !
>
> *Viva* 222-3

The language habitually employed by Adolfito is just one feature of his penchant for 'lo chulo' or 'lo jaque'. As Francisco Ynduráin has already indicated, indulgence in manners and words of Andalusia or of the 'barrios bajos' of Madrid is evident throughout the social range of the *Ruedo*.[4] What perhaps has not been made clear is the range of related language employed by the *chulos* or *jaques*, and the extent to which this is mingled with or kept distinct from the *caló* or *germanía* used by the Andalusian bandits.

An initial definition of terms may help here. Strictly speaking, *caló* is the 'jerga o lenguaje de los gitanos', a language originally self-contained, but which shows the effect of contamination from contact with Spanish. In general, the original vocabulary has been preserved, but is used within a Spanish grammatical

---

[4] Francisco Ynduráin, *Valle-Inclán: tres estudios*, (Santander, 1969) pp. 39-46. The phenomenon of interest in 'lo flamenco' by those living outside Andalusia is evident most particularly from the eighteenth century onwards. See Carlos Clavería, *Estudios sobre los gitanismos del español*, (Madrid, 1951), pp. 20-4.

context.[5] *Germanía*, or criminal slang, consists principally, according to María Moliner's *Diccionario del uso del español*, of 'palabras de sentido traspuesto, palabras españolas desfiguradas y otras extranjeras españolizadas'. The ways of the *chulo* are those of the 'clases populares de ciertos barrios de Madrid' (Moliner), while *jaque* does not signify either a particular regional origin or a necessary connection with the criminal world, but merely the ways of a domineering braggart, with a certain popular ostentatiousness of manner and speech. By the association of gypsies with the life of the underworld it is not surprising that one should find mixtures of *caló* and *germanía* occurring. There is moreover considerable confusion among those who have studied such linguistic phenomena as to the demarcations of particular jargons.[6] According to Clavería, *caló* has also come to mean a particular language which is unintelligible to those who do not speak it : he cites as example N. Estévanez, *Calandracas* (Barcelona, n.d.), page 57, who considers that the profession or mode of life of a person may be identified immediately by the type of language he employs. This particularism of *caló* runs counter to most of what is found in Clavería. Perhaps more significantly, it runs counter to the findings of Zugasti, whose work on *El bandolerismo* has been shown by Boudreau to be the principal source of the bandit episodes of the *Ruedo*.[7] According to Zugasti, (page 36), there are four *jergas* spoken by Andalusian bandits : *germanía* or criminal slang, a conventional language used in prisons by 'gente de la bribia', the *guasa diaria* of Andalusia, and *caló*, the language of the gypsies. He asserts that the 'gentes de mal vivir' mix words from all groups indiscriminately. In view of the above, the statement of Fernández Almagro that 'estos gitanos de *El Ruedo ibérico* traicionan su *caló* con la jerga de

---

[5] Clavería, p. 13, reports that A. F. Pott, who published in 1844 and 1845 the two volumes of the first fundamental book on gypsies and their language, *Die Zigeuner in Europa und Asien*, considered the language of Spanish gypies at the beginning of the nineteenth century as one of the most corrupt dialects which had received decisive influence from its contact with Spanish. Clavería's conclusion, p. 14, is that 'todo hace sospechar que la influencia del español se ha dejado sentir cada vez más sobre el caló y que lo que hoy en día hablan los gitanos no es más que la lengua de los españoles de la región en que los gitanos habitan, salpicada de un reducido número de voces gitanas'.

On the disappearance of the original grammar of the gypsies in Spain, see George Borrow, *The Zincali* (1841, 4th edition London, 1901), p. 332. Doubts have rightly been cast on Borrow's authority : Clavería, p. 10, delicately phrases it 'indoeuropeistas e historiadores de la literatura inglesa coinciden en reconocer el papel importante que desempeñó la fantasía en las elucubraciones filológicas . . . de Borrow'. But he also recognises the work as 'la única base y el constante punto de referencia en cualquier estudio del gitanismo español' (loc. cit.).

[6] Clavería, pp. 18-19, notes a common confusion between *caló* and *germanía* from the eighteenth century onwards, and that *caló* has come to signify the language of wrongdoers, and to be the 'denominación por excelencia del lenguaje popular'. He cites L. Besses, author of the *Diccionario de argot español; o Lenguaje jergal gitano, delincuente, profesional y popular* (Barcelona, 1906), as guilty of this type of confusion. Besses' work is however one of the more complete vocabularies, and often assists in elucidating parts of the *Ruedo* where other word-lists fail.

[7] H. L. Boudreau, 'Banditry and Valle-Inclán's *Ruedo ibérico*', *Hispanic Review*, XXXV (1967), pp. 85-92. The source, Julián de Zugasti, *El Bandolerismo: Estudio social y memorias históricas*, 10 vols., (Madrid, 1876-80) contains most of its linguistic information in vol. II. I shall be referring to the second edition (1876) here.

los barrios bajos de Madrid'[8] need not necessarily be taken as a motive for criticism.

To return to the text of the *Ruedo*, there are some general points to be made about Valle-Inclán's use of special language for the dialect of his bandits and gypsies. Firstly, his vocabulary range is such that one may easily be led to believe that his characters are using a particular jargon. Given the differences of opinion about whether certain words are *germanía, caló* or *popular*, one is driven to a rough rule of thumb in looking at this particular type of linguistic range. Out of a rough count of 133 unfamiliar words used in the Andalusian sections of the *Ruedo*, 74 were identifiable from some source as *caló*, and another 8, although unidentifiable, appeared by their form to be *caló*. Some idea of their rarity may be gained from the fact that only 61 of the total number of unfamiliar words were to be found in María Moliner, and this figure includes only 8 *caló* words, those in most common usage. Other words were mainly identifiable from Besses' dictionary as *popular* or *germanía*. Whatever Besses' shortcomings may be in his ability to distinguish between jargons, his *Diccionario de agrot español* is one of the most helpful in deciphering the Andalusian sections of the *Ruedo*.

Two different assertions have been made about the language of Valle-Inclán's bandits. Boudreau, having found that Zugasti was so clearly the source for much of the action and characterisation of the bandit sequences, states simply that 'most of the *germanía* and *caló* which occasionally confound the reader of the *Ruedo* is to be found in Zugasti II, with the more common Spanish equivalents provided'.[9] Clavería, on the other hand, while saying that Valle-Inclán was not a man who undertook serious study (and his preference of History over history bears this out), indicates (page 94) George Borrow's work, *The Zincali*, as a possible source. The two problems here are that Azaña, although, as Clavería points out, a friend and *contertuliano* of Valle-Inclán, did not publish his translation of *The Zincali* until 1932 (too late for the bandit sections of the *Ruedo*, the earliest, *Viva* V, having appeared as *Cartel de ferias* in 1925), and this did not contain the vocabulary of the gypsies contained in the first edition of the work. Even allowing for the possibility that Azaña, and via him, Valle-Inclán, had access to the first complete edition, even to one of the later English editions with a vocabulary, the argument is weakened. Clavería does, however, add : 'Consultó tal vez alguno de los vocabularios gitanos y de ahí sacó su pintoresco conocimiento del gitanismo.' Since he also (page 13) notes the suggestion of Brown that Borrow himself might have drawn on a previous vocabulary ('Most of the words he may well have collected himself, but there is considerable internal evidence that some were taken from an earlier work'[10]) one might be justified in supposing that Valle-Inclán had access to other sources still. Boudreau's claim for Zugasti as the main source is either an optimistic guess, or pre-supposes extraordinary knowledge on the part of the reader. Only 34 of the original 133 unfamiliar words can be found in Zugasti; Borrow (the vocabulary in the 4th edition, 1906) enlightens us on 56, Besses lists 85 of the words. Let it be said at once that some

---

[8] F. Almagro, *Vida y literatura de Valle-Inclán*, p. 257.

[9] Boudreau, art. cit., p. 90.

[10] The reference is to Irving Brown, 'The Vocabulary of the Zincali', a note in *Journal of the Gypsy Lore Society*, third series, 2, (1922), p. 192.

details seem clearly to mark Zugasti as one source. If we take absence from the dictionaries of Moliner and Besses as a sufficient indication of rarity, only Zugasti gives 'bulipen' (*Viva* 122) as 'engaño', 'cifra' (*Viva* 144) as 'astucia' and 'Grobelén' (*Viva* 142) as 'Gobierno' (although Borrow gives 'grobelar' as 'gobernar'). Reading the other way, only Borrow gives 'dosta' (*Viva* 123) as '¡basta !', and 'sonacai' (*Corte* 116, *Viva* 65) as 'oro'. Zugasti and Borrow both list 'quimbilia' (*Viva* 144), Borrow's translation of 'compañía' fitting the context better than Zugasti's 'sociedad'. To chase up overlap of contents of Valle-Inclán's bandit-language and the possible sources more than this would be little better than a tedious game of Mastermind. What is evident, however, is that his vocabulary range, even in this specialised area, is extraordinarily wide, and that several sources appear to have been used.

There is obvious concentration of this type of language in certain sections of the *Ruedo*. Indeed, it may be instructive first to look at an example of the use of isolated words, since the exception shows up, in part, the way Valle-Inclán intended to profit from this type of language in his social differentiations. Adolfito uses odd *caló* words with Segis : this is part of his 'flamenquismo', part of his aristocratic banditry, and also recognition of Segis' origins and connections. In the exchange where he discloses his financial difficulties to Segis, therefore, we have phrases such as 'Necesito a toca teja *parné*' and 'si tienes sindéresis puedes situarte muy ventajosamente para luchar en este *charní* de la vida' (*Corte* 224, *caló* in italics). This assumption of gypsy ways is shown in more elegant, but no less humorous form in Marqués de Bradomín who, according to Toñete, 'no cesa de recorrer el país y hablar con la gente, y aprender el gitano' (*Corte* 142). Even locals, such as Segis, are not genuine. When, with his retinue, he meets the Torre-Mellada party at the station, they are the city view of what is local and typical. Dressed 'con rodamonte y castoreño', 'tenían con tal avío un aire de bandoleros cantando zarzuela' (*Corte* 85).

Adolfito's movement of linguistic registers is in any case less accomplished than that of Tío Juanes, who utters cryptic isolated phrases with Juanilla : '¿Se halla más conforme con su cautiverio ese *palomino*?' (Besses gives 'palomo' as 'necio'); 'con que la familia apoquine el *loben*' (unidentified, but presumably 'ransom money'); '¿Es cierto que ha *merado* la vieja?' (Besses gives 'merar' as 'morir') (*Corte* 102). When faced by the Guardia Civil, he bursts into surprising eloquence :

Con franqueza, se me hacía extraño no haber antes tenido ocasión de saludarles. El Señor Marqués estimará mayormente – esa cuenta hago – que ustedes ronden por estos lugares, y vivirá más seguro cuando ustedes le hayan cumplimentado. En esos tiempos, con el hambre y las guerras, hay muchos desesperados que se han puesto al camino. Otros, sin tanto necesitarlo por vivir mejor y lucir y triunfar en francachelas, se les han juntado. (etc.)

Corte 139

High concentrations of *caló* and equally unfamiliar language occur in the Andalusian books of the *Ruedo*. *Corte* II, 'La jaula del pájaro', predictably contains a certain amount, but this is restricted to isolated phrases, some of the more unusual of which, such as 'apoquinar el loben', are repeated until the reader grasps the connection with, in this case, the ransom demand. Much play is made on the word 'pájaro' for prisoner, and implications of 'el mochuelo' and 'este nido hay que aburrirlo' (*Corte* 104) are self-explanatory. Words such as 'paripé' ('engaño') and 'gazuza' ('apetito') (*Corte* 105) are, in Besses' definition, *popular* rather than *caló*. Where it is clear from the context what is meant in a general way, greater concentrations of jargon occur. Thus at the bandits' protest against a lowering of the ransom demand, we find :

> – ¡Que el camastrón de su padre apoquine el loben !
> – ¡Que afloje la *zaina* !ᵃ
> – ¡Mi padre ya da lo que puede !
> – ¡Gandulazo, que te buscas un *finibusterre* !ᵇ
> El cutre de tu padre *abillela*ᶜ el *sonacai*ᵈ en tinajones.

ᵃ 'bolsa' (Zugasti), ᵇ 'patíbulo' (Zugasti), ᶜ 'tiene' (Zugasti, Borrow, Besses), ᵈ 'oro' (Borrow).

Corte 116

Much higher concentrations occur in *Viva* V. xii, xiii, xxviii, xxx.

Contrary to popular belief, Valle-Inclán does not intend to fox his reader entirely with his outlaws' language. Some phrases are given clear translation : '¡Dai de los Calés ! ¡Debel del Otalpe !' is followed by '¡Madre de los Gitanos ! ¡Dios del Cielo !' (*Viva* 142). The meaning of 'baria' (*Viva* 144) is explained by the context :

> El Curro y el Niño tomaban café con el Tuerto de la Chirlata. El Curro había convidado para cambiar la onza que recibiera del Señor Juan :
> – Vamos, pues, a descambiar la baria.

The succeeding dialogue, thick with *caló*, is again explained in advance : 'El Tuerto le conquería para que entrase con aquel dinero a repartir ganancias en la chirlata. Un negocio de hacerse ricos en las ferias de Portugal.' Problems of understanding the content of *Viva* V.xii (where Bernal Montoya goes with Linarejo to see Dona Quica) have been explained in *Viva* 66 : 'Y el galán verdino fue a sentarse con el Zurdo Montoya. Tramitaban engaños para la venta de un caballo loco.' There is a shift in linguistic register in *Viva* V.xii when Linarejo leaves Montoya to talk to Doña Quica. He renews conversation abruptly, using the *caló* term for 'mother' : 'Bata, ajorremos conversación.'

The chapters where the greatest difficulty in comprehension occurs are, luckily, those non-essential to the plot where a type of *costumbrista* display is made by the author. Thus there is relative confusion in these scenes, whereas the scenes concerning the bandits and their ransom enterprise are more clear. This is partly because the language used by the bandits is *popular*, or at the most *germanía* with a few words of *caló*. Some meanings of words are implied by repetition in particular contexts : 'finibusterre', for example, used in *Corte* 108, 116, 162, and *Viva* 80, may not have its precise meaning of 'horca' made clear, but its general meaning is shown by the context. When used at *Viva* 80, it is followed by 'No me asusta el presidio', which guides the reader in its implications. Partly also it seems fair to assume that it is more vital to the general under-

standing of the *Ruedo* that the bandit sections should be intelligible, whereas
the function of the gypsies is to appear as a picturesque group, antagonistic to·
the bandits, as shown by the central skirmish of *Viva*, but associated with them
in shady deals (as in *Viva* III.xx) and by minor linguistic overlaps (the bandits
use *caló* terms such as 'chachipé' (truth) (*Corte* 109), 'parné' (money) (*Corte* 111),
'sonacai' (gold) (*Corte* 116).

Viva V.xiii, following directly on the scene where Montoya bargains with
Doña Quica to obtain the drug to take a mad horse so that it may be sold, contains a high proportion of *caló*, but much of it has already appeared earlier on.
'Gachapla' ('copla') was introduced in *Corte* 159 ('Pues has oído la gachapla que
esta trae, dale respuesta'), 'charnin' (?=Borrow's 'chardi' (feria)) comes relatively clear from the context. Rather forced is the following phrase, 'Ostelinda,
deja el rebridaque, que el planoró trae su bulipen' and looks much as though
Valle-Inclán has pillaged and fused *coplas* from Zugasti :

> Si no gastas bulipénes,
> Y jabillas mis jacháres,
> Romandiñipen terquélo,
> Sin andar con rebridaques.

(Si no usas engaños, y comprendes mis tormentos, contigo me casaré sin andar
con más requiebros)

and

> Ostelinda, bien chanelo
> Que menda sis chororó;
> Pero aunque tú me bucháres,
> Sinaré tu planoró.

(María, bien conozco que yo soy un pobre; pero aunque tu me desprecies, seré
tu hermano.)

Zugasti II, 139–40

The chapter contains a simple but ostentatious use of *caló*, very little of which
appears to be drawn from Zugasti. The gypsies are made to identify themselves
linguistically thus :

    — Esa es la *chachipé*.[a]

    . . . .

    — Tío Ronquete, cállese usted esa palabra condenada, que es peor que
mentar la *filimicha*.[b] Un espanto apareja muchas ruinas.

    — Pues no sería raro, que hay siempre muchos *choríes*[c] con el ojo en eso.

    — Del Errate?

    — *Caloré*[d] y *busné*.[e]

    — *Jabilla*[f] usted más de la cuenta, Tío Ronquete.

    — Yo nada jabillo, que siempre camino por el *drunji*[g] (etc.).

[a] 'verdad' (Borrow), [b] 'horca' (Borrow), [c] 'cuchillo' (Borrow) or 'chorní' –
'ladrón' (Besses), [d] 'caloró' – 'gitano' (Borrow), [e] 'los gentiles' (Borrow)
[f] 'entiende' (Zugasti), [g] 'Camino real' (Borrow).

Viva 123

This *costumbrista* style of display (which no doubt would have been published with footnotes, had the author been Fernán Caballero) has a counterpart in *Viva* V.xxviii in the outburst at the news that a gypsy has died in prison ('¡Hay un planoró muerto en la trena!'). It is not entirely necessary for the reader to know that 'drupo' is 'cuerpo' (Zugasti) in order to understand 'nos zurrarán el drupo', and 'no le penela chi' ('no le dice nada') is neither here nor there. More vital is the meaning of 'caloré' ('gitano' – Borrow), since on this hangs the force of

– ¿Y por qué había el difunto de ser caloré?
– Es caloré, porque siempre pagamos los del Errate. Cuenta, si no, quiénes han ido al Estaribel.

Viva 142

(The meaning of 'estaribel' ('cárcel') is made more clear by the use of a capital here.)

The most densely packed chapter of *caló* is *Viva* V.xxx, which merits close attention because of a number of peculiarities. Firstly, two forms are given of one word: 'dunquendió' and 'duquendió'. They appear to have the same meaning of 'maestro' (Zugasti), and the variant may merely be due to carelessness. The first part of the exchange between el Curro, el Niño and el Tuerto de la Chirlata makes some sense, but not completely:

– Nosotros dos, y mejorando si se nos arrima una *chulana*[a] de buen trapío, como tengamos un tanto de *cifra*[b], alzamos un *curelo*[c] y *abelamos*[d] *jandoripen*.[e]
– ¡O vamos con la *quimbilia*[f] a la *trena*.[g]
– Ese *randiñó*[h] te puede caer donde menos lo *diqueles*.[i]
– *Jabillela*[j] sin fin de *chichís*[k] ese *burlo*.[l]
– *Dunquendió*[m] que *sicobamos*[n] para llenar la *zayna*.[o]

[a] 'mujer' (Zugasti), [b] 'astucia' (Zugasti), [c] 'negocio' (Borrow), [d] 'tenemos' (Zugasti), [e] 'dinero' (Zugasti), [f] 'sociedad' (Zugasti), [g] 'cárcel' (Besses – *popular*), [h] ? 'trabajo' (randiñar'='trabajar', Zugasti), [i] 'mires' (Besses) [j] 'entiende' (Zugasti), [k] 'caras' (Zugasti), [l] 'engaño' (Zugasti), [m] 'Maestro' (Zugasti), [n] 'sacamos' (Zugasti), [o] 'bolsa' (Zugasti).

Viva 144

By the time we reach '¡Curelo pesquibado! ¡Barbí! ¡Pirela bastaró!' ('¡Negocio probado! ¡Excelente! ¡Anda aflicción!' (?)) the link with a credible meaning seems remarkably tenuous. After this point the discussion returns to the more concrete and understandable issue of money, the only remaining query being at 'Chamullaremos callicaste'. One hopes Valle-Inclán was not relying on Borrow's 'ayer', but on Besses' version of 'ayer' or 'pasado mañana', otherwise the episode becomes totally surrealistic.

This last passage seems to point to an extensive though not total reliance upon Zugasti, heavier than in other sections of the *Ruedo*, and less successful. The reliance upon one main source was presumably the simplest means of producing a passage of concentrated *caló*. Although care has been taken by Valle-Inclán to introduce variety into his *caló* (he produces roughly 73 *caló* and 9 pseudo-*caló* terms, when Zugasti himself only lists approximately 125 words), his use of it as a linguistic register, although treated attentively in the changing language of a Tío Juanes or a Zurdo Montoya, is less skilful generally than his mastery of intonation and inference in more elevated social strata. Furthermore, his linguistic 'encrustación' is less successful in this area than his insertion and use of historical material.[11] The linguistic element here ranges from *costumbrista* ostentation to sheer clumsiness. One reliable effect, however, is that the reader, as *busné*, will find the *caló* as closed to him as it is intended to be to others. The world of the gypsies is a necessary social segment of the *Ruedo*, but not so closely involved as the world of the bandits with which it is tangentially associated. With the exception of those who, like Adolfito, try to adopt gypsy ways for show, the gypsy world remains relatively safe and impregnable. The gypsies are an isolated case both in the social structure of the *Ruedo*, and in the demonstration of Valle-Inclán's skill. Virtuosity there is certainly, but no assurance.

[11] 'En esta clase de obras históricas la dificultad mayor consiste en incrustar documentos y episodios de la época. Cuando el relato me da naturalmente ocasión de incrustar una frase, unos versos, una copla, un escrito de la época de la acción, me convenzo de que todo va bien. Pero si no existe esa oportunidad no hay duda de que va mal.' Interview with Luis Calvo, 'Don Ramón María del Valle-Inclán', *ABC*, 3 August 1930.

V

The Visual Impact of the *Ruedo*

Pero las estrellas se ríen a carcajadas, girando tranquilas en el
firmamento y reverberando sus plateadas luces sobre los insectos
que se mueven en el suelo con los pies hacia arriba.

Las Ánimas, 17 May 1869.

One is continually made aware of a concern for visual and plastic values in
Valle-Inclán's discussion of his process of composition. Of the creation of characters, he says :

Antes de ponerme a escribir necesito ver corpóreamente, detalladamente,
los personajes. Necesito ver su rostro, su figura, su atavío, su paso. Veo su
vida completa anterior al momento en que aparecen en la novela. De esa vida
que yo veo primero en el pensamiento, muchas veces es muy poco lo que utilizo
luego, al llevar el personaje a las cuartillas, donde a lo mejor sólo aparece una
escena. Cuando ya lo he visto completamente, lo 'meto', lo 'encajo' en la
novela. Después, la tarea de escribir es muy fácil . . .[1]

A similar attitude is shown in his statement made to Luis Calvo : 'Yo necesito
trabajar con mis personajes de cara, como si estuvieran ellos en un escenario;
necesito oírles y verlos para reproducir su diálogo y sus gestos.'[2] Even more committed to a plastic concept is his idea that 'todo el arte del estilo está en suplir la
palabra hablada . . . La capacidad del español es para el teatro por lo que el teatro
tiene de plástico, porque la Minerva española es más plástica que literaria.'[3]
Pictorial terms are consistently used in discussions of his aesthetic aims. Explain-
ing his intention in the *Comedias bárbaras*, he refers to a painter of centuries
earlier :[4] the first delineation of the aesthetic of the *esperpento* draws on another
painter.[5] Moreover, these preoccupations do not remain at the level of mere

[1] Francisco Madrid, *La vida altiva de Valle-Inclán*, p. 114. For an example of this reduction of a character see my article, 'The first fragment of *El ruedo ibérico*?', pp. 168-70.
[2] Interview with Luis Calvo, *ABC*, 3 August 1930.
[3] 'Una conferencia de don Ramón del Valle-Inclán', *El Sol*, 4 March 1932. It is possible
that Valle-Inclán envisaged the cinema as Spain's future artistic medium. See the article,
'Valle-Inclán y su opinión sobre el cine', *El Bufón*, (Barcelona), 15 February 1924 : 'El cine
habla a los ojos y nada más. Pudiéramos decir que la pantalla es lo plástico animado, en
donde el movimiento y el color son los dos únicos componentes.'
[4] 'Ahora en algo que estoy escribiendo, esta idea de llenar el tiempo como llenaba el
Greco el espacio, totalmente, me preocupa.' Letter to Alfonso Reyes, quoted in A. Reyes,
'Algo más sobre Valle-Inclán', *Tertulia de Madrid*, p. 76.
[5] 'El esperpentismo lo ha inventado Goya', *Luces de bohemia* (1920), *Obras completas*,
I, 939.

theory. The majority of Valle-Inclán's works, and in particular those of his maturity, demand comprehension in visual as well as in semantic terms. For Valle-Inclán, the world is what one perceives it to be, and individual visions of the world are as a result the means of gaining insight into the personality. There is no absolute or objective reality that one can neither perceive or imitate, only the reality of each individual which reveals itself through his concept of the world. It is this interpretative reality of the individual and of society that the artist must reflect or communicate.

One consequence of this strongly visual aesthetic of Valle-Inclán which moves quickly onto a plane of impersonality ('una superación del dolor y de la risa'[6]) is the distance the author introduces between himself and his creatures, and between the reader and the subject of his reading. Concrete objects act as a barrier to the establishment of empathy. Another consequence is the frequent shifting of focus and perspective which occurs on both the basic level of the plastic vision presented by his work, as well as on that of political or social interpretation. In the *Ruedo* we have more than a series of opposing opinions about the 1868 revolution : we have a solid, visual form given to such changes of perspective.

There is a paradox in the visual concept of the *Ruedo*. Valle-Inclán's aim was to present the events of 1868 as they had been viewed at the time, by the majority, and not just by historians. Hence his concern with informal and popular sources so that he could represent 'la sensibilidad española, tal como se muestra en su reacción ante los hechos que tienen una importancia.'[7] Yet an examination of the purely visual impressions in the *Ruedo* reveals that only a part of them derive from popular inspiration. For the rest a variety of sources can be perceived, among which the contrast between the visual worlds of Goya and Velázquez stands out clearly.

According to Ramón Sender, and this amplifies the statements which opened this chapter, visual impressions were more than just the result of Valle-Inclán's visual imagination. They constituted his starting point. For Valle-Inclán, Sender says, 'sus novelas y comedias nacían de un deseo casi físico, confuso y brillante y que cuando ese deseo era más vivo comenzaba a darles forma por combinaciones ideales de masas de color'.[8] Speaking of *Tirano Banderas* he is even more specific : 'La concepción era pictórica y plástica y en ella, como en los pintores venecianos, en el Greco y en los impresionistas modernos, era antes el color que la línea. La línea era subsidiaria del color y no existía por sí misma, como no existe, según parece, en la naturaleza.' Here too the principle of the 'masas de color' operated : 'cuando las *masas de color* de su primera inspiración tomaban forma en vacío, esa forma quedaba fijada con tonos permanentes en su conciencia y escribir después era lo de menos . . . El plan preconcebido era seguro. Sin embargo, ese plan era sólo una combinación de colores de cuyas proporciones dependía todo.'[9] In *Tirano Banderas* and the *Ruedo* the mixing and grouping of masses of colour leads to a succession of impressions and visions which highlight one another, an effect which Valle-Inclán likened to the technique used by El Greco. Of the

---

[6] *Los cuernos de don Friolera* (1921), *Obras completas*, I, 992-3.
[7] Francisco Madrid, op. cit., p. 112.
[8] Ramón Sender, *Valle-Inclán y la dificultad de la tragedia*, (Madrid, 1965), p. 23.
[9] ibid., p. 24.

Comedias bárbaras he said : 'en el *Enterramiento* sólo el Greco pudo meterlas [las figuras] en tan angosto espacio; y si se desbarataran, hará falta un matemático bizantino para rehacer el problema. Esta angostura de espacio es angostura de tiempo en las *Comedias*. Las escenas que parecen arbitrariamente colocadas son las consecuentes en la cronología de los hechos.' This treatment was not confined to the *Comedias bárbaras*; Valle-Inclán concludes : 'Ahora, en algo que estoy escribiendo, esta idea de llenar el tiempo como llenaba el Greco el espacio, totalmente, me preocupa.'[10] We may suppose that he was referring to the composition of the *Ruedo*.

The extent to which Valle-Inclán was in fact able to create 'angostura de tiempo' in the *Ruedo* is evident from the analysis of structure in Chapter II. The analogy with the work of El Greco may be pushed still further. If we think of Valle-Inclán's example, the *Enterramiento del Conde de Orgaz*, we note that the men standing around the corpse are not distinguished from the divine figures in the painting by colour, tone or perspective. The different planes of reality have been placed on a single level which at the same time retains certain areas of contrast. A simple parallel between this and Valle-Inclán's technique in the *Ruedo* is that here too widely differing social groups, royalty and bandits, courtiers and ruffians, are all submitted to the same techniques of presentation, are evoked by the same range of metaphors. Yet here too there are contrasts deriving from links with different types of graphic art.

A possible point of origin for the 'masas de color' of the *Ruedo* lies in the series of geographical and class contrasts outlined in Chapter II. This is what is suggested to us by the most explicit visual contrast, in the paragraph which describes Madrid at sunset. Here we see first the courtiers of Madrid, and then the *pueblo* :

Madrid, polvoriento de sedes manchegas, tenía un último resplandor en los tejados. Sobre la Pradera de San Isidro, gladiaban amarillos y rojos goyescos, en contraste con la límpida quietud velazqueña que depuraba los límites azulinos del Pardo y la Moncloa. La luz de la tarde madrileña definía los dos ámbitos en que se combate eternamente la dualidad del alma española.

Viva 218[11]

Other elements intervene in the system of the 'masas de color'. Although from the quotation above one might assume the echoes of Velázquez and Goya to be equal in the *Ruedo*, this is not the case. Goya dominates the aesthetic of the novels. Touches of Velázquez appear in *Corte* and *Viva*, but are absent from *Baza*. In *Viva* one is reminded periodically of the work of Gutiérrez Solana, although the first and last chapters of the book recall more than anything else the popular caricatures of the late 1860s. In *Baza* these popular impressions continue,

[10] Extract from a letter of Valle-Inclán published in *España*, (Madrid), X, no. 42, quoted by A. Reyes, *Tertulia de Madrid*, p. 68.

[11] The reference here to the Pradera de San Isidro, a geographical locality, but also the title of a painting by Goya, is a happy example of plastic-literary 'incrustación', a technique which Valle-Inclán defended when speaking of his inclusion of a passage of Casanova in the *Sonata de Primavera* : 'El procedimiento es completamente legítimo. Equivale a tomar un rincón del cuadro de las "Meninas" de Velázquez e incrustarlo en una tela mucho mayor, añadiéndole retazos por todos lados.' A. Reyes, *Tertulia de Madrid*, p. 68.

and in 'Alta mar' above all are added reflections of the type of illustrations that were found in melodramatic or sentimental novels of the period.

In discussing the nature of the visual impact of the *Ruedo* I propose to follow the example of Valle-Inclán, who believed in the adoption of empirical rather than perfect norms, whether it was a matter of writing novels or playing cards.[12] In equally arbitrary fashion, I do not propose to make a comprehensive survey of visual effects in the *Ruedo*, which are there for all to see, but to pick out those traces of echoes from painting and popular graphics which are especially significant in the creation of atmosphere and the stimulation of visual repercussions in the mind of the reader.

Goya

In the first instance, the influence of Goya in certain parts of the *Ruedo* can be identified by chromatic selection, with the use of strong contrast between colours of shadow and mystery and those of aridity and violence, 'Aires nacionales', the book which opens the series, is dominated by echoes of Goya with the 'horizonte incendiado', 'las rojas lumbres de las represalias', and 'las sedientas villas labradoras, negras de moscas . . . encendidas de sol' (*Corte* 17). Each detail, touched with unequivocal visual strokes, is further intensified by the addition of sound : 'Por la lontananza amarilla del rastrojo, moviéndose en hileras, fulgían brillos de roses y fusiles. Los pantalones colorados escalaban los cerros : Latían los gozques de corral sobre las bardas : Eran un clamoroso guirigay todos los gallineros' (*Corte* 16). Isolated details build up into a final crescendo, so that the panorama becomes a universal nightmare : 'Ladran los perros, innúmeros perros, nubes de perros : En fuga, cojeando, se expanden por la redondez del ruedo ibérico. Y sobre todos los horizontes, en el curvo límite, donde se juntan la tierra sin sembrar y el cielo, roses y pantalones colorados, brillo de bayonetas, fusilada y humo de pólvora' (*Corte* 19).

In addition to this we have Valle-Inclán's own qualification of his aesthetic as being that of Goya. It seems most probable that in his comments on the *esperpento*, Valle-Inclán had in mind principally the Goya of the *Caprichos*, the *Disparates*, and the *Desastres de la guerra* where, as in caricature, lines are reduced to a suggestive minimum in order to carry maximum impact. The process of artistic creation moves through reality to sketch out the artist's intuitive vision of what exists beyond or behind reality. In this sense one could regard any artistic representation which is not a replica copy as being a type of distortion. However, in the denuded sketches of caricature or the imaginative traces of Goya, full detail and background is blacked out in such a way that reality suddenly appears to be two-dimensional or less. Typically in the *Ruedo* characters are reduced to a mask or to their accessories. When we read 'El Marqués de Torre-Mellada – batín y pantuflas – acogió con severos chifles la presencia de don Segis' (*Viva* 50), Torre-Mellada is no more, and perhaps less, than the clothes he stands up in. In the description of two policemen, this technique is used with a more clearly defined moral intent : 'En la duda, esbirros de gorra y bastón paseaban día y

[12] 'Yo creo que hay metro para las novelas, y que cada novelista tiene el suyo. Un metro que probablemente no sirve para maldita la cosa, pero que no ilusiona, como las mil combinaciones a los jugadores de timba.' Interview given in 1925, reprinted in *Primer Acto*, no. 32, (1967), pp. 10-11.

noche las aceras del convento' (*Viva* 53). Here schematic and clinical wording emphasises the impersonal nature of the authority of the policemen. Another policeman materialises later on in *Viva*: 'Vino por la esquina un polizonte azul, sable de músico y bastón de autoridad'. Not even serious in his role, he is a figure of music hall fun. He meets Antonio Guzmán el Tuerto who has been badly beaten up and now resembles a corpse more closely than a human being ('la cabeza de cera, los ojos vidriados, la sien sucia de sangre'). The policeman tries to dismiss the tragedy by asserting that it should not have taken place, and certainly should not have presented such visible proof ('¡No están permitidos estos espectáculos en las calles céntricas!'). As the two have lost all trace of humanity, the only possible contact is between the shells of their caricature: 'El polizonte tocó el hombro del espectro con el puño dorado del bastón' (*Viva* 179). This process of reducing people to the absolute minimum of representative sign of their function is common to many caricaturists, but one salient example we might remember from Goya here is the painting of the '3 de mayo', in which the soldiers performing the execution are reduced to a line of guns at the side. A similar technique is used in 'No se puede mirar' of the *Desastres de la guerra*.

The rising of the Spanish people in the face of the Napoleonic invasion, which inspired Goya's '3 de mayo', is recalled repeatedly in the course of the *Ruedo*. A straightforward reflection of Goya's painting occurs in *Corte* 17: 'por las hispánicas veredas, con los últimos reflejos del día destellaban tricornios y fusiles.' It is used without undue emphasis to highlight the tragedy and violence of events that are politically absurd. More echoes of the painting and its associations are clustered in *Viva*. The brawl between gypsies and bandits in 'Cartel de ferias' is like a rehearsal for the revolution. Ironically, here it is Adolfito who is called the 'héroe de este Dos de Mayo' (*Viva* 132). In the words of the Niño de Benamejí, everything is confused and exaggerated, a caricatural preview of the revolution: '¡Han visto ustedes qué Dos de Mayo! ¡Estos sí que son toros de sangre!' (*Viva* 133). Later the irony of the comparison is accentuated by Valle-Inclán's comment at the end of the book: 'Toda España, en aquellos isabelinos amenes, gargarizaba para un Dos de Mayo' (*Viva* 133). Later still, in the response of Paúl y Ángulo to Rodena's declaration that he will answer for his 'leones de Cantabria', a note of jingoism is captured and deflated: '¡Eso tiene música de Dos de Mayo!' (*Baza* 45).

One technique which Goya uses frequently in the *Caprichos*, and which is echoed in the *Ruedo*, is to sketch in the shadow cast by a person, with the effects of distortion, dehumanisation and a range of suggestion that moves from the purely comic to the level of deep insight. Toñete as a character is grotesque in both appearance and manner: his transformation into a shadow makes him hover between reality and non-reality as he tries to escape from Gonzalón: 'Una sombra apareció en la biblioteca . . . y la sombra desapareció con una zapateta . . . La sombra se escurría por el corredor. Llevaba las manos en las posaderas . . . [Gonzalón] tendía el brazo sobre el pelele huidizo y engarraba la mano. La sombra desapareció por una puerta y corrió el cerrojo' (*Corte* 48). There are two main effects here. Toñete and Gonzalón both lose their humanity, and the former, who is shown to have hands, and the ability to bolt a door, seems to mock the latter, who is incapable of acting on the same plane of reality.

More ghostly is the vision of a wounded man on his horse travelling with barely recognisable silhouette across a landscape that is far from natural : 'El convoy perfilaba su línea negra por el petrificado mar del llano manchego. Trotaba detrás, enristrada la lanza, todo ilusión en la noche de luna, el yelmo, la sombra de Don Quijote : Llevaba a la grupa, desmadejado de brazos y piernas, un pelele con dos agujeros al socaire de las orejas' (*Corte* 83). Another example depends for its effect on the contrast of lines and a horrifying juxtaposition of life and death. Dalmaciana is close to the latter, her daughter an example of the former : 'Entre el cortejo labriego, era la sombra trenqueleante y caduca de una mujer adolecida, que se doblaba sobre un palo : Tras ella, la hija, moza lozana, abría el garbo de los brazos, atenta a sostenerla, con bermejo reír de manzana. La sombra trenqueleante, apretando la boca sin dientes, afirmaba en la estaquilla el pergamino de la mano' (*Corte* 96).

An extension of these shadows which make us doubt the validity of our perceptions is the technique of bringing a chapter to a close with a moment of visual madness, in which the play of angles and contrasts is strongly reminiscent of the bold lines of the *Caprichos*. *Corte* V.v is a scene of shadows, flashes and curves – Nature itself has exceeded its boundaries :

> Iba nublada la luna, y en el recato de las bardas se hacían un bulto el caducán y la bisoja . . . [*sic*] Y ha vuelto la luna, que tras el nublo saca un cuerno. La molinera ríe, desatándose con garbo tuno el pañolito del talle . . . Endrina, garbosa, tuerta, cenceña, ríe caprina y maligna. La sombra del viejo, socarrona y parda, proyecta otra sombra sobre las cales del tapial : Tiene brillos lilailos en el pecho, se comba y cimbra la comadre.

> *Corte* 103

The dialogue which ensues returns us to 'reality', but at the end of the chapter (not the end of the dialogue, which continues in chapter vi), Valle-Inclán reminds us of the initial echoes of Goya : 'La voz cazurra trascendía un sentido de rezo sacrílego entre la silueta que en el claro de luna cimbreaba su arabesco caprino y moreno' (*Corte* 104).

In the section on the flood, a turbulent reality symbolic of the possible chaos of the revolution, in which men and animals are reduced to the same level, there is no respite from Goya-like effects. The gestures reflected on the wall which had so frightened the prisoner in *Corte* V.xiv ('el tumulto de sombras, el guirigay de brazos aspados, ruedos de catite, mantas flotantes, retacos dispuestos') which remove him from chronological time ('Sentíase vivir sobre el borde de la hora que pasó, asombrado, en la pavorosa y última realidad de trasponer las unidades métricas de lugar y de tiempo, a una co-existencia plural, nítida, diversa, de contrapuestos tiempos y lugares') come to be, in *Corte* V.xv, a horrifying and direct reality of animal intensity. Nature is wholly and exaggeratedly vivified : 'Giraban las aspas del molino con un vértigo negro de pájaros absurdos. Huroneaba por los olivares el viento. La zorra aullaba al borde de la barranca y su hálito fosforecía en la nocturna tiniebla . . . Las aspas, negras y frenéticas, rodaban sus cruces sobre el repente de voces asustadas . . . Pronunciábase la gente de las quinterías con gritos y alarmas. Gatos y mujeres desnudas salían a los tejados. En los remansos de las vegas la luna multiplicaba su medalla' (*Corte* 117-18). The detail of the 'brazos aspados' which one might remember as the leit-motiv of *Los cuernos de don Friolera* here has reached a more mature and complete form in its integration into a total vision of chaos.

The twinkling of lights, impressionistic in effect, and symbolic of a mad world, could be seen as a minuscule version of Goya's use of mirrors. Emma Susana Speratti-Piñero has already given us some specific examples of Goya-like mirrors in Valle's work.[13] A mirror can fulfil two purposes : it can reveal us as we are, with our secret traits (a function of Goya's mirrors which produce distorted and animal-like reflections) or it can reveal us as others see us, often a false impression, but valid in its own way, since it reveals the person as he appears to function in the world. In the *Ruedo* real mirrors serve to reassure characters that their masks are correctly in place, but also, at a structural level, as shown in Chapter II, mirror effects from person to person reveal intimate truth after the manner of Goya.

As so few characters in the *Ruedo* are sure of the identity they have assumed or are assumed to have, the experience of looking in a mirror is frequently a disturbing one. Torre-Mellada, so made-up that there seems to be no human flesh beneath the face-powder, or the 'rosicleres de la alquimia', catches sight of himself in a mirror, and, perplexed and fascinated, cannot draw his gaze away : 'Su ánimo trenqueleante saltaba de una congoja a otra mayor, al contemplarse lacio, despintado, multiplicado en la desquiciada perspectiva de los tres espejos ... El Marqués se afligía versátil en la contemplación de su triple imágen' (*Corte* 190). Indicative of his superficiality is the way in which even distress is a self-consciously created visual impression. Monseñor Franchi, by contrast, looks in a mirror to remind himself of the perfection of his public image. When arranging for a letter to be handed over to Sor Patrocinio, he reassures himself of the perfection of his diplomatic attitude : 'pasó ante los espejos recogiéndose con estilo estatuario los pliegues del ropón' (*Viva* 204). Later he hardly has need to resort to the mirror since he knows himself to be infinitely superior to the humble Claret. We see him via the onlookers : 'Al salir, aún distinguieron la roja magnificencia del Nuncio de Su Santidad. Pasaba ante los espejos de un dorado salón, declinando saludos con elegante ceremonia' (*Viva* 211).

Another visual effect which is related to Goya, but equally also to popular graphic art of the period, is the technique of expressing an abstract notion through a humanoid or animal form – as in the *Desastres de la guerra* and the *Disparates*.[14] In this way an atmosphere of fear and tension is evoked admirably by the metaphor of a frightened woman : 'Valladolid estuvo tres días con tres noches tartamuda bajo las ráfagas del tiroteo, con las manos en las orejas, medio ojo abierto sobre la soldadesca tiznada de pólvora' (*Corte* 13). Another female figure appears at the end of *Viva* : 'Toda España, por aquel tiempo de dictaduras y trisagios, roncas y trapisondas marciales, vivía con las manos en las orejas, esperando que estallase el trueno gordo' (*Viva* 251). Admittedly much less complex than the *Disparates*, these images nonetheless are based upon similar principles.

[13] Speratti Piñero, *De 'Sonata de Otoño' al esperpento*, pp. 149-51, 154.

[14] e.g., 'Bobalicón' and 'Disparate conocido' in the *Disparates*, and 'El buitre carnívoro' and 'Fiero monstruo' in the *Desastres de la guerra*.

Velázquez

Echoes of Velázquez are presented almost always as a contrast to Goya, following here not just a general principle of contrast, but also a visual one, just as Delacroix used the surrounding crowd of the insane to heighten Tasso's spirituality in 'Tasso in the Madhouse'. Goya's influence, as we have seen, reveals itself in caricature, crazy lines and angles, silhouettes and shadows, garish colours and nightmare effect. Velázquez appears as an influence via soft-toned colours, blue and purple, by changes of perspective (less dramatic than Goya's mirror effects), a sense of space and expansion, and subtlety of psychological and political suggestions.

Scenes of high ceremony at court, and of Palace intimacy, recall Velázquez (*Corte* II.ii-ix : 'La Majestad de Isabel II tenía en el celaje de los ojos el azul de la mañana madrileña' (*Corte* 29); 'La clara luz de la tarde madrileña entraba por los balcones reales, y el séquito joyante de tornasoles, plumas, mantos y entorchados evocaba las luces de la Corte de Carlos IV' (*Corte* 31)). If the effect of Goya is to cause us anxiety by the crazy course of lines, and rough colour sensations, that of Velázquez is to introduce calm – ironically, a false calm, given the chaos we know to exist immediately below the surface of Palace life. Given the skill of Velázquez in introducing slightly discordant notes in structures of complex visual harmony, we have here another example of a correlation between painter and author.

Court scenes provide the ideal opportunity for exploring the possible perspectives in a situation, a technique of Velázquez that will be familiar to most from 'Las Meninas' or 'Las Hilanderas'. Such is the case in *Corte* II.vi, where the Queen, King Consort and Narváez are in conference in 'el hueco de un balcón, tan profundo y amplio, que parecía una recámara' (*Corte* 26). The balcony is bathed in natural morning light in contrast with the Salón Gasparini of which it is a part, and where the only light is reflected and symptomatic of the flagging moral climate within, since 'una gran mesa fulgente de cristal y argentería estaba dispuesta a fin que hubiesen reparo para sus fallecidos ánimos las ilustres personas que habían recibido el pan eucarístico en la solemne función de Capilla' (ibid.).

As in 'Las Meninas' a change of perspective is often introduced by means of mirrors. In this painting the dim mirror in the background was what most shocked the public of the day, since in it were sketched out two figures who appeared to be the King and Queen. There has been dispute about the identity of the two figures, but that they were royal was certainly possible, and the relegation to a position of relative unimportance was regarded as an insult. It changed the accepted order, since the small Infanta and the painter himself became the centres of attention. In the same way Valle-Inclán uses mirrors to focus our attention upon the concentration of power in quarters where it would seem to be inappropriate. Thus the machinations of the King Consort's *camarilla* are presented as being the more shady, the more secretive and the more inappropriate by the visual manner in which they are communicated to the reader. In the plot to extract a compromising letter from Isabel II to the Pope, the King consort, Sor Patrocinio and Padre Claret are gathered at one point, each hiding behind his mask of respectability of concern for the moral health of Spain. The last two have political and religious motives, but the King Consort is shown to be acting out of motives of personal rancour, blind to the manipulations of his co-plotters. As the meeting ends, the handing over of the letter is perceived in the unreal world of a mirror :

> Mueve sus velos la beata por el fondo de un espejo. Ha vuelto a sacar el doblado pliego, y lo pone en las reales manos. El Augusto Consorte, en el fondo del espejo se ha parado a leerlo. A escondidas, volviendo la cara, sorbe un polvo de rapé la Reverencia de Fray Fulgencio. El Rey se desvanecía por el fondo del espejo, con el papel en la mano. El Conde Blanc, famoso en las ruletas cosmopolitas, se inclinó ante los velos de la Seráfica.
> – ¡Qué rectitud de conciencia la del Tío Paco !

Viva 169

Two details cause concern here. Firstly, the appearance of Fray Fulgencio and the Conde Blanc (a secret supporter of the *camarilla*) puts the sincerity of Patrocinio and Claret into doubt. Secondly, the change of tense, from present to past, separates us from the reality of the action. It has already been accomplished, and does not exist as an ongoing experience. It might never have taken place, an impression reinforced by the fact that we only see it in the misty depths of a mirror.

On another occasion, the image alone of a mirror is used, again to divorce us from reality. *Baza* 'Alta mar' is the world in miniature, with all its problems. The *Omega* is the ship of the world, perhaps the proverbial ship of fools. After a heated discussion between Alcalá Zamora and Bakunin, Valle-Inclán uses a final image to highlight the unreality of the political theory just expounded : 'Con la proyección de los balances, el comedor columpiaba la quimera de haberse trasmudado la vida al fondo oblicuo de un espejo. Todo subía y bajaba con el ritmo del horizonte marino en el ojo de buey' (*Baza* 123-4).

More than anything, Valle-Inclán uses the touchstone of Velázquez to introduce a note of calm into the habitual chaos of the *Ruedo*. Thus all explicit references to Velázquez are concentrated into the figure of the Marqués de Bradomín, a character who belongs to no precise period, and who continues the old virtues of time gone by. He is 'muy velazqueño con atavíos de cazador' (*Corte* 119), 'velazqueño caballero' (*Corte* 120), he has a 'figura velazqueña' (*Corte* 123). The emphasis on 'Velázquez' qualities (serene and aristocratic) is introduced precisely at the time of the jarring episode when Feliche and Carolina meet the miller's wife.

Bradomín's elegance does not of course make him totally worthy, just as the skill of Velázquez was able to delineate weaknesses of character through facial features, while retaining lines of graceful composition. There is a strong contrast between the elevated conversation of Bradomín and Feliche on 'quijotismo' (*Corte* VI.xvi) and the previous chapter in which Adolfito mocks Torre-Mellada's loyalty to the Queen, and questions him about her superstitious practices. This does not mean that the section on Bradomín is straightforward or admiring in its approach : a discussion on quixotic action may be just as absurd as one on superstition. Irony is present, but set in a sophisticated framework and not the crude caricature of *Corte* VI.xv.

Other contrasts occur in *Corte* V, above all in the meetings between the Madrid aristocrats and the Andalusian bandits. The result is not necessarily fear or disgust. The ladies of the Torre-Mellada party take pleasure in the tales of Juan Caballero. The horror produced by the squinting miller's wife is converted into the relish of a tourist attraction : 'Del susto chillón habían saltado a la zalamería vocinglera, y jugando de los ojos bajo las mantillas, cercaban con apasionada intriga al novelesco salteador, que, garboso y marchoso, sobrio de ademanes y gestos, las enlabiaba con andaluces requiebros' (*Viva* 136). Caballero, within his type, is as aristocratic as Bradomín. It should be recalled however that, whatever the intended ironies here, the contrast between effects from Goya and Velázquez is rarely so strong as in *Viva* VIII.x, in the description of Madrid at sunset, and that nowhere are courtiers free from Goya-like caricature. Velázquez as source or inspiration appears in those moments when, if not dignity, at least style is apparent.

Popular graphic art

That popular graphic art of nineteenth-century Spain (that is, the illustrations which appeared in papers, broadsides and journals) should so closely show signs of influence from Goya, speaks both of his widespread recognition and of the realisation that his etchings had proved an excellent vehicle for contemporary political and social comment. Though it is hard to separate these two types of graphic influence, here I wish to concentrate on more general techniques of caricature than those mentioned above, discussing in particular the graphic ways adopted for political comment in the revolutionary period.

First, however, a word about the general patterns of graphic and pictorial influence in the *Ruedo*. To some extent, the influence of Velázquez is apparent in scenes of courtly dignity, and that of Goya in scenes of the *pueblo*, the bandits, and of the exposure of the folly of the aristocrats. Popular graphic art dominates in those scenes which provide a sweeping, kaleidoscopic panorama of revolutionary events (*Corte* 'Aires nacionales', *Viva* 'Almanaque revolucionario', *Baza* '¿Qué pasa en Cádiz?') or in those which deal most closely with revolutionary plots (*Viva* 'Barato de espadas', *Baza* 'Tratos púnicos' and 'Albures gaditanos'). Apart from these concentrations, the techniques of the graphic caricaturist are apparent throughout the series.

As usefully defined by Bergson, laughter may be provoked by any event which appears to run contrary to or interrupt the natural development of things : automatism, duplication, subjection to a geometric rule.[15] Hence the well-known technique of clowns who imitate the movement of puppets, or who move in unison, denying human individuality. On these principles we have the spectacle of Torre-Mellada and his cousin, made doubly ridiculous by the fact that they are identically ridiculous : 'Los dos, zancudos, pecosos y ojiverdes, muy angostos de mejillas, aguileños de narices tuertas. Los dos hablaban borroso, con un casi baladro, y eran por igual de gran linaje extremeño' (*Corte* 33). More tragic is the duplication of action between two policemen. At first differentiated by the

[15] Henri Bergson, *Le Rire*, (three essays published in the *Revue de Paris*, 1 and 15 February, 1 March 1899), reprinted *Oeuvres*, second edition, (Paris, 1963), pp. 383-5.

description of their physical appearance, they lose their identity on assuming an 'official' attitude : 'Los Señores Guardias, unánimes, se echaron el arma al hombro, unánimes inflaron la equis de las coreas [sic], y unánimes el tono, la palabra y el gesto, advirtieron : – ¡Ojo con torcerse, Tío Blases !' (*Corte* 141). There is humour in this sudden congruence, since the men *choose* to act identically (made clear by the four 'unánime's). Their warning to Tío Blas accentuates the ridiculous role officialdom forces them into, since even off-the-record comments are made to conform to a pattern which is a travesty of normal human reaction. Furthermore, there is obvious irony in their own strained rigidity and the warning to no 'torcerse'. A more complex form of reflection occurs in the description of the Coronela Sagastizábal. Her 'tristeza de carnales fuegos' is reflected in the triple image of her step-daughters who are like 'tres cirios que arden en un candelero con igual angustia de apagarse' (*Corte* 179). As yet their fires have no carnality, but not for long.

The graphic caricaturist frequently introduces a change of natural proportions in his figures, a technique emulated by Valle-Inclán, particularly in his portrayal of Isabel II. She becomes progressively more ponderous in scenes of political action. When she announces her intention to confer honours on Concha and Novaliches,[16] her figure grows out of all proportion as though this were the only way she could impose her will : 'Nuestra Augusta Señora . . . engordaba el labio borbónico . . . dio a sus mantecas un empaque altanero . . . inflaba la pechuga . . . Pomposa y mandona, se quitaba y ponía los anillos reales . . . no dejaba el mete y saca de los reales anillos. [sic] mirándose las manos de herpéticas mantecas, tan bastas y grandotas que podían manejar como un abanico el pesado cetro de Dos Mundos' (*Viva* 92-4). Again, when she is copying out the letter Patrocinio has given her to send to the Pope, her heavy hands impede every movement : covered in ink-stains, she is more like a clumsy child than a monarch. Slowly she inspects her inky fingers, upsets the ink-pot, and slowly Valle-Inclán watches her gaze at the results, reducing the pace of the narration by commas and use of the present tense : 'Considera con gran sobresalto la tinta en el pliego, en las manos, en el regazo' (*Viva* 170). Her slowness and perplexity, her child-like clumsiness, are out of keeping with her status and the importance of the letter. Her mind is clouded with the physical difficulties of the action, and thoughts of the implications of the letter are excluded, although they are probably the original cause of her clumsiness. It is a painful paradox that this action, so carefully and laboriously undertaken, is ill-conceived, and will lead to another scandal to shake the throne.

The overwhelming importance of physical presence of the characters leads at times to an impression of immobility and lack of spontaneity in scenes of dialogue, an effect further intensified by stylisation of speech. A dislocation then results between the impression of immobility and the action which theoretically is taking place. In dialogues where this occurs, the effect is one of a cartoon strip where we see a character and then read his words enclosed in a bubble, or alternatively

[16] José Gutiérrez de la Concha (1809-1895) was a fierce defender of the Queen, and was put in charge of defence by her at the beginning of the 1868 revolution. Novaliches, i.e. Manuel Pavía y Lacy (1814-1896), a *moderado*, took command of troops fighting the revolutionaries in 1868.

of an *aleluya* where couplet and illustrations must be perceived in different moments.

During the scene in the Casino where Adolfito is playing at the tables (*Viva* II.xiii), there is a sensation of developing paralysis as the likelihood of his losing a large sum of money increases. At the outset his appearance hints at disaster, and the feeling of vertigo is intensified by his sense of personal drama, heightened by the play : 'Apuntaba con fingida indiferencia, y poco pálido, frío y sonriente, gustando la fatua satisfacción de asombrar a los mirones, atraídos por la temeridad con que arriesgaba cuanto tenía delante' (*Viva* 41). The scene proceeds mechanically. The Niño de Benamejí leans over to counsel prudence, Adolfito continues his game. Again the Niño de Benamejí tries to draw him away and Adolfito 'siempre con los mismos faroles de tedio, repitió la maniobra, de empujar con la raqueta cuanto tenía delante, indiferente, sin darse la molestia de contar la puesta' (*Viva* 42). Valle-Inclán reminds us repeatedly in this section of Adolfito's attitude of boredom and indifference, and by a clever elaboration on 'gesto' stresses that it is all an act : 'Adolfito sonreía con el archigesto del tedio insoportable' (ibid). At a moment of particular tension we survey the onlookers as they comment :

– ¡Ya lo ve usted !
Corroboraba otro sabio del tapete verde :
– ¡Con cinco no se pide jamás !
Un erudito inicia una disertación :
– ¡En Monte Carlo, señores ! . . . [sic]
Un patriota :
– ¡No estamos en Monte Carlo !
Un filósofo :
– ¡Con cinco hubiera ganado !
El Barón de Bonifaz :
– ¡Señores, he preferido perder con nueve !

Viva 43

In this section the verbs of diction are gradually suppressed, thus producing a disjointed effect, similar to that of a comic strip. A character, such as 'un patriota', is pointed out, and his comment follows, with no bridging passage : there is a temptation, therefore, to see the comment almost as a physical projection of the character. Because the character stands alone, our attention centres upon him as a presence, independent of the normal progression of a narrative text. This passage, a verbal creation producing visual effect, is perhaps Valle-Inclán's answer to the silent cinema – a series of *estampas*.

At the same time as he exercises this verbal economy, Valle-Inclán reduces the scope of action. The two gestures made by the Niño de Benamejí : 'se echó atrás espantado [sic] los ojos . . . levantaba los brazos y se volvía a todos los vientos' (*Viva* 42), are made to continue throughout the comments on the inadvisability of Adolfito's actions. Thus his own comment is introduced by : 'Don Segis no bajaba los brazos del cielo' (*Viva* 43). We have the impression that the action has been suspended for a moment, and the fact that the gesture is still held after the comments it preceded, reinforces our appreciation of the cartoon-like qualities of the scene, and suggests that the rules of time have been broken. Adolfito himself breaks the atmosphere abruptly, so abruptly that it seems we have been moved on to the next drawing in the cartoon-strip : 'El Barón de Bonifaz se vendió con una súbita mudanza de voz y gesto : – ¡Por seguir la corazonada !' Movement in the scene approaches a more normal pace at this point, despite Adolfito's resumption of his original pose : 'Se recobró incontinenti, y por un rincón del bigotejo sacó ilesa la sonrisa de fatua indiferencia.' A strong visual impression of immobility is produced by the fact that Adolfito is able to 'take out' his 'sonrisa de fatua indiferencia' which has remained 'ilesa' despite his sudden betrayal of himself. This expression is re-established as a visual constant in the scene : 'Adolfito esbozó una mueca fría y desvergonzada'; 'Adolfito Bonifaz acentuaba su mueca cínica' (*Viva* 43).

This technique, which strongly resembles the Spanish broadsheet form of the *aleluya*,[17] is used to great effect in passages which evoke the many facets of a complex situation. In *Viva* 97-8 he surveys the attitudes of various parties to the marriage of the Conde de Girgenti and the Infanta Isabel Francisca. He introduces the passage with the comment '¡El prometido no es una ganga !' This is the opinion of the palace gossips, whose personification, or animalisation, as 'cornejas', is extended by the bird-like expression of their speech : 'repicaba con este rezo la castañeta de pico.' The exaggerated reaction of the Princesa de Beira to the marriage is pinpointed in the details Valle-Inclán supplies about the way she makes her views known, so that they are seen as a physical object : 'En un pliego, bajo cuatro obleas, por la posta certificada, habíale remitido su maldición con muchos borrones y el sello de sus armas.' We are presented with the picture of the Princess herself, 'fanática y mandona' and her energetic comments : '¡Dios está de nuestra parte! No puede ser de otra manera.' Her firm statements, with simple syntax, support the force of the portrait. The tenor of her speech echoes the comment of the King Consort's *camarilla*, whose superstitious fear is crystallised in fussy gestures to ward off evil : 'se arrugaba con el mismo melindre, garabatera de cruces.' The next illustration in the verbal cartoon-strip portrays the Apostolic party, which receives unfavourable treatment with the epithet 'de trashumancia carcunda', evocative of animal and herd-like qualities in its members.[18] The Carlist faction itself is shown to sneak in among the other groups of the right, in a concrete theatrical image : 'Asomaba entre cortinas la vieja tramoya, con el reconocimiento de los derechos que representaba la rama de Don Carlos María Isidro' (*Viva* 98). At the end of this survey of political attitudes there is another concrete image which expresses the character of the Vatican : 'Cautamente, en voz baja, sin salir de la sombra, la diplomacia vaticana acogía la posible regencia mancomunada de los Condes de Girgenti. El rojo solideo se inclinó con aparatosa cortesía : – Jamás olvidaré tan grata fiesta, que me ofrece el honor de saludar a sus Majestades' (ibid). With delicate ambiguity Valle-Inclán avoids stating whether this is in fact the description of a real representative of the Vatican, or whether it is a clever plastic

---

[17] See Chapter II, note 14.

[18] There may be a reflection here of popular cartoons in which Carlists were frequently portrayed as sheep in berets. See Plate V.

elaboration which shows the attitude and the 'manera de ser' of the Vatican representatives. The rapid change of scene within this short section combines with the epigrammatic résumé of attitudes to produce the cartoon-strip effect, at the same time as suggesting the melodramatic nature of a politics where participants hide in shadows to eavesdrop or to wait their chance.

In other sections there are explicit references to popular art which emphasise the stylisation of characters and our perceptions of them. The main effect is to increase the process of distancing between author and reader and to fix the action within the world of fiction. At times this technique is also used to remind the reader that he is dealing with history and not actuality. When the *Omega* arrives in London and arrests are made, we are told : 'Protestaban románticos, desde el botalón, los revolucionarios españoles, en grupo de girondinos. Las viejas litografías han perpetuado estos gestos' (*Baza* 156). In retrospect, we imagine the scene in the lines of the lithographs mentioned at the end, and in this way see the scene at one step removed. The slip from actuality to not just recorded but mythified past, begun by the stylisation implicit in 'románticos', is completed by the visual suggestion.

It is in *Baza* above all that this technique is used. Prim, as we have seen, is subjected to merciless satire, and is always locked in a plastic stylisation. From the first mention ('El General Prim caracoleaba su caballo de naipes en todos los baratillos de estampas litográficas' (*Corte* 11)) which introduces him as the character remembered by popular History, he remains within this framework throughout the narrative, although the lines of the caricature change. In *Viva* he appears in the office of *Gil Blas*, presiding 'con el ros ladeado, desde un marco de oralina' (*Viva* 164) : at one stroke here Valle conveys admiration of Prim by the journalists, but also their stylised conception of him. When Prim meets Cabrera, the action is clearly set back into recorded history : 'El Héroe de los Castillejos escorzóse en el sillón con saludo de litografía, al Héroe de Morella' (*Viva* 236).

There are many other specific echoes of popular graphic art in the *Ruedo*, usually included as brief detail that is telling of the author's acquaintance with his informal sources. Montpensier, brother-in-law to Isabel II and a pretender to the throne, appeared to cultivate a deliberate image of bourgeois stolidity and respectability to present a clear contrast with the throne's previous occupant. These pretensions were seized on and ridiculed by the press. A caricature in *El Caos* of 4 July 1870 summarised all the points of criticism, showing him growing as an orange, an umbrella for his hair, galoshes for his moustache, Topete for an eye and papers for his forehead.[19] Thus were exposed the foibles of the nobleman who sold the oranges of his estate, adopted the ostentatiously humble dress of Louis-Phillippe and suborned both the revolution and the press. Valle-Inclán repeatedly includes references to his orange-groves of San Telmo (e.g. *Baza* 125, 180, 195, 209), and a description in *Viva* clearly reflects the graphic caricature :

Las tardes de la primavera vasca, cuando hacía claro, salían a pasear por

---

[19] See Plate VI. Topete's connexion with Montpensier is indicated obliquely in *Baza* 30 : 'Don Juan Bautista era un gigante curtido de soles y vendavales, con un Karma de cielos estrellados y luces de San Telmo.' The 'luces de San Telmo' may either be read as a plain reference to St. Elmo's fire, or a hint at his financial backer.

las mojadas carreteras, y la revolución con bufanda, paraguas, chanclos de goma, se asomaba sobre la frontera de España.

Viva 13

A brief glimpse in *Viva* I (a panorama of popular impressions) shows us González Bravo making paper birds in a council meeting (*Viva* 22-3). The resemblance between this and a caricature by Ortego in *Jeremías* on 31 January 1869 of a meeting between Isabel, the King Consort, Carlos VII and González Bravo is made by the occupation of the King Consort, again occupied with crude origami.[20] The glimpse of Rivero, described with a companion 'con trancas de nudos, calañés y capa' (*Viva* 56), is close to the Rivero of illustration 15 of the *aleluya D. N. M. Rivero*, although the type of hat is different.[21]

The visual effects to be found in other parts of Valle-Inclán's works are present still in the *Ruedo* : the means of suggesting atmosphere by lighting (the aristocracy normally appear in artificial light); characters are left poised with arms 'en aspa'. But other depths have been added. The range of visual sources and influences extends between two extremes of Spanish art : from those painters most skilled in portraying subtleties of human character and situation, most skilled in the use of tone and colour, to those who inherited their tradition in the nineteenth century, major cartoonists like Ortego. With the exception of the *aleluyas*, pictorial references do not reflect the art of the *pueblo*, but of the more cultured, of the man versed in the politics of his time, although even 'cultured' cartoonists are not above using crude visual statement to press home a point, just as Goya previously had exposed with insistence the frailty and vanity of man in the *Caprichos* and the *Desastres*. Here too, then, Valle-Inclán maintains a perception that is both aristocratic and critical, a mode of contemporary reportage that uses the most direct sense, that of sight, to communicate the emotions, changes of atmosphere and crude ways of understanding, imagining or rationalising that were those of participants and onlookers of the 1868 revolution.

[20] See Plate VII.
[21] See Plate VIII.

Conclusion

The commentary of *El ruedo ibérico* given in the preceding pages could have been pursued at far greater length, so closely-knit is the network of resonance and reference based on the History of the mid-nineteenth century. That Valle-Inclán should have based his series of historical novels on the 'reacción del pueblo' is not surprising : the wealth and depth of his knowledge of such sources, however, goes well beyond one's expectations. Knowledge and awareness of the *política callejera* or the jests of the populace about the supposed events of politics had been present in many of his preceding works, but here the texture and concentration of this element is over-powering. Furthermore, the choice of reading matter has been a catholic one. The notion that Valle-Inclán's interests were restricted to papers or documents of a republican and revolutionary nature is patently false. If any element of choice has been present, it is shown in the relative neglect of the anti-Carlist press, or rather of the typical contemporary attacks on Carlos VII (as 'el enano de la venta' or the 'rey alcornoque'). It should be added at once, however, that Carlism is not put forward as a pure or admirable form of politics which outstrips the others. The pretender may be preferable to the reigning monarch in some respects, but *Baza* at least hints at a king of widespread affections who in his own right gives cause for gossip.

The *Ruedo* maintains a line of merciless attack on all aspects of social and political life in Spain at the time of the revolution of 1868. The attack is not that of the social didact, but of the man who sees the pretentiousness and shallowness of most supposed human aspirations. Here, instead of creating from nothing the *bufonada* to puncture the bubble, he adopts and records the *bufonadas* of the time. The process of *encrustación*, a practice repeatedly defended by Valle-Inclán, results in neither a clumsily pasted collage, nor in a disruption of the fundamental artistic unity of the *Ruedo*. This is because the popular material, although clearly identifiable, has been subjected to change in order that it should fit within the author's concept of novelistic and human credibility. This is partly achieved by the categorisation of material into pure rumour and surmise, gossip or rumour which is shown to have some foundation, and material which is transmitted directly to the reader by the author, thus acquiring the status of fact in which the author wishes us to believe. It is also achieved by selection of detail, so that attacks upon the reader's sensibility remain within the confines of Valle-Inclán's intention, and are not dictated by the frequently more outrageous levels of press comment.

It will no doubt be argued that I have over-stressed the extent to which Valle-Inclán tempered and restrained his original material. I recognise that there is a danger, when turning from *El Cencerro* or *El Centinela del Pueblo* to the *Ruedo*, that one might see the latter as a relatively anodyne romp. Nonetheless, it is necessary perhaps to overstate the case of temperance and taste in the *Ruedo* in order to counter-balance previously held beliefs that the *Ruedo* was a scandalous and unparalleled attack on the Spain of Isabel II. An attack it is, and in more concentrated and sustained form than one finds in either the popular press or contemporary historical accounts, but its statements and suggestions are more subtle than those of its sources. Isabel II is seen with one lover, not a dozen; she is stupid, vulgar, and patently a menace to the good reputation of the Spanish monarchy, but she is not malevolent; she is unthinking and capricious, rather than wilfully cruel or violent. Her husband is a laughable fop, but not a pervert whose contact must lead to corruption. Sor Patrocinio is scheming and fraudulent, Claret blinkered and irresponsible in his position as confessor to the Queen : their misdemeanours reside however in abuse of their position of confidence, rather than in flagrant contravention of the commandments. The portrayal of Prim is close to the original : in both accounts, concentration is upon the super-ego, the political astuteness and ambitions. The dangers of the military man turned politician have changed little in the years between the historical event and its novelistic re-creation. Valle-Inclán's attack is less outrageous in its form, but the criticism contained is more far-reaching and bitter. The vestige of hope that there may be some more worthy form of politics (not to be confused with the nineteenth-century predications of new political credos, all expressed in the same bombastic language, and attaining the same level of overkill and disenchantment as advertisements for soap-powder do) adds particular poignance to the criticism. The satirical press of 1868-70 retained few illusions. Some sixty years later Valle-Inclán has difficulty in retaining his, but the tone is of world-weariness, rather than of involvement in the games of the carnival and the competition to see who could relate the most scandalous stories.

The welding of subject matter into a homogeneous rather than a heterogeneous whole is revealed on other levels. The language of the *Ruedo*, so often claimed to be typical of the *esperpento*, is also typical of the historical period, and is one of our best guides through the social tangles of the novels. Similarly the visual force of the *Ruedo*, partly an inevitable element in a man whose *acotaciones* reveal an intense preoccupation for the impact of shape and colour on the eye, also shows detailed awareness of contemporary caricature. The division of style and colour tonality into the artistic worlds of Goya and Velázquez at times reinforces more formal aspects of the structure, at times moves in counterpoint.

One last point should be touched upon, especially since it concerns recent discussion on the possible meanings of some of Valle-Inclán's work. The extent to which Valle-Inclán exerted himself in the concealment of less than obvious meanings below the obvious verbal statements of the text is debatable. Hypotheses of hidden allegory are attractive, but are undermined by certain careless and capricious composition habits of the author. In the case of the *Ruedo*, the author seems to be exceptionally well-documented, and to have used his material with both delight and discrimination. To seek detailed allegory here would surely be to 'buscarle tres pies al gato'. The supposed dedication of the *Farsa y licencia de la reina castiza* does remind us that there might be parallels between the reigns of Alfonso XIII and Isabel II, and it is true that the greater part of the *Ruedo*'s text was composed before Alfonso's departure from Spain in 1931, from which it could be argued that any comment on the king would need to be veiled for the sake of tact and safety. But it should be remembered that the cycle was intended to cover the period up to the death of Alfonso XII, a fact which would presumably disturb carefully woven allegories between the reigns of Isabel II and Alfonso XIII. What is much more credible is that the reader should be intended to grasp the general political analogies between Spain of 1868, Spain of 1888 and Spain of 1928 or 1931. Constitutional monarchy, as a form of unsatisfactory government, did not alter radically over the years. The problems besetting politics in one century continued to menace political development in the next. As ever the *pueblo* were to remain as underdogs, seeking ideals of social and political justice undreamed of by those who ruled. The *Ruedo* has full coherence within its own limitations, and in the traditions of the best literature leads naturally from the detailed to the general, from an individual revolution doomed to failure to the static nature of a society which decrees such failure. The awareness that the turnings of the wheel of fortune are bound to be non-revolutions is what provokes sober thought, the only stimulus that can lead us to break out of what has become a vicious circle.

Bibliography

(There is not space in this bibliography to give full account of all critical works on Valle-Inclán, or of all historical books and papers which are relevant to the period of history covered by the *Ruedo*. Only the works which are most directly relevant have been selected.)

For the most complete published accounts of work on and by Valle-Inclán, the reader is referred to three bibliographies:

Rubia Barcia, José, *A Biobibliography and Iconography of Valle-Inclán, 1866–1936*, (Berkeley, 1960).

Doménech, Ricardo, 'Contribución a la bibliografía de Valle-Inclán', *Estudios Escénicos*, no. 15, (July, 1972), pp. 10–29.

Lima, Robert, *An Annotated Bibliography of Ramón del Valle-Inclán*, (Pennsylvania State University Libraries, 1972).

I. WORKS BY VALLE-INCLAN

I. BOOKS

Femeninas, (Pontevedra, 1895).

Epitalamio, (Madrid, 1897).

Cenizas, (Madrid, 1899).

Sonata de otoño (Memorias del marqués de Bradomín), (Madrid, 1902).

Jardín umbrío, (Madrid, 1903).

Corte de amor: Florilegio de honestas y nobles damas, (Madrid, 1903).

Sonata de estío (Memorias del marqués de Bradomín), (Madrid, 1903).

Sonata de primavera (Memorias del marqués de Bradomín), (Madrid, 1904).

Flor de santidad: Historia milenaria, (Madrid, 1904).

Sonata de invierno (Memorias del marqués de Bradomín), (Madrid, 1905).

Jardín novelesco, (Madrid, 1905). (Second edition, enlarged, Madrid, 1908).

Historias perversas, (Barcelona, 1907).

Aguila de blasón: Comedia bárbara, (Barcelona, 1905).

Aromas de leyenda, (Madrid, 1907).

El marqués de Bradomín: Coloquios románticos, (Madrid, 1907).

Romance de lobos: Comedia bárbara, (Madrid, 1908).

Una tertulia de antaño, (Madrid, 1908).

Los cruzados de la causa: La guerra carlista, I, (Madrid, 1908).

El yermo de las almas, (Madrid, 1908).

El resplandor de la hoguera: La guerra carlista, II, (Madrid, 1908–9).

Gerifaltes de antaño: La guerra carlista, III, (Madrid, 1908–9).

Cofre de sándalo, (Madrid, 1909).

Cuento de abril, (Madrid, 1910).

Las mieles del rosal, (Madrid, 1910).

Voces de gesta, (Madrid, 1911).

La marquesa Rosalinda, (Madrid, 1913).

El embrujado, (Madrid, 1913).
La cabeza del dragón, (Madrid, 1914).
La lámpara maravillosa, (Madrid, 1916).
La media noche, (Madrid, 1917).
Mi hermana Antonia, (Madrid, 1918).
La pipa de kif, (Madrid, 1919).
Cuentos, (México, 1919).
Farsa de la enamorada del rey, (Madrid, 1920).
El pasajero, (Madrid, 1920).
Divinas palabras, (Madrid, 1920).
Farsa y licencia de la reina castiza, (Madrid, 1922).
Cara de plata: Comedia bárbara, (Madrid, 1923).
Luces de bohemia: Esperpento, (Madrid, 1924).
La rosa de papel y La cabeza del Bautista, La novela semanal, (Madrid, 22 March 1924)
Los cuernos de don Friolera: Esperpento, (Madrid, 1925).
Tablado de marionetas para educación de príncipes, (Madrid, 1926).
El terno del difunto, (becomes *Las galas del difunto* when published in *Martes de Carnaval*), (Madrid, 1926).
Zacarías el Cruzado o Agüero nigromante, La novela de hoy, no. 225, (Madrid, 3 September, 1926).
Tirano Banderas, (Madrid, 1926).
Retablo de la avaricia, la lujuria y la muerte, (Madrid, 1927).
La hija del capitán: Esperpento, La novela mundial, (Madrid, 28 July, 1927).
Teatrillo de enredo, Los novelistas, I, no. 16, (Madrid, 28 June 1928).
Claves líricas, (Madrid, 1930).
Martes de Carnaval: Esperpentos, (Madrid, 1930). This included *Las galas del difunto, La hija del capitán* (1927), *Los cuernos de don Friolera* (1925). The Austral reprint of *Martes de Carnaval,* (Madrid, 1968) included another *esperpento, ¿Para cuándo son las reclamaciones diplomáticas?* (1922).

'EL RUEDO IBERICO' AND ITS FRAGMENTS

La corte de los milagros: El ruedo ibérico, I, (Madrid, 1927). Reprinted and enlarged, *El Sol,* 20 October–11 December 1931. Reprint of second edition, Madrid: Austral, 1968.
Viva mi dueño: El ruedo ibérico, II, (Madrid, 1928). Reprinted with some alterations, *El Sol,* 14 January–25 March, 1932. Reprint of second edition, Madrid: Austral, 1969.
Baza de espadas (incomplete vol. of *El ruedo ibérico, III*), *El Sol,* 7 June–19 July, 1932. Reprint in book form, Barcelona: AHR, 1958.

Cartel de ferias, La novela semanal, V, no. 183, (Madrid, 10 January, 1925).
Ecos de Asmodeo, La novela mundial, (Madrid, 1926).
Fin de un revolucionario, Los novelistas, I, no. 1, (Madrid, 15 March, 1928).
Teatrillo de enredo, Los novelistas, I, no. 16, (Madrid, 28 June 1928).
Las reales antecámaras, La novela de hoy, VII, no. 335, (Madrid, 12 October, 1928).
Otra castiza de Samaria, La novela de hoy, no. 392, (Madrid, 15 November, 1929).
Vísperas de la gloriosa, La novela de hoy, no. 418, (Madrid, 16 May, 1930).
Correo diplomático, Ahora, 12, 19 March, 1933.
El trueno dorado, Ahora, 19 March–23 April, 1936.
La jaula del pájaro, Enciclopedia pulga, no. 308, (Barcelona, 1957). (Presumably a reprint of an earlier edition.)

II.   ARTICLES BY VALLE-INCLAN REFERRED TO IN THE TEXT

'Palabras de mal agüero', *El Universal*, (México), 11 June, 1892. Reprinted in William Fichter, *Publicaciones periodísticas de Don Ramón de Valle-Inclán anteriores a 1895*, (México, 1952), pp. 163–7.

'Un libro sugeridor', *Ahora*, 18 June 1935.

'Sugestiones de un libro (*Amadeo de Saboya*) II', *Ahora*, 26 June, 1935.

'Sugestiones de un libro (*Amadeo de Saboya*) III', *Ahora*, 2 July, 1935.

'Sugestiones de un libro (*Amadeo de Saboya*) IV', *Ahora*, 11 July, 1935.

'Sugerencias de un libro (*Amadeo de Saboya*) V', *Ahora*, 19 July, 1935.

'Sugerencias de un libro (*Amadeo de Saboya*) VI', *Ahora*, 26 July, 1935.

'Paúl y Ángulo y los asesinos del general Prim I', *Ahora*, 2 August, 1935.

'Paúl y Ángulo y los asesinos del general Prim II', *Ahora,* 13 August, 1935.

'Paúl y Ángulo y los asesinos del general Prim III', *Ahora*, 16 August, 1935.

'Paúl y Ángulo y los asesinos del general Prim IV', *Ahora*, 28 August, 1935.

'Paúl y Ángulo y los asesinos del general Prim V', *Ahora*, 20 September, 1935.

'*Mi rebelión en Barcelona*: nota literaria', *Ahora*, 2 October, 1935.

III.   INTERVIEWS ETC.

Interview of 1925 reprinted in *Primer Acto*, no. 32, (1967), pp. 10–11. (Source unknown.)

'Valle-Inclán y su opinión sobre el "cine" ', *El Bufón*, (Barcelona), 15 February, 1924, p. 2.

'Una conferencia de don Ramón del Valle-Inclán', *El Sol*, 4 March, 1932.

'Don Ramón María del Valle-Inclán', interview with Luis Calvo, *ABC*, 3 August, 1930.

Martínez Sierra, G, 'Hablando con Valle-Inclán', *ABC*, 7 December, 1928.

Rivas Cherif, Cipriano, interview with Valle-Inclán, *El Sol*, 3 September, 1920.

2.   WORKS OF CRITICISM ON VALLE-INCLAN

Bary, David, 'Un personaje de Valle-Inclán. ¿Quién es el Barón de Benicarlés?', *Insula*, XXIV, no. 266, (January, 1969), pp. 1, 12.

Bermejo Marcos, Manuel, *Valle-Inclán: introducción a su obra*, (Madrid, 1971).

Boudreau, Harold L., 'Banditry and Valle-Inclán's *Ruedo ibérico*', *Hispanic Review*, XXXV, no. 1, (January, 1967), pp. 85–92.

Boudreau, Harold L., 'The circular structure of Valle-Inclán's *Ruedo ibérico*', *Publications of the Modern Languages Association*, LXXXII, no. 1, (March, 1967), pp. 128–35.

Boudreau, Harold L., 'Materials toward an analysis of Valle-Inclán's *Ruedo ibérico*', unpublished PhD dissertation, (University of Wisconsin, 1966).

Boudreau, Harold L., 'The metamorphosis of the *Ruedo ibérico*', *Valle-Inclán: An Appraisal of his Life and Works*, ed. Anthony N. Zahareas, pp. 758–76. (Hereafter referred to as the Zahareas *Appraisal* . . .)

Boudreau, Harold L., 'The moral comment of the *Ruedo ibérico*', Zahareas *Appraisal* . . ., pp. 792–804.

Cardona, Rodolfo, 'Los cuernos de don Friolera: estructura y sentido', Zahareas *Appraisal* . . ., pp. 636–71.

Díaz-Plaja, Guillermo, *Las estéticas de Valle-Inclán*, (Madrid, 1965).

Enguídanos, Miguel, 'Las raíces históricas del esperpentismo', *Insula*, XXVII, no. 305, (April, 1972), pp. 1, 10, 14.

Fernández Almagro, Melchor, *Vida y literatura de Valle Inclán,* (Madrid, 1943).

Fichter, William L, *Publicaciones periodísticas de Don Ramón del Valle-Inclán anteriores a 1895*, (México, 1952).

Franco, Jean 'The concept of time in *El ruedo ibérico*', *Bulletin of Hispanic Studies*, XXXIX, (1962), pp. 177-87.

García de la Torre, José Manuel, *Análisis temático de 'El ruedo ibérico'*, (Madrid, 1972).

Gómez Marín, J. A., *La idea de sociedad en Valle-Inclán*, (Madrid, 1967).

Gómez de la Serna, Gaspar, 'Las dos Españas de don Ramón María del Valle-Inclán', *Clavileño*, III, no. 17, (September-October, 1952), pp. 17-32.

Gómez de la Serna, Gaspar, 'Sus dos Españas', *Entrerramones y otros ensayos*, (Madrid, 1969).

Hormigón, Juan Antonio, *Ramón del Valle-Inclán: La política, la cultura, el realismo y el pueblo*, (Madrid, 1972).

Madrid, Francisco, *La vida altiva de Valle-Inclán*, (Buenos Aires, 1943).

Marías, Julián, *La imagen de la vida humana y dos ejemplos literarios: Cervantes, Valle-Inclán*, (Madrid, 1971).

Marías, Julián, *Valle-Inclán en el Ruedo ibérico*, (Madrid, 1966).

Reyes, Alfonso, 'Apuntes sobre Valle-Inclán: III: Las 'fuentes' de Valle-Inclán', 1922; reprinted in *Tertulia de Madrid*, (Buenos Aires, 1949) pp. 67-70.

Reyes, Alfonso, 'Apuntes sobre Valle-Inclán: La parodia tragica', *Tertulia de Madrid*, pp. 79-88.

Reyes, Alfonso, 'Apuntes sobre Valle-Inclán: Algo más sobre Valle-Inclán', *Tertulia de Madrid*, pp. 74-77.

Risco, Antonio, *La estética de Valle-Inclán en los esperpentos y en 'El ruedo ibérico'*, (Madrid, 1966).

Rubia Barcia, José, 'The *esperpentos*: a new novelistic dimension', *Valle-Inclán Centennial Studies*, ed. Ricardo Gullón, (Austin, Texas, 1968), pp. 65-96.

Rubia Barcia, José, review of Fichter, *Publicaciones periodísticas . . .*, *Romanic Review*, XLVII, no. 1, (1956), pp. 48-52.

Salper de Tortella, Roberta, 'Don Juan Manuel Montenegro: the Fall of a King', Zahareas *Appraisal . . .*, pp. 317-33.

Seco Serrano, Carlos, 'Valle-Inclán y la España oficial', *Revista de Occidente*, XV, nos. 44 and 45, (November-December, 1966), pp. 203-24.

Sender, Ramón, *Valle-Inclán y la dificultad de la tragedia,* (Madrid, 1965).

Sinclair, Alison, 'The first episode of *El ruedo ibérico*?', *Bulletin of Hispanic Studies*, XLIX, (1972), pp. 165-74.

Sinclair, Alison, 'Nineteenth-century popular literature as a source of linguistic enrichment in Valle-Inclán's *Ruedo ibérico*', *Modern Language Review*, LXX, no. 1, (January, 1975), pp. 84-96.

Smith, Verity A., '*Fin de un revolucionario* y su conexión con el ciclo ibérico', *Revista de Literatura*, XXVI, nos. 51-52, (1964), pp. 61-88.

Speratti Piñero, Emma Susana, *De 'Sonata de otoño' al esperpento: (Aspectos del arte de Valle-Inclán)*, (London, 1968). This includes the articles: 'Como nació y creció *El ruedo ibérico*', pp. 243-48; 'Acerca de *La corte de los milagros*', pp. 249-72; 'La aventura final de Fernández Vallín', pp. 273-93; '¿Un nuevo episodio de *El ruedo ibérico*?', pp. 295-312; 'Las últimas novelas de Valle-Inclán', pp. 313-27.

Speratti Piñero, Emma Susana, *El ocultismo en Valle-Inclán,* (London, 1974).

Ynduráin, Francisco, '*La corte de los milagros*: Ensayo de interpretacion', *Cuadernos Hispano-Americanos (Homenaje a Valle-Inclán)*, nos. 119-200, (1966), pp. 322-46.

Ynduráin, Francisco, *Valle-Inclán: Tres estudios*, (Santander, 1969).

Zahareas, Anthony N., 'The absurd, the grotesque and the esperpento', Zahareas *Appraisal . . .*, pp. 78-108.

Zahareas, Anthony N., editor, *Ramón del Valle-Inclán: An Appraisal of his Life and Works*, (New York, 1968).

Zamora Vicente, Alonso, *La realidad esperpéntica: Aproximación a 'Luces de Bohemia'*, (Madrid, 1969).

Zavala, Iris M., 'Historia y literatura en *El ruedo ibérico'*, *La revolución de 1868: Historia, pensamiento, literatura*, ed. Clara E. Lida and Iris M. Zavala, (New York, 1970), pp. 425–49.

The following works provide a useful background for the study of the plastic in Valle-Inclán. Criticism on individual painters has not been included.

Baudelaire, Charles, 'De l'essence du rire, et généralement du comique dans les arts plastiques', (Paris, 1855); reprinted in *Oeuvres Complètes*, (Paris, 1954), pp. 710–728.

Díaz-Plaja, Guillermo, *Cuestión de límites*, (Madrid, 1943), pp. 139ff, 191ff, 225ff.

Díaz-Plaja, Guillermo, *Modernismo frente a noventa y ocho*, (Madrid, 1951), pp. 235–40.

Durán, Victorina, 'Escenografía y vestuario: Valle-Inclán con sus acotaciones en verso', *La Voz*, (20 January, 1936).

Gómez de la Serna, Gaspar, 'Velázquez y el 98', *Villa de Madrid*, no. 14, (1960); reprinted in *Entrerramones y otros ensayos*, (Madrid, 1969).

Lafuente Ferrari, Enrique, 'La pintura española y la generación del 98', *Arbor*, XI, no. 36, (December, 1948), pp. 449–64.

Lyon, J. E., 'Valle-Inclán and the art of the theatre', *Bulletin of Hispanic Studies*, XLVI, no. 2, (1969), pp. 132–52.

Mesa, Enrique de, *Apostillas a la escena*, (Madrid, 1929).

Nieva, Francisco, 'Virtudes plásticas del teatro de Valle-Inclán', *Primer Acto*, no. 82, (1967).

Pérez de Ayala, 'Sobre los escritores universales', *Nuevo Mundo*, (3 July, 1915).

Risco, Antonio, *La estética de Valle-Inclán en los esperpentos y en 'El ruedo ibérico'*, (Madrid, 1966), p. 235ff.

Salinas, Pedro, article in *Heraldo de Madrid*, (6 January, 1936), p. 3.

Torrente Ballester, *Literatura española contemporánea (1898–1936)*, (Madrid, 1949), pp. 233–34.

3. GENERAL BIBLIOGRAPHY

Angelón, Manuel, *¡Flor de un día!*, (Barcelona, 1862).

Azaña, Manuel, *Mi rebelión en Barcelona*, second edition, (Bilbao, 1935).

Ballesteros y Beretta, Antonio, *Historia de España y su influencia en la historia universal*, 9 vols., (Barcelona, 1918–41).

Baroja, Pío, *Memorias de un hombre de acción*, (1913–35), published in *Obras completas*, 8 vols., (Madrid, 1946–51).

Bergson, Henri, *Le Rire*. Three essays published in the *Revue de Paris*, 1, 15 February, 1 March, 1899, reprinted in *Oeuvres*, second edition, Paris, 1963.

Bermejo, Ildefonso Antonio, *La estafeta de Palacio: Historia del último reinado*, 3 vols., (Madrid, 1871–2).

Besses, L., *Diccionario de argot español*, (Barcelona, 1906).

Blasco, Eusebio, *¡A la humanidad dolente!! Juicio del Año 1868 . . .*, (Madrid, 1868).

Blasco, Eusebio, *El joven Telémaco*, (Madrid, 1866).

Blasco, Eusebio, *Los novios de Teruel*, (Madrid, 1867).

Blasco, Eusebio, *Pablo y Virginia*, (Madrid, 1867).

Borrow, George, *The Zincali*, (1841), fourth edition (London, 1901).

Brown, Irving, 'The vocabulary of the Zincali', *Journal of the Gypsy Lore Society*, third series, 2, (1922), p. 192.

Brown, Reginald, *La novela española, 1700–1850*, (Madrid, 1953).

Cambronero, Carlos, *Isabel II, íntima: Apuntes histórico-anecdóticos de su vida y de su época*, (Barcelona, 1908).

Cánovas del Castillo, A., 'Discurso primero del Ateneo', *Problemas contemporáneos*, 3 vols., (Madrid, 1884–90), I, 5–52.

Carr, Raymond, *Spain, 1808–1936*, (1966), Spanish edition, corrected and enlarged, *España, 1808–1936*, (Barcelona, 1969).

Cipolla, Carlo, *Literacy and Development in the West*, (London, 1969).

Claret y Clará, P. Antonio, *La llave de oro o serie de reflexiones que, para abrir el corazón cerrado de los pobres pecadores, ofrece a los confesores nuevos el Excmo. e Illmo. Sr. D. Antonio María Claret*, (Barcelona, 1960).

[Claret], *Biografía del Padre Claret por O * * **, colaborador de *La Iberia* de Calvo Asensio, (Madrid, 1869).

[Claret], *San Antonio María Claret: Escritos autobiográficos y espirituales, Biblioteca de Autores Cristianos*, Vol. 188, (Madrid, 1859).

Clavería, Carlos, *Estudios sobre los gitanismos del español*, (Madrid, 1951).

Coupe, William Arthur, *The German Illustrated Broadsheet in the Seventeenth Century: Historical and Iconographical studies*, 2 vols., (Baden-Baden, 1966–7).

'Crónica de don Sancho el bravo', *Crónicas de los reyes de Castilla. I. Biblioteca de autores españoles*, Vol. 66, (Madrid, 1875).

Deleito y Piñuela, José, *Origen y apogeo del género chico*, (Madrid, 1959).

Elorza, Antonio, *La utopía anarquista bajo la segunda república española*, (Madrid, 1973).

Estévanez, N., *Calandracas*, (Barcelona, n.d.).

Ferreras, Juan Ignacio, *Los orígenes de la novela decimonónica, 1800–1830*, (Madrid, 1973).

Ferreras, Juan Ignacio, *La novela por entregas, 1840–1900*, (Madrid, 1972).

Garrido, Fernando, *Historia del reinado del último Borbón de España: De los crímenes, apostasías, opresión, corrupción, inmoralidad, despilfarros, hipocresía, crueldad y fanatismo de los gobiernos que han regido a España durante el reinado de Isabel de Borbón*, 3 vols., (Madrid, 1868–69).

Gaspar, Enrique, *Las circunstancias*, (Madrid, 1867).

Guzmán de León, Antonio, *El último Borbón: Historia dramática de Isabel II desde sus primeros años hasta su caída del trono*, 2 vols., (Barcelona, 1868–9).

Hartzenbusch, Juan Eugenio, *Los polvos de la madre Celestina*, (Madrid, 1840).

Harvey, W. J., *Character and the Novel*, (London, 1965).

Herrero Salgado, Félix, *Cartelera Teatral Madrileña, II: años 1840–1849, Cuadernos bibliográficos*, no. 9, (Madrid, 1963).

Holt, Edgar, *The Carlist Wars in Spain*, (London, 1967).

Ixart, José, *Arte escénico en España*, (Barcelona, 1894).

Jarnés, Benjamín, *Sor Patrocinio, La monja de las llagas*, (1929), reprinted (Madrid, 1930).

Kendrick, T. D., *St. James in Spain*, (London, 1960).

Klingender, F. D., *Goya in the Democratic Tradition*, (1945), reprinted, (London, 1968).

Lastra, Ruesga and Prieto, *Vivitos y coleando*, (Madrid, 1884). Music by Chueca and Valverde.

López de Ayala, Adelardo, *Un hombre de estado*, (Madrid, 1851), reprinted in *Obras Completas de D. Adelardo López de Ayala, I, Colección de Escritores Castellanos: Dramáticos*, (Madrid, 1881).

Maluquer de Motes Bernet, J., 'El problema de la esclavitud y la revolución de 1868', *Hispania* (Madrid), no. 117, (1971).

Miquel i Vergés, J. M., *El General Prim, en España y México*, (México, 1949).

Montesinos, José F., *Introducción a una historia de la novela española en el siglo XIX*, (Valencia, 1955).

Olivar Bertrand, R., *El Caballero Prim: Vida íntima, amorosa y militar*, 2 vols., (Barcelona, 1952).

Ortega y Gasset, José, *Ideas sobre la novela, Obras completas*, 11 vols., (Madrid, 1957–69); III, fourth edition, (Madrid 1957).

Picón, José, *La corte de los milagros*, second edition, (Madrid, 1863).

Pí y Margall, Francisco, and Pí y Arsuaga, *Historia de España en el siglo XIX*, 7 vols., (Barcelona, 1902–3).

Pérez Galdós, Benito, *Montes de Oca*, (1900), *Los Ayacuchos*, (1900), *Bodas reales*, (1900), *Los duendes de la camarilla*, (1903), *La revolución de Julio*, (1903–4), *O'Donnell*, (1904), *Aita Tettauen*, (1904–5), *Carlos IV en la Rápita*, (1905), *Prim*, (1906), *La de los tristes destinos*, (1907), *España sin rey*, (1907–8), *España trágica*, (1909), *Amadeo I*, (1910), *La primera república*, (1911), *De Cartago a Sagunto*, (1911), *Cánovas*, (1912), (*Episodios nacionales* of third, fourth and last series, published in *Obras completas*, 6 vols., (Madrid, 1967–9)).

Pott, A. F., *Die Zigeuner in Europa und Asien*, 2 vols., (Halle, 1844–5).

Répide, Pedro de, *Isabel II, reina de España*, (Madrid, 1932).

Romanones, Conde de, *Amadeo de Saboya, el rey efímero: España y los orígenes de la guerra franco-prusiana de 1870*, (Madrid, 1935).

Rubio, Carlos, *Historia filosófica de la revolución española de 1868*, 2 vols., (Madrid, 1869).

Sainz de Robles, F. Carlos, *Historia y estampas de la Villa de Madrid*, 2 vols., (Madrid, 1933).

Sánchez Alonso, B., *Fuentes de la historia española e hispanoamericana*, 3 vols., (Madrid, 1952).

Stone, J. S., *The Cult of Santiago*, (London, 1927).

Stern, P. J., *On Realism*, (London, 1973).

Vicens Vives, J., *Historia económica de España*, third edition, (Barcelona, 1964).

Villarasa, E. M. and Gatell, J. L., *Historia de la revolución de setiembre*, (Barcelona, 1875).

Young, Sir Charles, *Ornaments and Gifts Consecrated by the Roman Pontiffs*, (London, 1860).

Zugasti, Julián, *El Bandolerismo: Estudio social y memorias históricas*, 10 vols., (Madrid, 1876–80).

4. BIBLIOGRAPHY FOR THE POPULAR PRESS, INCLUDING EPHEMERAE

Information on newspapers contained in this part of the bibliography is compiled from a number of sources. The best work of reference for newspapers of the nineteenth century is Juan Eugenio Hartzenbusch, *Apuntes para un catálogo de periódicos madrileños desde el año 1661 al 1870*, (Madrid, 1894). Hartzenbusch included in his work not only the newspapers which were in his care at the Biblioteca Nacional in Madrid, but also those contained in various private collections, and a certain number of which he had report only. As this is the case, his *Apuntes* are not necessarily the best guide for the reader wishing to locate newspapers in Madrid. Of more practical help in this respect, perhaps, is the *Catálogo de las publicaciones periódicas existentes en la Hemeroteca Municipal de Madrid*, (Madrid, 1933), published by Antonio Asenjo, Director of the Hemeroteca at the time. This unfortunately does not list the newspapers which were published outside Madrid. The information that is given about provincial newspapers in this bibliography is based on papers seen in the Hemeroteca Municipal Madrid, and the Instituto Municipal de Historia in the Casa del Arcediano in Barcelona, the main depository for Barcelona publications of this type. The information on Madrid newspapers has been amended where the published guides did not agree with what was found in the libraries.

General information about Spanish newspapers and journalism may be obtained from the following:

Agulló y Cobos, Mercedes, *Madrid en sus diarios*, 5 vols., (Madrid, 1961–1972).

Gómez Aparicio, Pedro, *Historia del periodismo español, I: Desde la 'Gaceta de Madrid' (1661) hasta el destronamiento de Isabel II*, (Madrid, 1967). *II: De la revolución de Septiembre al desastre colonial*, (Madrid, 1971). *III: De las guerras coloniales a la Dictadura*, (Madrid, 1974).

Martínez Olmedilla, Augusto, *Periódicos de Madrid: Anecdotario*, (Madrid, 1956).

Schulte, Henry F., *The Spanish Press 1470–1966*, (University of Illinois Press, 1968).

Zavala, Iris M., 'La Prensa ante la revolución de 1868', *Románticos y socialistas*, (Madrid, 1972), pp. 179–205.

Eguizábal, José Eugenio, *Apuntes para una historia de la legislación española sobre imprenta desde el año de 1480 al presente*, (Madrid, 1873).

Newspapers are, almost by definition, ephemeral, and some of the ones which appeared in the first burst of release when censorship was lifted after the September revolution disappeared almost immediately, so that it is difficult to have very precise information about them. This bibliography can therefore only be an approximate and not an exhaustive description of the papers referred to. In the interest of brevity it is restricted to the papers mentioned in this study. There is still much to be done on the general study of the Spanish press of the period.

Papers in Valle-Inclán's library at Pontevedra are marked with an asterisk.

Las Ánimas. Periódico joco-serio y algún tanto reaccionario. Madrid, 1 March, 1869–26 July, 1869. Valle-Inclán's library contains nos. for 12 April, 1869 and 3 May, 1869. Imp. de F. Gamayo y en la de E. de la Riva.

El Anticristo. Predicará hasta la conversión de los neos, o sea hasta el juicio final. Madrid, Sermón 1, 26 November, 1868. Satírico. Imp. de J. Noguera.

La Campana de Gracia. Barcelona, 8 May, 1870–11 October, 1934. This appeared to be published in alternation with *L'Esquella de la Torratxa*. Both papers, founded by Inocencio López Bernagossi, were anti-clerical, republican and *catalanista*. For details see Gómez Aparicio, op. cit., II, 355.

El Caos. Confusión semanal. Madrid, 8 April, 1870–11 July, 1870, or later. Republican federalist. Imp. de J. Pena; Imp. de J. Noguera.

El Capitán Araña. Diario de circunstancias. Madrid, 26 November, 1868. Satírico. Imp. de Orga.

El Cascabel. Periódico para reír, política, poca, pero buena, Madrid, October 1863–2 April, 1891, or later: the 3rd época began on this date according to the catalogue of the Hemeroteca Municipal. Political comments started to appear in this paper after February 1866. Anti-Moderado; then anti-Amadeo. Imp. de M. Minuesa; Imp. de D. Valero; Imp. de Viuda e Hijos de la Riva.

El Cencerro. Periódico, político, satírico, burlón y camorrista. Organo oficial del club de los maldicientes. Cordoba, 5 December, 1869–20 March, 1870; Madrid, May 1870–1912? Republican, anti-clerical. Imp. de M. Tello; Oficina Tipográfica del Hospicio.

El Centinela del Pueblo. Periódico liberal. Madrid, 23 July, 1868; 5 August, 1868; Supplement to no. of 19 August, on 21 August, 1868; 1 September, 1868; 20 September, 1868; Supplement 29 September, 1868; Supplement to no. of 30 December, 1868 (no. 77). The above numbers are the ones I have seen in the Hemeroteca Municipal, Madrid. *La Correspondencia de España* of 7 October, 1868 reports the first date of publication as 23 June, but this must be an error, as 23 July was the date on which

No. 1 was published. The same paper on 5 July, 1870 announced that the *Centinela* was going to stop publication. Gómez Aparico op. cit., II, 29, notes the paper's enthusiasm for the Duque de Montpensier and concludes that he possibly financed it.

El Cohete. Periódico revolucionario. Barcelona, 1 October, 1868–14 November, 1868.

El Cohete, Periódico satírico. Pese a quien pese, dale que dale. Madrid, 27 October, 1872–2 March, 1873. Imp. a cargo de J. E. Morete y la de C. García León.

La Comedia Política. Satirical supplement to no. 65 of *La Independencia Española*. Madrid, 31 May, 1865.

La Correspondencia de España. According to Hartzenbusch, originally the *Carta Autógrafa*. Madrid, 1848–70. It took the name of *La Correspondencia de España* in 1859. According to the catalogue of the Hemeroteca Municipal, *La Carta Autógrafa* was published 1848–27 June, 1925, and was a news organ taking news from papers of all parties.

Las Cosa Pública. Madrid, 26 November, 1868–4 July, 1869, or possibly June 1870 acc. Hartzenbusch. Montpensierist. Gómez Aparico, op. cit., II, 44, inaccurately gives the date for no. 1 as 27 November, 1868: this was the date of no. 2. Imp. de F. Hernández.

La Democracia. Periódico político, cuyo título indica el partido a que pertenecía. Madrid, 18 March, 1856–14 June, 1856. Imp. de *La Democracia*.

La Democracia. Madrid, 1 January, 1864–21 June, 1866. Publication was suspended for political reasons 13 January, 1866–18 March, 1866. It proclaimed all liberties, and had altercations with *La Discusión*. Imp. de Minuesa; Imp. Universal.

El Despertador. El que quiera comer, que trabaje. Gobierno poco y barato. 14 October, 1868. It declared support of 'Soberanía nacional y todas las libertades'.

Diario Español. Político y literario. Madrid, 1 June, 1852–1923. Hartzenbusch describes it as a 'periódico principalmente político de la unión liberal'. Imp. de A. Babi, finally Imp. de P. Andrés.

Don Diego de Noche. Revista crítico literaria. Madrid, 18 April, 1868–September 1868, then incorporated into *El Eco de España*. Imp. de Cuevas y Minuesa.

La Diosa Razón. Periódico satírico político, bajo la dirección de tres ciudadanas. Madrid, 25 November, 1868. Shortlived. Imp. de M. Tello.

*Don Quijote. Diario político satírico. Saldrá en busca de aventuras los días . . . Madrid, 5 January, 1869–25 July 1869. Valle-Inclán's library contains all numbers up to 10 July, 1869. Establecimiento tipográfico de R. Vicente; Imprenta de R. Moreno.

La Época. Madrid, 1 April, 1849–1936. Publication was interrupted 4 May, 1852–18 June, 1852, when it reappeared with the title *La Época Actual*. It retained this title till 30 June, 1852, and had no political nature for the period. Publication was also interrupted 27 June, 1854–4 July, 1854. For some time it was a paper of the Unión Liberal, then of the *moderados*, and then Alfonsine after the revolution of 1868. Imp. de Aguirre y Cía; Imp. de J. Juanes y Cía.

La Esperanza. Periódico monárquico. Madrid, 10 October, 1844–December, 1873. Absolutist, carlist. Imp. de *La Esperanza*.

L'Esquella de la Torratxa. Barcelona 5 May, 1873. Appeared as continuation of *La Campana de Gracia*, and alternated with it. See *supra* on *La Campana de Gracia*.

La Flaca. Barcelona, 27 March 1869–4 October, 1873. Suspended 3 September, 1871, reappeared with the title of *La Carcajada*, 17 January, 1872. It reverted to the title of *La Flaca*, 7 November, 1872. Attacked all parties though was mainly republican and federalist in attitude. Its treatment of Isabel II, Prim, Serrano and others belies the intention expressed in the first number: 'no rebajaremos hasta la personalidad ni mucho menos nos valdremos de chanzas pesadas para ridicularizar este o aquel partido, tal o cual institución, esa o esotra manifestación particular'.

La Flora. Peródico satírico y literario. Madrid, February 1868? Short-lived. Imp. de C. Moliner y Cía.

Fray Tinieblas. Periódico Político, progresista, enciclopédico, serio-jocoso, crítico burlesco, escrito en fuerte y flojo. Defensor de la revolución de julio. Madrid, 1 May, 1855–10 September, 1855. Imp. de M. Minuesa; Imp. de L. García.

La Gaceta de Madrid. The first Spanish newspaper, still in publication under the title *Boletín Oficial del Estado* which it assumed in 1939. Its original subtitle in 1661 was 'Relación o gazeta de algunos casos particulares, assí políticos como militares, sucedidos en la mayor parte del mundo, hasta fin de Diciembre de 1660'. Main function to carry official news, decrees etc.

El Ganso. Periódico satírico. Organo oficial de la gansocracia española. Madrid, 7 November, 1868.

*El Gato. Periódico Ministerial hasta cierto punto. Madrid, 19 November, 1868–20 April, 1870, or to end of that year. On 7 August, 1869 the subtitle was 'Periódico rabiosamente ministerial'. Publication was suspended 31 August, 1869–7 December, 1869, after which the 2ª época began with the subtitle 'Periódico antirrevolucionario'. Valle-Inclán's library contains *El Gato,* 19 November, 1868–5 July, 1869. Imp. de F. G., Soldado 4; Imp. de A. Moreno.

Gil Blas. Periódico político, satírico. Madrid, 3 November, 1864–6 October, 1872. The last number announced that the paper preferred to make a voluntary suspension rather than to buy off the necessary politicians. Publication was suspended 16 June, 1866–4 October, 1866. The dates given by both the catalogue of the Hemeroteca Municipal, Madrid and Gómez Aparicio, op. cit., II, 551ff are misleading and at variance with the editions of the paper available at Colindale Newspaper Library, London. *Gil Blas* was mainly republican in politics, with a tendency to federalism. Imp. de J. García; Imp. de R. Labajos.

*La Gorda. Periódica [sic] Liberal. *La Gorda,* enemiga de 'La Gorda,' 10 November, 1868–30 June, 1870. Suspended 30 July, 1869–15 November, 1869. Highly critical of the revolutionary regime, it came under attack from the Partido de la Porra. Valle-Inclán's library contains *La Gorda,* 10 November, 1868–15 June, 1869. Imp. del Norte; Imp. de la Viuda de Martínez; Imp. de J. Noguera.

El Guirigay. Periódico popular del mediodía. Madrid, 1 January, 1839–7 July, 1839. Suspended by Royal decree. Editor González Bravo, known as Ibrahim Clarete. Imp. de *El Guirigay.*

El Guirigay. Periódico satírico. Madrid, 22 July, 1965 for at least 10 numbers. Imp. de Fortanet.

La Iberia. Diario liberal. Madrid, 15 June, 1854-1896. The paper had the title *La Nueva Iberia* 2 January, 1868–29 September, 1868. An economical edition of the paper began in 1859, and a satirical weekly edition appeared 22 December, 1862-7 September, 1863 (seen by Hartzenbusch). A 'periódico progresista', founded by Calvo Asensio, its directors included Sagasta and Carlos Rubio. Imp. de *La Iberia;* Imp. de J. de Rojas.

El Imparcial. Diario liberal. Madrid, 16 March, 1867–1930. Valero; Imp. de *El Imparcial.*

La Independencia Española: two papers of this name are listed by Hartzenbusch, neither of which seems to be the paper referred to in Chapter VI.i, note 47, dated 1865. They were published 15 April, 1858–5 March, 1859, possibly September 1859, (Imp. de Noguera; Imp. de P. Núñez).

El Jaque-Mate. Periódico maldiciente. Madrid, 1 September, 1872–8 June, 1873. Anti-Amadeo. Imp. de la Asociación general del Arte de Imprimir.

Jeremías. Periódico político, literario y gazmoño. Madrid, 1 April, 1866–21 June, 1866; 4 April, 1869–5 August, 1869. Republican, anti-Carlist, anti-Montpensier, anti-

Inquisition, pro freedom of religion. Imp. de F. Beltrán; Imp. de *La Victoria*; Imp. de M. Tello.

El Juego. Periódico descolorido. Madrid, 1868.

La Linterna. Periódico liberal, serio, y concienzudo, creado para combatir el santonismo, la licencia, el retraimiento y a todos los enemigos de la idea liberal. Madrid, 18 September, 1868, no. 4, 1 November, 1868, no. 6. Imp. de J. Morales y Rodríguez.

El Loro. Revista semanal de colores rabiosos, escrita por una sociedad de pajarracos. Sevilla, 1869.

*La Mano Oculta. Madrid, 10 January, 1869–11 July, 1869. Carlist. Valle-Inclán's library contains numbers up to 17 February, 1869. Imp de R. Ramírez; Imp. de R. Anoz.

El Monaguillo de las Salesas. Periódico serio-satírico. Madrid, 15 December, 1868. Short-lived. Imp. de Noguera.

El Mono Rey. Periódico festivo, de carácter republicano. Madrid, 21 March, 1870. Imp. de P. Abienzo.

El Murciélago. Periódico nocturno. Madrid, June, 1864. Imp. de J. A. Artigosa.

Neo. Periódico satírico con ínsulas de beato y puntos de republicano. Huesca, 1868.

Los Neos sin Careta. Periódico satírico. Plasencia, 23 April, 1870, no. 2 – 20 August, 1870. The Director, José García Mora, is named as the founder of the Iglesia Cristiana Liberal de Villanueva de la Vera.

El Niño Terso. Organo expresivo del derecho divino y obligado del humano. Madrid, 15 December, 1868. Short-lived. Anti-Carlist. Imp. de C. Moliner.

Las Novedades. Madrid, 14 December, 1850-1870, or later. A 'periódico progresista' which included Galdós among its contributors. Gómez Aparicio, op. cit., I, 365, considers this paper the most important organ of the revolution of July 1854.

La Nueva Iberia: see *La Iberia.*

*El Padre Cobos. Periódico de política, literatura y artes. Madrid, 24 September, 1854–30 June, 1855; 5 September, 1855–30 June, 1856; 25 February, 1869–25 November, 1869. A paper of opposition to the 'Bienio Liberal', which gained a reputation for its 'indirectas'. It continued with conservative criticism in its 3ª época : Imp. de R. Vicente.

El Palitroque. Periódico republicano federal. Barcelona, 22 November, 1868, no. 1, 20 December, 1868, no. 5.

El Papagall. Semanario Bilingüe, satíric y plorós. Valencia, 28 April, 1868–30 November, 1868.

El Papel de Estraza. Periódico ecléctico dedicado a la posteridad. Valencia, 21 April, 1866, no. 2 –25 May, 1866.

El Papelito. Periódico para reír y llorar, Madrid, March 1868, número muestro –29th January, 1871. Fiercely Carlist. Imp. de *El Cascabel*; Imp. de M. Tello.

El Paraguas de Montpensier. Periódico honesto, redactado por una asociación de tunos. Madrid, 20 June, 21 July, 1870, or later. Anti-Montpensier. Imp. de J. Noguera; Imp. de J. Vercher.

La Píldora. Medicina nacional propinada al público. Madrid, 22 November, 1868–May or June, 1869. Imp. de F. Hernández.

El Quijote. Periódico satírico. Began Madrid, January, 1868. Organ of the *Bufos Madrileños.*

El Relámpago. ¡Abajo los Borbones! ¡Viva la soberanía de la nación! Madrid, 13 January, 1867–14 July, 1867, 6 numbers. Clandestine. Published by Luis Blanc and Felipe Fernández.

La Revolución. Diario Republicano. Madrid, 14 November, 1868, no. 2 –23 December, 1868, then later again. Imp. de C. Minuesa.

Rigoleto. Periódico (progresisto [sic]). Madrid, 1 December, 1869–5 March, 1872.

Carlist, anti-Montpensier, anti-Amadeo. Imp. de R. Vicente; Imp. de J. J. de las Heras.

La Saeta. Periódico más que revolucionario: republicano. Barcelona, 25 October, 1868.

El Sainete. Madrid, 19 February, 1867–14 December, 1867. Imp. de C. Moliner y Cía.

Satanás. Organo ministerial/de la región infernal/redactado en el este suelo/y que va a tomar el pelo/a la corte celestial. Madrid, began February 1886. Establecimiento tipolitográfico.

La Seca. Periódico verdirrojo. Madrid, 22 November, 1868. Imp. de J. Sanabria.

Semanario Pintoresco Español. Madrid, 3 April 1836–20 December 1857. Weekly of general and cultural interest. Imp. de Jordán; later imp. de Gómez.

La Soberanía Nacional. Diario liberal. Hartzenbusch believes it began in May 1868. Imp. de L. Paiz, a cargo de D. José María Velasco, Bendición de Dios, núm 4.

El Telégrafo. Diario de avisos, noticias y decretos. Barcelona, 1864-68.

El Trancazo. Pasmo semanal contemporáneo. Began publication 5 January, 1868, continued for at least 16 numbers. Imp. de C. Moliner y Cía.

El Vigía. Hartzenbusch only mentions a paper of this name for 1855, and nothing for 1879.

La Voluntad Nacional. Madrid, must have begun September, 1868, and was still being published at the beginning of 1869. Imp. de A. Moreno.

The *aleluyas* mentioned in the text were all found in the Museo Municipal, Madrid. Some others are to be found in the Hemeroteca Municipal, Madrid, the other good collections being in Barcelona, in the Biblioteca Central, and the Instituto Municipal de Historia.

Aleluyas madrileñas. n.p., n.d. 20 illustration. Museo Municipal, 7.713.

D.N.M. Rivero. es propiedad. Madrid, 1869. 30 illustrations. Museo Municipal, 4.693.

Historia de una cualquiera que no es Dª – Bal-Domera. Primera parte. Es propiedad. Unico depósito y despacho «El Arca de Noe» Corredera baja 39. 48 illustrations. Museo Municipal, 4.997.

Historia de la gloriosa per un *xicot* del estudi del Mestre Titas. n.p., n.d. 48 illustrations. Museo Municipal, 4.960.

El Joven Telémaco. Aleluyas de teatros. Madrid, 1868. Ferrer y compañía, c. de la Magdalena num. 17. Imp. a cargo de R. Ramírez, c. de San Marcos num. 32. 48 illustrations. Museo Municipal 12.160.

El Padre Clarinete. Madrid, 1869. 30 illustrations. Museo Municipal, 4.961.

Vida de Guzmancito. Madrid, 1869. Es propiedad de J.E.P. Lechuga 2–3°. 30 illustrations. Museo Municipal, 4.958.

All of the following broadsides were found in the Hemeroteca Municipal, Madrid.

A la caída de los Borbones. Madrid, 1868. Hemeroteca Municipal, A/1275.

Carta del Diablo al Padre Santo. Dated 'En el Tártaro a 10 de Diciembre de 1868'. Madrid. Hemeroteca Municipal, A/1207.

La culebra de Borbon en Pau. Españoles. n.p., 17 October, 1868. Hemeroteca Municipal A/1276.

Disparos, de un marino, a Isabel de Borbón. Es propiedad de su autor, n.p., 1869. Hemeroteca Municipal, A/1274.

España pendiente de un hilo. n.d. Propiedad de P. de Torres. Imp. a cargo de Diego Valero. Hemeroteca Municipal, A/1454.

Juicio de Isabel de Borbón. Madrid, 1868. See Chapter III.i, n. 19. Hemeroteca Municipal, A/1278.

La rosa que regaló el Padre Santo a Isabel de Borbón. Signed R.T.R. n.p. Bought 6 November, 1868? Hemeroteca Municipal, A/1277.

Colección Támesis

SERIE B – TEXTOS